SPATIAL PLANNING, URBAN FORM AND SUSTAINABLE TRANSPORT

To my family

Spatial Planning, Urban Form and Sustainable Transport

Edited by

KATIE WILLIAMS
Oxford Brookes University, UK

ASHGATE

Published by
Ashgate Publishing Limited
Gower House
Croft Road
Aldershot
Hampshire GU11 3HR
England

Ashgate Publishing Company
Suite 420
101 Cherry Street
Burlington, VT 05401-4405
USA

Ashgate website: http://www.ashgate.com

British Library Cataloguing in Publication Data
Spatial planning, urban form and sustainable transport. -
   (Urban planning and environment)
   1. Transportation - Planning 2. Sustainable development
   3. City planning 4. Transportation and state
   I. Williams, Katie
   388'.0684

Library of Congress Cataloging-in-Publication Data
Spatial planning, urban form and sustainable transport / edited by Katie Williams.
       p. cm. -- (Urban planning and environment)
   Includes bibliographical references and index.
   ISBN 0-7546-4251-8
   1. City planning. 2. Urban transportation. 3. Sustainable development. 4. Land
use, Urban. 5. Spatial behavior. I. Williams, Katie. II. Series.

   HT166.S636 2005
   307.1'216--dc22

                                                                        2004030116

ISBN 0 7546 4251 8

Printed & bound by MPG Books Ltd, Bodmin, Cornwall

Contents

List of Figures

List of Tables

List of Contributors

Professor David Banister is Professor of Transport Planning at University College London, UK.

Carey Curtis is a Senior Lecturer in the Department of Urban and Regional Planning, Curtin University, Western Australia.

Professor Frans M. Dieleman is a Professor in the Department of Human Geography and Planning at Utrecht University, The Netherlands.

Dr Martin Dijst is a Senior Lecturer in the Department of Human Geography and Planning at Utrecht University, The Netherlands.

Robin Hickman is Associate Urban Planner with the Halcrow Group Ltd, London, UK.

Taichiro Ikeda is a Civil Engineer at the Bureau of Waterworks, Hiroshima City Government Office, Japan.

Dipl.-Ing. Birgit Kasper is a Researcher in the Department of Transport Planning at the University of Dortmund, Germany.

Birgit Krausse is a Research Student at the Institute of Energy and Sustainable Development at De Montfort University, Leicester, UK.

Nicholas Low is Associate Professor in the Faculty of Architecture, Building and Planning at the University of Melbourne, Australia.

Kees Maat is a Senior Researcher at OTB Research Institute for Housing, Mobility and Urban Studies at Delft University of Technology, The Netherlands.

Dr John Mardaljevic is a Senior Research Fellow at the Institute of Energy and Sustainable Development, De Montfort University, Leicester, UK.

Dr Rocky Piro is Principal Growth Management Planner with the Puget Sound Regional Council in Seattle, USA. He also teaches Land Use Planning at the University of Washington in Seattle and Tacoma.

Dr Joachim Scheiner is a Researcher in the Department of Transport Planning at the University of Dortmund, Germany.

Dr Tim Schwanen is a Lecturer in the Department of Human Geography and Planning at Utrecht University, The Netherlands.

Dr Dominic Stead is a Senior Researcher at OTB Research Institute for Housing, Mobility and Urban Studies, Delft University of Technology, The Netherlands.

Dr Mamoru Taniguchi is a Professor in the Department of Environmental Science and Technology, Okayam University, Okayama, Japan.

Hans Tindemans is a Research Assistant in the Department of Geography at Ghent University, Belgium.

Dries Van Hofstraeten is a Research Assistant in the Department of Transport and Regional Economics at the University of Antwerp, Belgium.

Professor Dr Ann Verhetsel is Professor of Human Geography in the Department of Transport and Regional Economics, University of Antwerp, Belgium.

Dr Katie Williams is Reader in Urban Sustainability at the Oxford Institute for Sustainable Development, School of the Built Environment at Oxford Brookes University, UK.

Professor Dr Frank Witlox is Assistant Professor of Economic Geography in the Department of Geography at Ghent University, Belgium.

Preface

The purpose of this book is to advance the debate on the relationship between urban form and sustainable transport, and to investigate the associated role of spatial planning. In all, twelve chapters present new research findings, debates and lessons from planning practice on these issues. The aim in compiling the book was to present new thinking on the links between urban form and sustainable transport from a number of different perspectives. The contributors come from a range of professional and disciplinary backgrounds, including human geography, urban planning, civil engineering, urban design, growth management, environmental planning, and transport research. The book is international in scope, with chapters from the UK, Australia, the USA, Belgium, The Netherlands, Germany and Japan. This highlights both differences and similarities in transport planning contexts and debates.

The book forms one of a series produced under the auspices of the International Urban Planning and Environment Association (IUPEA). The aim of the series is to share research findings and current best practice on a number of aspects of environmental planning. The books are devised to present and critically assess a variety of initiatives to improve environmental quality. The other books in the series are: *Urban Environmental Planning: Policies, Instruments and Methods in an International Perspective* (Miller and de Roo, 2004); *Integrating City Planning and Environmental Improvement: Practicable Strategies for Sustainable Urban Development* (Miller and de Roo, 2004); and *Compact Cities and Sustainable Urban Development: A Critical Assessment of Policies and Plans from an International Perspective* (de Roo and Miller, 2000). All are published by Ashgate.

In editing this book, I have had help from a number of people. The contributors to the book have been professional and enthusiastic throughout the project and I thank them for that. The staff at Ashgate have also been helpful and accommodating from the start. I would like to thank Daniel Kozak and Seema Dave for preparing many of the figures and tables, and Nic Dempsey for editorial assistance. I would also like to acknowledge the support of my colleagues at the Oxford Institute for Sustainable Development: Elizabeth Burton, Carol Dair, Lynne Mitchell, Mike Jenks, Sarah Taylor and Andy Hudson.

I also greatly appreciate the assistance of the Dutch Ministry of Housing, Physical Planning and Environment for supporting the preparation of this book, in particular, Jaap van Staalduine. Finally, I would also like to thank my IUPEA colleagues, and particularly the book series editors, Gert de Roo and Donald Miller for setting the series in motion. I would also like to acknowledge the contribution of the late Professor Mike Breheny to the International Urban Planning and Environment Association, and to research and scholarship on urban form and transport planning. Mike was an active and enthusiastic member of the IUPEA and is greatly missed.

Katie Williams, August 2004

Chapter 1

Spatial Planning, Urban Form and Sustainable Transport: An Introduction

Katie Williams

Introduction

The ways in which we travel are having a huge impact on the sustainability of the planet. There is general agreement that current levels of car use, fuel consumption and emissions are unsustainable. The issue which this book addresses is the relationship between travel patterns and the physical form of cities. It considers how urban form affects mobility, and the role of spatial planning in that relationship.

The debate about whether particular urban forms, in terms of their shape, density, configuration and so on, can have an impact on the sustainability of cities has a relatively long and rich history (see for example, Breheny, 1992; Williams *et al.* 2000; de Roo and Miller, 2000). Within this debate, researchers and planning practitioners have considered the impact of urban form on a number of elements of sustainability, such as social equity, accessibility, ecology, economic performance, pollution and health. However, the issue which has attracted the most attention both academically and in practice is the impact of city form on transport and mobility. In particular, this field of enquiry has concentrated on the 'best' urban forms to facilitate sustainable transport solutions, generally seen as reducing trip lengths and times, reducing reliance on the car, enabling efficient public transport, encouraging walking and cycling and reducing transport-related emissions, pollution and accidents.

The outcome of much of this research is an advocacy of 'contained', compact, urban layouts, with a mix of uses in close proximity: i.e. a move away from functional land use zoning and a reduction of urban sprawl. The reasoning is that such forms reduce travel demand because people can work near their homes and make use of local services and facilities. Such forms can also provide population densities high enough to support public transport services and, through improved urban design, encourage cycling and walking. Variations on this model, with concentrations of high density developments around public transport nodes, or in local neighbourhoods within a city, are also advocated. In Europe such models have become common in planning strategies. They are now also becoming more widely accepted elsewhere, particularly in Asia, the USA and Australia.

However, as with all issues in the sustainability debate, the reality is not as straightforward as this 'compact city' solution would suggest. There are three key areas of debate, and these form the focus of this book. First, there is considerable uncertainty about the extent to which spatial planning or the manipulation of urban form can contribute to sustainable mobility *at all* in the face of broader socio-economic and cultural trends. Clearly, a number of forces shape travel patterns and transport options: economic activity and related production trends, structural socio-demographic changes, trade flows, technological change, consumer choice and income levels all have a significant impact (OECD, 1999). Currently, such forces are leading to increases in vehicle numbers, travel frequencies and trip lengths. Given this context, it is almost impossible to isolate the benefits of planning.

What is clear, however, is that currently almost all transport indicators world-wide are moving in an unsustainable direction. Since the 1980s, the majority of industrialised countries have experienced increases in the proportion of trips made by car compared with public transport (*ibid*), and overall the car accounts for around 80 per cent of passenger kms travelled. In most countries, road and motorway network densities (i.e. the proportion of land given over to road infrastructure) are also steadily increasing (*ibid*). Perhaps unsurprisingly the amount of traffic and the number of motor vehicles owned are also rising, with some of the largest recent percentage increases for industrialised nations in counties such as Korea, Poland and Turkey. Although, highest per capita car ownership rates are still in the USA, Canada, Australia and Western Europe. Along with these trends are increases in fuel consumption and emissions. Given these indicators, the extent to which changes in urban form, facilitated through spatial planning, can have an impact on sustainable transport is rightly questioned.

Second, there are still uncertainties about whether the compact form, as opposed to other urban layouts, is the most effective city form in terms of sustainable transport (Breheny, 1995; Rickaby 1987; Feitelson and Verhoef, 2001). Some have questioned whether the 'compact city' does actually lead to the desired effects of reduced car-use and increased walking, cycling and public transport patronage. There are also uncertainties about whether it can contribute to wider sustainable travel patterns, for example regional and intra-regional travel (Headicar, 2000; Newman and Kenworthy, 2000). Further, some researchers have claimed that the compaction model relies on an over-simplification of complex travel behaviour, especially in terms of live-work co-location (Breheny, 2004). In the light of these criticisms, other city forms such as 'corridor developments' and multi-centred cities are also suggested as having significant transport benefits (Williams *et al.*, 2000).

Third, even if it is possible to find a consensus on which urban form is the most beneficial in terms of sustainable transport, there are still questions about our ability to implement substantial changes in the physical fabric of cities through the planning system. Existing urban form changes relatively slowly, and opportunities for newly planned towns and cities are limited in most developed countries. In Europe, many of the most significant transport problems are found in historic towns which are bound by strict conservation policies, and where opportunities for further compaction are rare. The compact city solution may be beneficial where there is vacant land ready for development within urban boundaries, but all too often urban intensification is experienced as 'town cramming' and is unpopular with existing urban residents. In fact, many measures to promote sustainable transport through planning, such as higher densities and mixed uses are, paradoxically, disliked at the local level. In the UK, plans for such forms of development are regularly stymied by local politicians. For these reasons, and others such as lack of resources, in many developed countries measures to temper travel demand through planning have not worked as effectively as hoped. In the UK, for example, the Government has had to acknowledge that its ambitious plans for sustainable transport have all but failed. In a recent overview of the Government's record on sustainable transport Docherty and Shaw (2003) concluded that while there were genuinely good intentions, the outcomes were minimal and the performance disappointing.

This said, advocates of planning would view this critique as unduly pessimistic. Clearly, there *is* a relationship between the way that space is planned and used and how people and businesses can access the services and facilities they need. Physical form, in terms of buildings and infrastructure, may change very slowly, but certain types of development, in certain locations, can have a major impact on travel patterns over long time periods (see Hickman and Banister, this volume). There are also examples of good practice in spatial planning that have made progress in stemming some unsustainable trends (for example, the UK's policy of restricting further out-of-town retail developments and European and Australian neighbourhood planning to encourage walking and cycling). However, there remain many gaps in our understanding of how to deliver urban forms that genuinely contribute to sustainable mobility.

The chapters in this book are arranged into three parts, which pick up on the three areas of debate outlined above. The first part (Part A) considers the impact of urban form, *in combination with other factors*, on sustainable transport. The authors consider the inter-relationships between, for example, urban form and socio-demographic characteristics and lifestyles. They also explore relationships between different physical form elements and various trip purposes and temporal aspects of travel behaviour for different sectors of the population. This research can be seen as a progression from some of the earlier urban form and transport research which either did not consider the impact of wider factors on the relationship between urban form and travel, or treated them as contextual rather than inter-related.

The second part of the book (Part B) addresses the relationship between *different aspects of urban form* and sustainable transport. For example, the contributors cover the relationship between transport infrastructure and employment development, the impact of a range of urban form features (such as density and topography) on petrol consumption, and the impact of road layouts on pollution levels. These contributions add depth to previous research by clarifying our understanding of the role of individual elements of city form on a number of specific aspects of sustainable mobility.

The third part of the book (Part C) addresses the more *practical implementation issues* surrounding spatial planning policies aimed at engendering sustainable transport. This section broadens out the debate to consider not only what planning practitioners should be doing, but what is hindering progress towards implementing sustainable transport policies. It gives examples of good practice in policy development and implementation from Australia and the USA, and offers some cause for optimism about the role of spatial planning in delivering sustainable mobility.

A summary of the chapters is presented below. However, first it is useful to consider what is meant by 'sustainable transport' and how it is interpreted in the contributions that follow.

A Definition of 'Sustainable Transport'

The concept of 'sustainability' is now so widely used that repeating common definitions here is unnecessary. However, it is important to be specific about the term 'sustainable transport'. A review of some alternative definitions developed by researchers and organisations involved in transport policy gives useful comparisons.

Richardson (1999, quoted in VTPI, 2004) describes a sustainable transport system as: 'One in which fuel consumption, emissions, safety, congestion, and social and economic access are of such levels that they can be sustained into the indefinite future without causing great or irreparable harm to future generations of people throughout the world.' In a similar vein, the Environmental Directorate of the Organisation for Economic Co-operation and Development define 'environmentally sustainable transportation' as:

> ... transportation that does not endanger public health or ecosystems and that meets the needs for access consistent with (a) use of renewable resources that are below their rates of regeneration, and (b) use of non-renewable resources below the rates of development of renewable substitutes (*ibid*).

The World Business Council for Sustainable Development defines sustainable mobility as: 'the ability to meet society's need to move freely, gain access, communicate, trade, and establish relationships without sacrificing other essential human or ecological values, today or in the future' (WRI, 2004). And the European Union Council of Ministers describe a 'sustainable transport system' as one that:

- Allows the basic access and development needs of individuals, companies and society to be met safely and in a manner consistent with human and ecosystem health, and promotes equity within and between successive generations.
- Is affordable, operates fairly and efficiently, offers a choice of transport mode, and supports a competitive economy, as well as balanced regional development.
- Limits emissions and waste within the planet's ability to absorb them, uses renewable resources at or below the rates of development of renewable substitutes, while minimizing the impact on the use of land and the generation of noise (quoted in VTPI, 2004).

These definitions display a great degree of commonality. They refer to sustainable transport systems providing a basic requirement to *meet society's and the economy's mobility needs* (although, in practice, there is considerable disagreement about how mobile society needs to be). They also refer to *social equity* elements of sustainability, i.e. that transport systems should be affordable, accessible and safe. In addition, the definitions share references to *environmental impacts*, both in terms of operating within carrying capacities and avoiding pollution of natural resources, such as air and land. Although each of these aspects of sustainability is complex and contested, they form the basis for a common understanding of sustainable transport shared by the majority of contributors to this book.

A Summary of the Chapters

Part A: The Impact of Urban Form, in Combination with other Factors, on Sustainable Transport

In the first chapter, Tim Schwanen and his colleagues take as their starting point the hypothesis that urban form affects travel behaviour, but that socio-demographic factors are equally, if not more, important. The authors stress the value of taking account of the interactions between urban form and socio-demographic characteristics, because constraints imposed by the physical environment may be compensated for, or reinforced by, an individual's circumstances. Hence, they argue that urban form impacts may not be equally important for all sectors of the population. Given this position, they seek to answer the research question: 'Does the direction and/or magnitude of the influence of urban form on travel vary across different household types?' The authors then present research findings for a number of types of trips across six different types of household living in different residential contexts. The results they obtain vary markedly according to the kind of trip, household and purpose of travel: hence the answer to their research question is 'yes'. This leads the authors to conclude that it may be useful to develop land use policies aimed at different sectors of the population. For example, building high-rise developments near public transport facilities in larger cities may be a sensible policy for single workers and two-worker couples, but concentrating new development in compact suburban locations may be a better strategy for one-worker couples or retired households. Overall, the research shows that the complex interplay of socio-demographic factors, physical elements and travel behaviour requires a sophisticated planning approach, as straightforward relationships between urban form and travel behaviour can not be assumed given heterogeneous urban populations.

Following Schwanen *et al.*, Joachim Scheiner and Birgit Kasper continue to investigate the importance of additional factors in combination with urban form in influencing mobility. In this case, they are interested in the impact of different lifestyles on both residential mobility and travel behaviour. They start by citing recent sociological research which describes the fragmentation of society (via individualism, differentiation and pluralisation of lifestyles). They assert that not only are new lifestyles emerging, but also different 'mobility styles'. Their basic thesis is that different lifestyle groups are characterised by specific forms of mobility, and from this they seek to address how the built environment can meet the needs of less predictable ways of life in the future.

The authors present a pilot study of empirical research in which they developed six lifestyle groups or categories. Research was then carried out in three different neighbourhoods. The conclusions they present are that: development of mobility in relation to individualism and pluralisation of lifestyles is increasingly resistant to planning regulation (evidenced by growing dispersal of spatial development, and the limited success of supply-oriented planning). Hence, an approach to spatial planning which connects mobility behaviour, lifestyles, social and spatial structures is required for sustainable development. For planning, the challenge is to connect this differentiation of lifestyles with traditional requirements for planning. This may mean a fundamental change for planning if it is to be truly integrated.

The next chapter, by Hans Tindemans and colleagues, is a report of travel demand research. The authors adopt an 'activity-based' approach in their work which focuses on the need to understand activities before attempting to determine travel behaviour (i.e. viewing travel as derived demand). The authors are specifically interested in 'trip-chaining' where multiple activities are carried out. The chapter presents results of the 'SAMBA' (Spatial Analysis and Modelling Based on Activities) research project which considers these activity chains and their spatial dimension in Belgium. Detailed information is presented on the different patterns of trips undertaken by different sectors of the population and variations in modes of travel used. Also, data on modes used for different stages of the trips is evaluated. An analysis is also presented of activities taking place at different times (during the week and at weekends, and during different times of the day). This data is to be the basis for further spatial modelling. However, the findings already demonstrate the importance of understanding how, when and why people travel, and highlight the sophistication required in devising appropriate planning policies.

In Chapter Five, Birgit Kasper and Joachim Scheiner concentrate on one sector of the population (older people) and one type of trip (leisure). They argue that, due to changing demographics, if sustainable patterns of mobility are to be devised then older people need to be considered in mobility planning far more than at present. The authors report on the findings from a research project (entitled 'FRAME') which aims to help develop environmentally friendly, socially balanced and economically sound mobility options for seniors. They point out that sometimes there may be conflicts with traditional sustainability aims (e.g. reduced travel demand, a modal shift away from the car, and optimising traffic flows). But these have to be complemented by 'mobility maintenance' for older people to be socially sustainable and equitable.

The chapter presents research which questioned seniors in three study areas in Germany about their travel demands. The research was carried out in three types of area: city, suburb and rural. This research was then followed up by workshops and interviews with experts in the fields of seniors' leisure and travel. Overall, the authors found that leisure mobility patterns for older people are diverse, although there are specific constraints. In relation to transport options, use of public transport was found to be problematic. If older people were in a position to choose, they tended to use their cars or walk. The research also found that seniors' leisure activities tended to be very locally-oriented, with most taking place within their own neighbourhood. For this reason, small-scale urban design considerations are very important. However, the authors concluded that transport planning measures are probably not the most important way to improve leisure mobility for elderly people. Issues such as management of public transport, ensuring security, and providing very localised facilities are also key. This led to the conclusion that an integrated response is required which includes public transport providers, spatial planners, leisure facility professionals, housing developers and others.

The next chapter, by Robin Hickman and David Banister, considers integrated land use and transport planning, particularly the scope for using land use planning to reduce travel by car. The authors question the extent to which the built environment affects how people travel, and whether the land use and transport interaction relationship changes over time (i.e. do people modify their travel behaviour as households and workplaces co-locate?). Following from this, they question whether land use policy and planning can be strategically and locally applied to reduce car use. The authors begin by presenting a useful overview of the literature in this field, highlighting the knowledge gaps and pointing out contradictions in existing research findings. A number of issues have had considerable coverage in the literature: namely the influence of population size, density, mix of uses, location of development, and balance of jobs and housing. But the authors seek to broaden the debate to look at change over time, pointing out that even though urban form changes at a rate of only 1-2 per cent per year (in the UK), major developments such as housing estates, and employment and leisure developments may have a disproportionate impact on travel behaviour from one time period to another. The authors stress how little is known about the interaction of urban form (density, size etc.) and socio-economic variables (house value, income, attitudes to travel behaviour) and travel behaviour.

The chapter presents evidence from two household surveys of new houses in Surrey (UK) over a three year period to see if people in various household categories ('stayers', 'in-movers' and 'out-movers') modified their travel behaviour over time. They found that, even over a short period of time people had made changes to their behaviour, but the results varied across household types. The authors also analysed the findings in relation to urban form features (including density and household location) and found variations by different households, in different circumstances, over time. A very general finding is that people do seem to modify their behaviour to reduce energy consumption. However, the authors' main message is that 'time' must be factored into any analysis of urban form and travel behaviour. It is crucially important to understand that people do modify their behaviour, and the extent and nature of this modification should be key considerations for spatial planners.

Part B: The Relationship Between Different Aspects of Urban Form and
Sustainable Transport

As stated above, this part of the book explores how different *elements* of urban form affect sustainable transport. Chapter Seven, by Kees Maat and Dominic Stead, investigates the impact of transport infrastructure on employment development in the Netherlands. The authors' starting point is that the focus of employment development in urban centres has shifted to a clustering around transport infrastructure (e.g. near motorways and major transport interchanges). However, they point out that very little is known about the extent and nature of the impact of transport infrastructure as a draw for employment. Hence, the chapter presents empirical evidence from research on the location of employment along a transport corridor (the A12) in the Netherlands, which stretches from the Hague to the German boarder. The chapter examines recent spatial patterns of employment change in relation to transport infrastructure. Overall, the research found that proximity to transport infrastructure does have some effect on employment, although the effect is not particularly strong. Employment growth is high within very close proximity to transport infrastructure, i.e. within 1km of a motorway or a motorway junction. However, proximity to existing employment areas is more significant, confirming the concept of employment 'clusters'. The authors suggest that there are likely to be different results for different employment sectors.

In the next chapter, Mamoru Taniguchi and Taichiro Ikeda turn to the widely researched issue of urban compaction and sustainable transport. They point out that while there has been much work on the virtues of the 'compact city' for sustainable transport, little (with a few notable exceptions) has been based on empirical evidence or statistical analyses. The authors therefore undertake empirical research in Japan that will form the basis of precise design guidelines. Their chapter presents findings from a research project which aims to define which factors of urban form affect petrol consumption. The analysis is undertaken at two scales: the city and the neighbourhood. The research uses thirty explanatory variables related to urban layout, land use, historic and geographical context and transport conditions, which were correlated with data on petrol consumption.

The authors found that, at the city scale, population density was a very important factor in relation to fuel consumption, but so was transport infrastructure (e.g. the number of railway stations in a city). Topographical factors were also significant (e.g. linear port cities with physical and land use restrictions seemed to discourage car use). Also, cities within large metropolitan areas had lower petrol consumption, as did historic cities. Interestingly though, those cities damaged in the Second World War and subsequently rebuilt had higher petrol consumption levels, probably due to car-orientated highway planning. At the neighbourhood level, the research found that, as at the city scale, population density was the most significant explanatory variable for petrol consumption, but the neighbourhood's location in relation to the city centre was also important: consumption was lower closer to the centre. The availability of public transport infrastructure was also important in keeping fuel consumption low. Further, residential and neighbourhood zoning tended to increase petrol consumption. The authors point out how useful these findings are in developing guidelines for future planning and design strategies which maximise the benefits to sustainable transport of urban layouts.

The next chapter, by Birgit Krausse and John Mardaljevic, introduces two additional elements of sustainable transport planning: pollution and health. Specifically, the authors investigate exposure to air pollution by car drivers. They relate this to urban form by researching the impact that various road layouts have on pollution levels inside the car. Other studies have concluded that non-driving commuters are exposed to different pollution levels depending on transport infrastructure and road layouts (e.g. motorways, small urban roads etc.), but until now attention on car drivers has been minimal.

The research focuses on an inner area of Leicester, a medium-sized city in the UK, where pollutant levels would be expected to be high. Records are taken of air quality inside a van at peak commuter times on three different routes with different road layouts (e.g. dual carriageways, residential streets, one-way systems and roads with bus lanes). The findings confirm that road specific parameters are very important in affecting drivers' exposure to pollutants. In particular, layouts that lead to queuing traffic are a real problem. This research is an important contribution to the sustainable transport debate as it raises issues of equity. It confirms that drivers, and presumably other road users and urban residents, are exposed to pollutants with harmful effects, and that highway planning can have an impact on levels of pollutants. This is a health and equity issue for drivers where no transport options other than using their car exist: but is also relevant for cyclists and pedestrians who have little choice other than to experience exposure to pollutants.

Part C: Sustainable Transport Policies and their Implementation

The final part of the book concentrates on planning policies to facilitate sustainable mobility and their operation. It starts with a chapter by Nicholas Low which presents research addressing sustainable transport policy and planning inertia in Australia. Low's argument is that not only is it crucial to understand what sustainable transport development is, but it is also important to understand what stops it being implemented. He takes a look at barriers related to discourse and institutions that lead to a 'knot of story-lines' among transport professionals which, he asserts, are continuously reinforced at the expense of sustainable transport development. Low points out the importance of the institutional context in Australia, which has seen a vast imbalance in federal expenditure in favour of roads over urban public transport. This has resulted in real environmental concerns in Australia, and a likely 67 per cent increase in emissions in the transport sector above 1990 levels by 2010.

The bulk of the chapter concentrates on 'discursive barriers'. The analysis is derived from research on transport policy literature produced in Sydney and Melbourne since the early 1960s. The researchers drew out dominant arguments from the perspective of engineers, economists and town planners to gain an understanding of how transport problems and solutions have been framed. They found that the engineers favoured the 'predict and provide' ethos, based on modelling trends and providing transport systems to fit these trends. They were also consistent in their quest for 'free-movement' of traffic, 'integrated' or 'balanced' transport, and the need for further road building. The economists 'story-line' was very much related to market economies and to individual freedoms. The car is seen as the enabler of mobility: 'travel as opportunity'. It is also related to economic prosperity. But Low points out that a result of this is that anyone who opposes road building is seen as opposing freedom, self-expression and economic growth. Planners were found to base their policy actions on three intertwined 'story-lines': that low density development can only be served efficiently by road transport; that people should not be disadvantaged because of where they live (locational equity); and that there should be a balance between mobility and amenity.

Low questions where these dominant story-lines leave prospects for sustainable transport policies. He observes that, more recently, the language of sustainability has been adopted in Australian planning policy, but that it has not yet penetrated the transport establishment. There is still also both implicit and explicit stigmatisation of opposition to road building, and the road construction industry and road service organisations continue to have considerable power. Low concludes that a better understanding of institutions, discourses and the dynamics of human society are required if real progress is to be made.

In the penultimate chapter, Carey Curtis reports on good practice in developing and implementing sustainable traffic management guidelines in Western Australian. She starts by acknowledging that even though policies for sustainable transport have been in place for some time, achieving better integrated land use planning and transport exposes tensions between the professionals involved and their traditional ideologies. In particular, the dominant road safety objectives of traffic management, car-centric engineering standards of street layouts, and conventional designs of intersection controls can be a challenge to those seeking more sustainable solutions.

Curtis focuses on the need for co-ordination of agencies and services and a better understanding of different professionals' objectives in devising and implementing better practice, which she suggests should be a total package of measures rather than fragmented solutions. As she explains, the old ways of working have led to functionally separated land uses, and residential areas developed with little or no consideration of pedestrians or other non-car users.

The chapter presents the work carried out for the Western Australian Government on the development of new traffic management guidelines aimed at creating liveable streets. It explains how these guidelines differ from 'conventional' traffic management practice in Australia, and examines the development of the new approach which focuses on the creation of 'liveable neighbourhoods'. Curtis concludes that a move from the conventional approach to a new approach focusing on inter-connected and permeable street networks, and appropriate traffic and access functions, land uses and intersection controls, allows for the creation of active and liveable streets and neighbourhoods. Whilst it is too early to test the effectiveness of the guidelines described, Curtis cites evidence from schemes built to similar principles elsewhere as good indications for success. She also stresses the importance of multi-disciplinary working in moving towards more sustainable transport solutions.

Finally, Rocky Piro concludes the book with an overview of the processes and thinking behind integrating land use policies in regional transport planning in the central Puget Sound Region of Washington State, USA. Piro explains how an innovative approach used traditional urban transport modelling, but incorporated land use and growth management policy in the most recent update of the Metropolitan Transport Plan. The benefits at both regional and local levels of linking land use policy with regional transport planning are discussed.

In common with other contributors to the book, Piro emphasises the importance of wide stakeholder involvement in the development of the plans, and in the analysis of plan options and alternatives. Perhaps the most significant aspect of the Plan, however, is its prescription for spatial development. It sets out a policy to develop urban centres in the Region (in all 21 locations were officially designated as such centres). These areas are to be the focus for future regional growth in compact communities that serve as the urban framework for developing a multi-modal transport network. This 'centres-based' approach is pioneering in the USA, and early evidence suggests that the regional plan is being favourably received locally.

Emerging Themes

So, what can be learnt from reading these chapters? It does not seem appropriate to try to develop general conclusions from such a diverse range of contributions, but it is useful to try to draw out some emerging themes with a view to identifying common messages and guidance for further research and practice. The following general observations can be made:

- First, there is a need to know more about the interaction of urban form (for example density, size, topography, and road layouts) and socio-economic and cultural variables (for example household types, income levels, attitudes to travel behaviour). Several authors stressed that urban form has uneven impacts on different sectors of society. For example, households comprising older people with low incomes may be highly affected by the form and facilities in their local neighbourhood, whereas more wealthy, single person households may be far less constrained. This varying impact has not been adequately researched or addressed in policy.

- The importance of broad socio-cultural trends, such as increased leisure time, changing lifestyles, variable wealth patterns and an ageing society, also need to be fully understood when devising future strategies for spatial planning to reduce travel demand.

- Following these first two points, it may be time for a more detailed exploration of planning solutions targeting particular sectors of the population. If the impacts of urban form fall differently on different population sectors then perhaps the common 'planning for all' approach needs reviewing. Many of the authors suggest that there is a need to move away from planning based on simplistic relationships between form and travel behaviour, to a more complex approach reflecting the increasingly diverse nature of society.

- More attention needs to be paid to the incorporation of 'time' as a variable in urban form and travel research. There is a need to consider both how land uses and behaviour adapt, but also to acknowledge how long it may take for benefits of spatial planning to be seen. Several authors address how travel patterns are adapted in different urban locations over time. The question of how people modify their behaviour, whether travelling on certain days of the week, peak and off-peak times, or over longer time periods is under-researched.

- Many of the authors refer to conflicts or trade-offs between sustainable mobility and other sustainability aims. In many instances what is beneficial for fuel efficient mobility or socially equitable travel may be at odds with other urban sustainability objectives. For example, for older people there are environmental and social sustainability conflicts with respect to maintaining mobility. To stay active and involved in society the only viable option may be to use a car, however in terms of environmental impacts this is not desirable. Currently there is little clarity on how to deal with these sorts of trade-offs.

- There is a need for practical advances in sustainable transport policy and implementation. Currently there is a lack of monitoring of the effectiveness of policies, and there are few detailed investigations into what works and what does not. There is undoubtedly a role for spatial planning in delivering sustainable urban transport, but currently information about what planners should do is not clear. Practitioners are often faced with inconclusive and conflicting research findings and with making difficult decisions about trade-offs.

- In terms of planning practice, more inter-disciplinary working is required. If integrated solutions to unsustainable mobility patterns are to be implemented then new coalitions are required that deal simultaneously with physical planning and design and transport management. Action needs to be taken to close the wide gulf between professionals such as transport planners, highway engineers, urban designers and housing officers, as well as employers, facilities managers and end users. This is both a technical and professional challenge.

These observations demonstrate that there is still far more to learn about the effects of urban form on sustainable mobility and the role of spatial planning in that relationship. By presenting the chapters that follow, the aim of this book is to advance understanding of this complex issue.

References

Breheny, M. (1992) *Sustainable Development and Urban Form*, Pion Ltd, London.

Breheny, M. (1995) 'Compact Cities and Transport Energy Consumption', *Transactions of the Institute of British Geographers*, vol. 20(1), pp. 81-101.

Breheny, M. (2004) 'Sustainable Settlement and the Jobs-Housing Balance', in C. H. Bae and H. Richardson (eds) *Urban Sprawl in Western Europe and the United States*, Ashgate, Aldershot.

De Roo, G. and Miller, D. (2000) *Compact Cities and Sustainable Urban Development: A Critical Assessment of Policies and Plans from an International Perspective*, Ashgate, Aldershot.

Docherty, I. and Shaw, I. (2003) *A New Deal for Transport? The UK's Struggle with the Sustainable Transport Agenda*, Blackwell Publishing, Oxford.

Feitelson, E. and Verhoef, E. (2001) *Transport and Environment: In Search of Sustainable Solutions*, Edward Elgar Publishing Ltd, London.

Headicar, P. (2000) 'The Exploding City Region: Should it, Can it, be Reversed?', in K. Williams, M. Jenks and E. Burton (eds) *Achieving Sustainable Urban Form*, E and F N. Spon, London.

Newman, P. and Kenworthy, J (2000) 'Sustainable Urban Form: The Big Picture', in K. Williams, M. Jenks and E. Burton (eds) *Achieving Sustainable Urban Form*, E and F N Spon, London.

OECD (Organisation for Economic Co-operation and Development) (2002) *Policy Instruments for Achieving Sustainable Transport*, OECD, http://www.oecd.org.

Richardson, B. (1999) 'Towards a Policy on a Sustainable Transportation System', *Transportation Research Record*, vol. 1670, pp. 27-34.

Rickaby, P. (1987) 'Six Settlement Patterns Compared', *Environment and Planning B*, vol. 14, pp. 193-223.

Transportation Research Board (1999) *Toward a Sustainable Future: Addressing the Long-term Effects of Motor Vehicle Transportation on Climate and Ecology*, National Academy Press, http://www.trb.org.

VTPI (Victoria Transport Policy Institute) (2004) *Sustainable Transportation and Travel Demand Management: Planning that Balances Economic, Social and Ecological Objectives*, http://www.vtpi.org/tdm/tdm67.

Williams, K., Jenks, M. and Burton, E. (2000) *Achieving Sustainable Urban Form*, E and F N Spon, London.

World Commission on Environment and Development (1987) *Our Common Future*, Oxford University Press, Oxford.

WRI (World Resources Institute) (2004) *Sustainable Cities, Sustainable Transportation*, http://www.earthtrends.wri.org/features.

Part A:
The Impact of Urban Form in Combination with Other Factors on Sustainable Transport

Chapter 2

The Relationship between Land Use and Travel Patterns: Variations by Household Type

Tim Schwanen, Martin Dijst and Frans M. Dieleman

Introduction

Transport researchers have traditionally considered the relationships between urban structure and travel patterns at the aggregate level. During the 1960s, they recognised, however, that for a better understanding of such relationships it is necessary to consider the travel behaviour of individuals (Chapin and Hightower, 1965). Since then numerous studies employing disaggregated data at the individual or household level have been undertaken in which the influence on travel behaviour of characteristics of the built environment is modelled alongside a range of other determinants, mostly socio-demographic variables, such as gender, employment status and income.

While most studies in this field have suggested that urban form affects individual travel patterns, a consensus seems to have developed that socio-demographics are more important for the explanation of travel behaviour (Stead, 2001). Because of this, and the fact that households with a given socio-demographic profile are not distributed uniformly across urban space, it has become standard practice to include socio-demographics as control variables in studies investigating the impact of urban form on travel behaviour. Although this approach is superior to not considering socio-demographic variables at all, we believe that the empirical analysis of the impact of urban form on travel patterns can be taken one step further by taking account of the interactions of urban form and socio-demographic characteristics. This is partly because constraints imposed by the physical environment can be compensated for, or reinforced by, personal conditions. For instance, individuals with limited time budgets who lack access to a car are at least in theory more dependent on their direct residential environment than those with more time or access to a car.

Few empirical studies have investigated the extent to which the impact of urban form on individual travel patterns varies across household types. Exceptions include the work of Herz (1982) and Snellen (2001), who have shown that built environment characteristics are not equally important for different population sectors. The same conclusion can be drawn from studies in the domains of gender, racial and ethnic differences in commuting patterns (McLafferty and Preston, 1997; Wyly, 1998) and space-time accessibility modelling (Dijst *et al.*, 2002; Kwan, 2000). While providing valuable insights, the empirical evidence in these studies is either restricted to specific dimensions of travel behaviour (McLafferty and Preston, 1997; Wyly, 1998), is based on empirical data from only one or a limited number of urban areas (Dijst *et al.*, 2002; Kwan, 2000; Snellen, 2001), or is rather dated (Herz, 1982).

In this chapter we therefore address the following question: Does the direction and/or magnitude of the influence of urban form on travel vary across *different* household types? If the answer is 'yes', we can suggest the existence of interaction effects in the impact of urban form. If, on the other hand, the analysis shows no differences in the impact of urban form, this suggests that household types display similar responses to urban form, irrespective of their personal situation. In particular, we investigate differences in the effect of urban form, or residential context, on trip frequency and travel time across six household types: single workers, two- and one-worker couples, two- and one-worker families and senior households. The analysis of travel time is segmented by trip purpose: we differentiate between commuting times, 'maintenance' times (e.g. trips running household errands, moving goods, shopping, giving lifts to people etc.) and leisure travel times, for several reasons. First, this broader perspective permits us to obtain better insights into the impact of urban form on travel patterns than a focus on commuting alone. Second, the number of both maintenance and leisure trips is larger than that of commuting trips in the Netherlands (Schwanen *et al.*, 2001a). The data used for this analysis is derived from a nationally representative sample of the Dutch population, and stems from the 2001 Netherlands National Travel Survey.

The remainder of this chapter starts with the hypotheses underlying the empirical analysis. This is followed by two sections presenting the operationalisation of concepts and the data respectively. We then turn to a description of the distribution of household types and residential contexts, followed by the results for trip frequency and travel time. The chapter ends with a summary and discussion of the results.

Study Background and Hypotheses

The starting point for this study is that a household's longer-term residential location choice is not only related to considerations about the quality of the neighbourhood and social status of the community, but also about activities outside the home and travel. This idea has long been articulated in urban geography and urban economics literature. For instance, the household trade-off between dwelling space and commuting costs lies at the very heart of the monocentric model (Alonso, 1964), and remains important in its contemporary modifications (Clark, 2000). In addition, empirical research about residential location decision making commonly conceptualises residential location choice as a trade-off of housing characteristics, neighbourhood characteristics and accessibility considerations (Van de Vijvere *et al.*, 1998; Weisbrod *et al.*, 1980). This implies that households, *ceteris paribus*, choose a location that maximises access to relevant spatial opportunities. Various studies have produced evidence of such access maximising behaviour, see for example Bhat and

Guo (2004) for the case of shopping opportunities. Because residential preferences vary across household types (Clark and Dieleman 1996; Champion, 2001), we may expect the relative importance of specific accessibility considerations to differ by households type. Access to high-quality primary schools will be most relevant to households with young children. In contrast, small households, and especially one-person households, are attracted to city neighbourhoods, because these are close to urban leisure facilities such as cinemas and restaurants, where they can meet and interact with friends and other people (Brun and Fagnani, 1994).

Such differences in accessibility considerations may not only result in an uneven distribution of household types within urban areas, they may also affect the travel patterns of individuals belonging to the same household type, but residing in different parts of those areas, and hence to differences in the impact of urban form across household types. For example, a worker without a partner living in a suburban, lower-density environment may visit urban facilities, such as cinemas or theatres and restaurants, less frequently than a counterpart living in an urban neighbourhood. This expectation is based on prior empirical studies, which have shown accessibility to a given set of opportunities to be positively correlated with trip frequency (see Handy, 1996 and Meurs and Haaijer, 2001 for shopping travel and Schwanen and Mokhtarian, 2003 for trips for dining and other leisure purposes). Empirical evidence is equivocal, however, because various authors have found (virtually) no effects of built environment characteristics on trip frequency (Hanson and Schwab, 1987; Sun *et al.*, 1998). None of these studies has, however, considered differences in the impact of built environment factors on trip frequency *across* households types.

The amount of effort required to access destinations (travel distance or time) may also vary across households of the same type in different residential settings. Given that the suburban one-person households in the previous example have chosen to visit urban leisure facilities, they have to travel longer and may select a different transport mode than urban residents. Numerous studies have shown that travel distance tends to be higher among suburban residents (see Dieleman *et al.* 2002 for a review). For travel time, this relationship is less clear-cut because lower travel speeds, which are a result of the wider use of public transport, and more walking and cycling, combined with congestion and parking problems, may offset the impact of shorter distances in cities (Levinson and Kumar, 1997). Nevertheless, we *a priori* expect one-person households living in the suburbs to spend more time on travelling to leisure facilities than their urban counterparts.

Although we have so far concentrated the discussion on one-person households, we can formulate hypotheses for several household types. For two-worker couples we expect largely similar results as for one-person households, because these are also known for their above-average preference for urban living (Brun and Fagnani, 1994). Travel times are thus hypothesised to be lower, and trip frequency higher, in large cities than in suburban or low-density areas. At the other end of the continuum we find household types with a strong preference for suburban or low-density living; these are households with young children. For them, we expect inverse relationships: travel times will be shorter, and trip frequencies higher in low-density or suburban settings.

Research Design

Household Types

To classify households we have chosen a series of criteria associated with households' time budgets: the number of adults in the households; the number of employed adults; and the presence of children younger than twelve. The following household types have been defined:

- Single worker: an adult aged 30 or over living without a partner who is formally employed; he/she does not live with any children.
- Two-worker couple: a household consisting of two partners without any children or other dependants living with them; both partners are aged 30 or over and are formally employed.
- One-worker couple: a household consisting of two partners without any children or other dependants living with them; both partners are aged 30 or over but only one is formally employed.
- Two-worker family: a household consisting of two partners with at least one child younger than twelve living with them; both partners are aged 30 or over and are formally employed.
- One-worker family: a household consisting of two partners with at least one child younger than twelve living with them; both partners are aged 30 or over but only one is formally employed.
- Retired household: a single adult aged 55 or over and retired from the labour force, or two adults each aged 55 or over and no longer formally employed.

While time availability is the overriding motivation behind the classification, we also concentrate on these groups because they will remain or become important in the future. At least in the Netherlands, the trends of the ageing of the population, the decrease of the average household size, and the rise in the number of people who combine paid employment with household maintenance will continue during the coming decades. The minimum age of 30 years is used because younger individuals and households are often still 'settling down': they frequently hold temporary jobs and/or have not yet made stable commitments regarding co-habitation or marriage. This is exemplified, for instance, by the fact that starters in the housing market are responsible for a large share of all residential moves; the propensity to relocate declines rapidly after the age of 35 (Clark and Dieleman, 1996).

Residential Setting

Urban form or residential context is operationalised in this study through a categorisation of municipalities in the Netherlands. It combines several interdependent dimensions related to the spatial configuration of land uses and infrastructure, thus capturing possible synergies among the following factors: density; land-use mix; distance to the urban centre; the mono/polycentric orientation of an urban area; and city size. The classification is based on two criteria: the location of a municipality within or outside the Randstad (the economic and cultural heartland of the Netherlands located in the western, heavily urbanised part of the Netherlands); and its level of urbanisation. Within the Randstad we distinguish the *three major cities* (Amsterdam, Rotterdam, The Hague), the *medium-sized cities*, and *suburbs*. A fourth category is the *growth centres*. These are the Dutch equivalent of the English New Towns. These new communities were expressly designed in the 1970s and 1980s to attract suburbanising households and firms. Outside the Randstad, municipalities are split into *more urbanised* and *less urbanised*.

Data

The data employed for this study stems from the 2001 Netherlands National Travel Study (NTS). Implemented in 1978, this is a continuous survey into the travel behaviour of Dutch households. Since 1995, data has been available for 70,000 households, or 130,000 persons, annually. Every month a random sample of households living independently (that is, excluding nursing homes, children's homes, etc.) is drawn from the Municipal Basic Administration (GBA in Dutch). All members of a selected household over the age of six are requested to complete a travel diary for a single day, in which they have to report the purpose, transport mode, distance, starting and ending time, and origin and destination location of all their trips. Households are allocated a specific day to ensure that all days of the week and months of the year are represented in the final data set. In addition to the travel diary, respondents are asked to fill out several surveys, including one on socio-demographic variables, one on trips undertaken by public transport and one on trips undertaken by children below the age of six (Statistics Netherlands, 2002).

From the 2001 data we have only selected individuals who belong to one of the six household types introduced previously and whose daily travel and activity pattern starts and ends at their home location. Further, only data of male and female heads of households are used; grown-up children are excluded from the analysis to enable sound comparisons between households in different residential settings. Moreover, for each of the dependent variables, travellers with the 0.5 per cent highest values were excluded from the empirical analysis to reduce the influence of out-liers on the final results. The value of 0.5 per cent was arbitrarily chosen. It can be considered a compromise of minimising the impact of extreme values and including as many individual cases as possible in the analysis (to prevent any selectivity bias in the outcomes).

The data collected from the travel diaries has been used to construct the following dependent variables for each individual:

- Total daily number of trips;
- Daily number of non-work trips, excluding the mandatory trip purposes of commuting, work-related and education;
- Daily travel time for commuting trips;

- Daily travel time for maintenance trips, i.e. trips for shopping, giving lifts to passengers, moving goods and doing personal business; and
- Daily travel time for leisure trips, i.e. trips for social visits, sports or hobbies, entertainment or recreation.

Spatial Distribution of Household Types

As an introduction to the analysis of travel behaviour, we start with a brief overview of the distribution of the household types over the six types of municipalities (Table 2.1). In line with our expectations, single workers exhibit the strongest orientation towards city living. Comparing across household types, we find that they form the highest shares in the large and medium-sized cities within the Randstad and the more urbanised municipalities outside the Randstad. At the other end of the spectrum, the family households are the most suburban and rural oriented. This is even more so for one-worker than two-worker families. These results are also consistent with the existing literature on residential location choice (Brun and Fagnani, 1994; Champion, 2001). The two- and one-worker couples and retired households occupy the middle ground between these extremes. Two-worker couples are more concentrated in the Randstad than one-worker couples and households consisting of seniors.

Table 2.1 Distribution of household types across residential settings (per cent)

	Single worker	Two-worker couple	One-worker couple	Two-worker family	One-worker family	Retired household
R[a] 3 big cities	22.2	10.7	9.6	8.5	5.6	11.3
R medium-sized cities	11.3	8.1	7.0	8.4	5.9	7.8
R suburbs	14.7	20.2	19.6	20.0	22.0	18.6
R growth centers	5.4	7.1	5.6	7.8	6.5	4.9
Rest NL more urbanised	31.4	28.9	30.7	27.5	28.2	31.1
Rest NL less urbanised	14.9	25.0	27.5	27.8	31.7	26.4

[a] Randstad
NL = Netherlands

Trip Frequency

Having established that differences exist in the distribution of household types across residential settings, we now proceed with analysing the extent to which the relationship between trip frequency and residential setting varies among household types. Table 2.2 summarises the results for the daily number of trips per person. For the two family groups and the retired, the average daily trip frequency varies

Table 2.2   Daily number of trips per person, by household type and residential context

	Single worker		Two-worker couple		One-worker couple		Two-worker family		One-worker family		Retired household	
	Mean	S.D.	Mean	S.D.	Mean	S.D.	Mean	S.D.	Mean	S.D.	Mean	S.D.
R three big cities	3.42	2.05	3.13	2.04	3.02	2.26	3.68	2.28	3.55	2.61	2.15	2.10
R medium cities	3.45	2.04	3.17	2.10	3.01	2.29	3.89	2.47	3.32	2.48	2.29	2.19
R suburbs	3.49	2.31	3.09	2.06	3.10	2.39	3.80	2.47	3.86	2.66	2.39	2.24
R growth centres	3.27	1.96	3.04	2.09	2.86	1.99	3.79	2.52	3.82	2.77	2.18	2.06
Rest NL more urbanised	3.56	2.20	3.29	2.24	2.87	2.22	3.92	2.50	3.77	2.67	2.24	2.18
Rest NL less urbanised	3.36	2.31	3.17	2.17	2.90	2.23	3.71	2.51	3.67	2.63	2.18	2.15
ANOVA (F-ratio)	1.4		2.1		2.1		2.3[a]		3.5[b]		5.4[b]	

[a] Statistically significant at $\alpha = 0.05$
[b] Statistically significant at $\alpha = 0.01$

statistically significantly among residential settings, although these variations do not show a particular character (Table 2.2). While this might suggest that built-environment characteristics are not true determinants of trip frequency, it may also imply that the relationships between urban form and trip frequency are not as straightforward as hypothesised. Ranking residential settings from high to low in terms of the total number of trips per person, per day, for the one- and two-worker families and elderly, we notice considerable differences across household types. A common finding is that the three big cities have low scores for these household types. This does not mean that living in a city is always associated with a lower trip frequency for these households; the mean is high for the medium-sized cities in the western part of the country and the more urbanised municipalities outside the Randstad (with the exception of one-worker families in the medium-sized cities).

For three of the population sectors (the single workers and the one- and two-worker couples) ANOVAs (Analysis of Variance between groups) indicate that the differences between residential settings in the daily trip frequency are not statistically significant (at the 5 per cent level). Post-hoc Bonferroni tests indicate that none of the pair-wise differences between residential settings are statistically significant for these households.

To gain further insights into the relationship between trip-making propensity and residential setting, we have also analysed the number of non-work trips (that is, excluding the mandatory trip purposes of commuting, work-related and education) per residential setting for each of the six population sectors (Table 2.3). By leaving out the activity types which are least flexible in space and time, we may be better able to capture any influence of urban form on trip frequency. Only for the one-worker couples and retired households do we find statistically significant variations across residential contexts. Because these household types appear to be least affected by time pressure, the number of trips by individuals in these groups may be more sensitive to differences in urban context. In particular, a suburban environment in the Randstad appears to stimulate the trip-making propensity for non-work purposes for these groups. On the other hand, the average frequency is rather low in the growth centres and the more and least urbanised municipalities outside the Randstad. The number of non-work trips is also low among elderly households in the three big cities. An explanation for this last result might be that car availability and ownership tend to be lower in urban areas. Elsewhere, we have argued that car ownership is an important condition for remaining mobile among older seniors (Schwanen *et al.*, 2001b). Perhaps the lower car ownership rate among elderly people in the large cities means they make few non-work trips. In short, while we do find statistically significant differences in the number of non-work trips by residential context for some household types, the results do not support our hypotheses that trip frequency varies statistically significantly between urban and suburban environments, and that the direction of this difference depends on household type.

Table 2.3 Daily number of non-work trips[a] per person, by household type and residential context

	Single worker		Two-worker couple		One-worker couple		Two-worker family		One-worker family		Retired household	
	Mean	S.D.	Mean	S.D.	Mean	S.D.	Mean	S.D.	Mean	S.D.	Mean	S.D.
R three big cities	2.12	2.08	1.76	2.05	2.29	2.32	2.64	2.43	2.63	2.72	2.11	2.08
R medium cities	2.05	2.04	1.83	2.03	2.30	2.31	2.78	2.51	2.60	2.55	2.24	2.16
R suburbs	2.06	2.34	1.81	2.09	2.36	2.40	2.64	2.55	2.95	2.84	2.30	2.20
R growth centres	1.83	2.04	1.80	2.04	2.18	2.04	2.69	2.61	2.95	2.95	2.12	2.04
Rest NL more urbanised	2.15	2.20	1.93	2.15	2.10	2.16	2.76	2.58	2.92	2.79	2.17	2.15
Rest NL less urbanised	1.89	2.15	1.86	2.12	2.08	2.19	2.62	2.56	2.81	2.74	2.12	2.12
ANOVA (F-ratio)	2.0		1.1		3.5[b]		1.0		2.0		5.0[b]	

[a] Non-work trips include all trip purposes except commuting, work-related and education
[b] Statistically significant at $\alpha = 0.01$

Travel Time

For each of the trip purposes considered (commuting, maintenance and leisure), we start by comparing mean travel times and testing whether observed differences are statistically significant. Because variations around the average values are generally large, we also pay detailed attention to the travel time distributions through the estimation of 'survival' functions: a technique specifically developed for the exploratory analysis of duration processes and adopted quite frequently in travel demand analysis (Bhat, 2000).

A survival function gives the proportion of individuals spending an equal amount (or more) time on travelling, than a specified time (t). It can be used to calculate the cumulative probability of surviving beyond the jth time, t: where n_j is the number of individuals still travelling at time t_j, and q_j is the total number of travellers who end travelling at t_j.

$$\hat{S}(t_k) = \prod_{j=1}^{k} \frac{n_j - q_j}{n_j}$$

Graphically, a survival curve appears as a step with a drop at each discrete time (t_j) a person stops travelling. Because individuals filling out a travel diary tend to round off travel times to five- or even ten-minute intervals, we have grouped travel times in five-minute intervals: $t_1 = 2.5$, $t_2 = 7.5$, $t_3 = 12.5$ and so on. Beyond a certain t_j, observations are grouped together in a single class, because otherwise their number becomes too low for reliable analysis. These cut-off points have been set arbitrarily at 147.5 minutes for commuting; 117.5 for maintenance; and 197.5 for leisure. For each of the three trip purposes, and all household types, we have calculated cumulative survival probabilities for travellers in all residential settings, and tested whether the pair-wise differences between each combination of two residential settings are statistically significant (using Wilcoxon tests).

Commuting

Comparing average commuting times per residential setting, we find statistically significant differences *within* all five population sectors examined (Table 2.4). (retired households are left out of this analysis). Differences *across* the five sectors seem to be minor. However, the lowest average travel times can consistently be found in the more and less urbanised municipalities outside the Randstad, whereas the highest value is always associated with the growth centres in the Randstad. Moreover, for all household types, the differences between the residential settings with the highest and lowest mean are large. Dividing the highest by the lowest average, for each household category, yields ratios in the range 1.27-1.37, which indicates that the maximum difference in average commuting times between residential sectors within a household type is between 27 and 37 per cent. When we repeat this calculation, but compare household types within a single residential

Table 2.4 Daily commuting time per person, by household type and residential context[a]

	Single worker		Two-worker couple		One-worker couple		Two-worker family		One-worker family	
	Mean	S.D.	Mean	S.D.	Mean	S.D.	Mean	S.D.	Mean	S.D.
R three big cities	54.1	35.7	50.6	32.0	52.0	32.9	50.6	32.4	53.5	32.7
R medium cities	52.0	36.4	57.1	37.3	55.2	37.5	49.6	37.1	52.2	36.3
R suburbs	48.3	31.0	53.7	36.3	50.4	33.2	45.3	32.8	50.1	34.4
R growth centres	55.5	33.8	59.1	36.4	59.6	40.6	53.5	37.0	58.9	35.9
Rest NL more urbanised	42.0	30.8	44.2	31.5	43.7	29.1	39.5	29.0	46.2	31.3
Rest NL less urbanised	43.0	31.8	44.2	30.3	46.2	31.7	42.0	30.9	43.3	30.0
ANOVA (F-ratio)	13.1[b]		21.8[b]		6.8[b]		15.3[b]		8.2[b]	

[a] Only travellers making at least one commuting trip are considered
[b] Statistically significant at $\alpha = 0.01$

setting, we find ratios in the range of 1.07-1.18. This suggests that differences in average commuting time between residential settings are larger than those between population sectors.

To gain further insights in the differences between and within household types we have estimated cumulative survival functions. Figure 2.1 depicts survival curves for single workers (A) and two-worker families (B). Regarding the former category, Figure 2.1 shows that until t_{13} (62.5 minutes) the curves of the growth centres, and to a lesser degree the three big cities in the Randstad, clearly lie above the other lines. This means that single workers commuting up to 62.5 minutes per day are under-represented in these residential settings. Further, we notice that between t_7 and t_{20} (or 32.5 and 97.5 minutes) the curves for the more and less urbanised municipalities outside the Randstad clearly lie below those for the Randstad areas. These results suggest that single workers outside the Randstad tend to commute less than their counterparts in the Western Netherlands. The fact that the curve for the Randstad suburbs drops below those for the growth centres and big and medium-sized cities in the Randstad in Figure 2.1 (A) indicates that differences exist between residential settings within this part of the Netherlands. Reasons for the relative absence of long commutes in the suburbs appear to be the lower inclination to travel by public transport in general, and by train in particular, as well as the less severe parking problems and congestion on the local road network (Dieleman *et al.*, 2002; Schwanen *et al.*, 2002).

The graph for the two-worker families, Figure 2.1 (B) differs in various respects from that for the single workers. First of all, the lines tend to decline more steeply in the range between t_{10} and t_{20}, indicating that fewer members of two-worker families commute between 47.5 and 97.5 minutes per day (the averages in Table 2.4 are also consistent with this conclusion). This finding should not be surprising given that women in two-worker families tend to have shorter commutes than single females, because the former often have to combine commuting, frequently to a part-time job, with household and childcare duties (Turner and Niemeier, 1997). Second, the variation between residential settings is larger for two-worker families than for single workers. Third, patterns of over- and under-representation of commuting durations per residential setting differ markedly between the two population sectors. From t_6 (22.5 minutes) onwards the curve for the Randstad suburbs lies below the others; the same is true for the line for the less urbanised municipalities outside the Randstad beyond t_8 (32.5 minutes). Because these two area types are characterised by the lowest residential densities, we may conclude that the inverse relationship between density and car commuting time found to be valid for the general population of commuters (Schwanen *et al.*, 2003) seems transferable to the commuting times of the subgroup of two-worker households. In contrast, cumulative survival probabilities are high until t_{10} for the three big cities, which means that individuals from two-worker families residing there tend to have longer commutes. The cumulative survival plots further reveal that the conditional probability of staying in the commuter group is rather high for workers from the growth centres and medium-sized cities in the Randstad beyond t_{10} and t_{14}, respectively. In other words, there is an over-representation of persons from two-worker families commuting extensively in these two municipalities (see also Table 2.4).

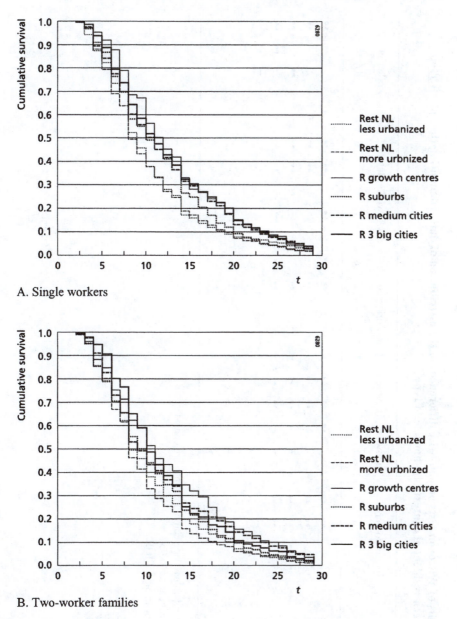

A. Single workers

B. Two-worker families

Figure 2.1   Survival curves for daily commute time per person, by residential context

Table 2.5 **Results of Wilcoxon tests on pair-wise differences in the distribution of daily commuting time per person between residential contexts, by household type[a]**

	Single worker					Two-worker couple					One-worker couple					Two-worker family					One-worker family				
	2	3	4	5	6	2	3	4	5	6	2	3	4	5	6	2	3	4	5	6	2	3	4	5	6
1 R three big cities	–	–	–	••	••	–	••	••	••	••	–	–	–	••	••	–	••	••	••	••	–	–	–	•	••
2 R medium cities		–	–	••	••		–	–	••	••		–	–	••	••		–	–	••	••		–	–	–	••
3 R suburbs			•	••	••			–	••	••			–	••	••			–	••	••			•	–	••
4 R growth centres				••	••				••	••				–	••				••	••				–	••
5 Rest NL more urbanised					–					–					–					–					–
6 Rest NL less urbanised																									

[a] Only travellers making at least one commuting trip are considered

• Statistically significant at α = 0.05

•• Statistically significant at α = 0.01

Table 2.6   Daily travel time for maintenance trips per person, by household type and residential context[a]

	Single worker		Two-worker couple		One-worker couple		Two-worker family		One-worker family		Retired household	
	Mean	S.D.	Mean	S.D.	Mean	S.D.	Mean	S.D.	Mean	S.D.	Mean	S.D.
R three big cities	32.2	27.8	35.6	27.9	38.6	29.5	36.4	26.4	38.5	26.8	37.8	27.7
R medium cities	31.4	26.0	31.0	25.4	31.0	25.1	34.8	26.8	35.0	28.2	35.3	25.2
R suburbs	29.7	25.0	32.4	27.3	33.4	26.7	33.6	26.0	35.2	26.4	32.7	26.0
R growth centres	33.4	30.8	35.6	29.0	40.5	30.4	34.4	26.7	36.5	23.8	34.1	25.8
Rest NL more urbanised	27.8	23.6	30.2	23.5	31.2	24.5	33.5	25.5	35.1	26.0	33.4	25.3
Rest NL less urbanised	26.2	22.5	32.9	27.3	32.2	26.3	29.7	24.2	32.8	25.5	31.5	25.1
ANOVA (*F*-ratio)	3.0[b]		2.6[b]		5.9[c]		5.9[c]		2.3[b]		10.7[c]	

[a] Only travellers making at least one maintenance trip are considered
[b] statistically significant at $\alpha = 0.05$
[c] statistically significant at $\alpha = 0.01$

With Wilcoxon tests we have tested whether the pair-wise differences in the distributions of daily commuting times are statistically significant (Table 2.5). The results clearly illustrate that the distinction between the Randstad and the rest of the Netherlands prevails: for the single workers and those from two-worker couples and families all pair-wise differences concerned are statistically significantly different at the 1 per cent level. Differences between the more and less urbanised municipalities outside the Randstad are not statistically significant at the 5 per cent level for any of the population sectors considered. In addition, only 6 out of 30 of the pair-wise differences *within* the Randstad are statistically significant. These patterns hold more or less for all five household types.

With respect to our hypotheses, the analysis suggests that the role of the residential context in determining commuting times does not differ much across household types. For all groups, commuting times tend to be highest in the growth centres, followed by the cities in the Randstad. Yet, commuting trips comprise a mere one-fifth of all trips in the Netherlands and are outnumbered by the number of shopping and leisure trips (Schwanen *et al.*, 2001a). We will therefore also consider travel times for maintenance and leisure activities.

Maintenance Travel

As for commuting, all of the ANOVAs for the average travel time for 'maintenance' yield statistically significant results (Table 2.6). Yet, the differences between the Randstad and the rest of the Netherlands are less pervasive than in the case of commuting. The maximum variation between residential settings is also smaller. Ratios of the highest and lowest average per household type fall between 1.18 for the one-worker families and 1.28 for the single workers, suggesting that the spatial variation in mean maintenance travel times varies between 18 per cent and 28 per cent. The maximum variation between household types in a single residential context falls in a comparable range (14-27 per cent). Thus, the variation between residential settings in average travel time for maintenance activities is no larger than that between household types.

Ranking residential settings from the highest to the lowest average travel time yields considerable differences between household types. For the one- and two-worker families and retired households the average travel time tends to increase with the level of urbanisation. The growth centres and the big cities in the Randstad are associated with the highest mean values for the one- and two-person households.

Given the large variation around the mean values, we have again considered travel time distributions. Those for one-worker couples and retired households are depicted in Figure 2.2. Consistent with Table 2.6, the cumulative survival curves for the three big cities and the growth centres lie above those for the other residential settings, indicating that travel times tend to be longer for residents of these two municipality types. Differences between the other four residential settings are limited.

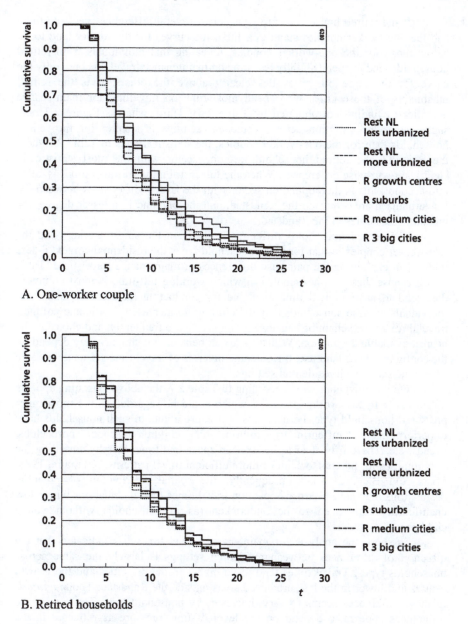

A. One-worker couple

B. Retired households

Figure 2.2   Survival curves for daily travel time for maintenance trips per person, by residential context

If the retired households are considered, several differences between them and the one-worker couples stand out. First, the curves for the former tend to lie below those for the one-worker couples, revealing that individuals from retired households tend to spend slightly less time on maintenance travel. Second, only the curve for the three big cities lies clearly above the others; it is the retired inhabitants of those cities who spend most time on travelling for maintenance activities (a finding corroborated by Table 2.6). Third, whereas Figure 2.2 may suggest that the variation across residential settings is smaller for the retired households than for the one-worker couples, the statistical tests in Table 2.7 show the opposite: the retired households are the sector with the most statistically significant pair-wise differences. When the full distribution of travel times is taken into account, this is the population sector with the largest differences between the less urbanised areas outside the Randstad, and the big, and to a lesser degree, the medium-sized cities in the Randstad.

The retired households differ markedly from the single workers and the two-worker couples in that for those household types the residential context is less relevant in explaining the pair-wise differences in maintenance travel time (Table 2.7). Because these are households in which working full-time is most common, they tend to have limited time available for conducting maintenance activities. Individuals in these households may therefore try to increase the efficiency of their travel through 'trip chaining', using a private car more frequently, and choosing the nearest available destination. Whilst the exact behavioural strategy may depend on the configuration of land use, the outcome in terms of travel time seems to be more or less the same in all residential settings.

One may wonder why, according to Table 2.7, the above reasoning appears not to apply to two-worker families, which could be regarded as the most time-pressured household type. Perhaps this is because adults in such households have to perform many chauffeuring trips to bring young children to school, sports clubs, friends, etc. These trips tend to be fixed in space and time, thereby curtailing the opportunities for parents to achieve more efficient travel patterns (Kitamura, 1983; Misra and Bhat, 2000). Consequently, the spatial distribution of potential destinations may have a larger impact on travel times than in situations where few chauffeuring trips need to be undertaken (as in households without young children).

In short, the analysis for maintenance travel times has indicated that the *direction* of differences between residential settings is largely the same across households types. Travel times tend to be higher in the big cities and the growth centres and lower in the less urbanised areas outside the Randstad. The *magnitude* of these differences seems to vary, however, by household type. The size of the differences appears to depend on the level of time pressure as reflected in the number of hours worked per week, combined with the types of maintenance activity conducted.

Table 2.7 **Results of Wilcoxon tests on pair-wise differences in the distribution of daily travel time for maintenance trips per person between residential contexts, by household type[a]**

	Single worker					Two-worker couple					One-worker couple					Two-worker family					One-worker family					Retired household				
	2	3	4	5	6	2	3	4	5	6	2	3	4	5	6	2	3	4	5	6	2	3	4	5	6	2	3	4	5	6
1 R three big cities				•					•		••	•		••	••	••				••		•		•	••		••	••	••	••
2 R medium cities	--				•	--					--				••	--				••	--				•	--	••	••	••	••
3 R suburbs	--	--				--	--				--	--	••			--	--			••	--	--				--	--		•	
4 R growth centres	--	--	--			--	--	--			--	--	--	••	••	--	--	--		••	--	--	--		•	--	--	--		••
5 Rest NL more urbanised	--	--	--	--		--	--	--	--		--	--	--	--		--	--	--	--		--	--	--	--		--	--	--	--	
6 Rest NL less urbanised	--	--	--	--	--	--	--	--	--	--	--	--	--	--	--	--	--	--	--	--	--	--	--	--	--	--	--	--	--	--

[a] Only travellers making at least one commute trip are considered
• Statistically significant at α = 0.05
•• Statistically significant at α = 0.01
-- redundant comparison

Leisure Travel

The discussion for leisure (social visits, sports and hobbies, entertainment and recreation) is restricted to some key findings, because many results reinforce the conclusions for commuting and maintenance travel. As Table 2.8 indicates, the variation across residential settings is statistically significant for all population sectors with the exception of two-worker couples. Note, however, that the ANOVA *F*-ratio is also low for the single-worker group, suggesting that differences are small for these households. Contrary to expectations, the 'means' for singles in the big and medium-sized cities of the Randstad are higher than elsewhere. For the one- and two-worker families, the average travel time for leisure activities is highest in the growth centres. Again this is not as expected, given that the percentage of families residing there is higher than for other household types (Table 2.8).

In comparison with commuting and maintenance travel times, the impact of residential setting on travel times, per household type, for leisure trips is larger, but difficult to interpret. Nonetheless, the conclusion that the magnitude of the differences in travel time (when taking account of the number of observations and the size of the standard deviations) is a function of time availability, and type of activities conducted, also appears to hold for leisure travel.

Conclusions and Discussion

In this chapter we have considered the question of whether the influence of built environment characteristics on trip frequency and travel time for commuting, maintenance and leisure purposes differs across household types. We hypothesised that family households, because of their over-representation in suburban and lower-density areas, would experience shorter travel times for commuting, maintenance and leisure activities and higher trip frequencies, as the level of urbanisation of their residential environment is lower. In contrast, we expected travel times for every trip purpose to be lower and the number of trips higher as the level of urbanisation increases for single workers and two-worker couples.

The descriptive analysis presented here has produced many statistically significant differences among residential contexts, stressing the general significance of urban form to the understanding of differences in travel patterns. That is not to say, however, that the impact of urban form always differs by household type. For maintenance travel, and certainly for commuting, the conclusion should be that the impact of residential setting on travel time is characterised more by similarity than by differences across household types with respect to the *direction* of the influence. Thus we find that, for most household types, travel times for these purposes are higher in the cities and growth centres and lower outside the Randstad in general and in the less urbanised municipalities in particular. Nonetheless, the *magnitude* of the differences between residential settings varies across household types for maintenance travel time. The differences

Table 2.8 Daily travel time for leisure trips per person, by population segment and residential setting[a]

	Single worker		Two-worker couple		One-worker couple		Two-worker family		One-worker family		Retired household	
	Mean	S.D.	Mean	S.D.	Mean	S.D.	Mean	S.D.	Mean	S.D.	Mean	S.D.
R three big cities	57.8	46.3	58.2	45.5	58.4	44.5	51.6	42.9	51.3	46.9	64.8	50.9
R medium cities	55.5	52.8	61.6	48.9	66.1	52.7	49.6	42.4	48.8	41.2	63.4	53.8
R suburbs	51.9	44.6	58.5	50.5	61.5	51.3	45.0	42.3	46.0	40.9	58.0	49.3
R growth centres	50.5	43.1	64.0	58.0	53.5	45.4	55.1	46.9	57.5	49.3	64.2	52.3
Rest NL more urbanised	50.1	45.6	56.6	53.3	53.2	45.8	43.7	38.7	42.9	39.9	58.7	49.9
Rest NL less urbanised	45.7	42.5	55.1	48.1	49.6	53.6	45.7	43.8	42.7	39.7	55.1	48.2
ANOVA (F-ratio)	2.7[b]		1.4		3.4[c]		3.8[c]		4.9[c]		7.7[c]	

[a] Only travellers making at least one leisure trip are considered
[b] Statistically significant at $\alpha = 0.05$
[c] Statistically significant at $\alpha = 0.01$

tend to be larger for household types with larger time budgets, such as retired households and one-worker couples. Presumably because of the adoption of various behavioural strategies to increase the efficiency of travel patterns, variations in travel time by residential setting are small for working singles and two-worker couples.

The travel time for leisure purposes and the non-work trip frequency are also statistically significantly associated with urban form in a number of instances. Nevertheless, these differences tend to be less systematic than for commuting and maintenance travel time. Perhaps some of this variation could be explained by taking account of other factors which have not been considered here, such as socio-economic condition, car availability, and lifestyle.

While we do find that single workers are concentrated in the cities of the Randstad and more urbanised municipalities in the rest of the Netherlands, and that families are gravitating towards suburban and low-density living, the analysis suggests that opportunities for efficient travel or easy access to relevant destinations seem to be of modest importance in decisions about where to live. It appears that those household types have other, non-transport and accessibility-related motivations when choosing a residential location, such as the availability of suitable housing or the prevalence of a certain lifestyle. Similar arguments have been made in other studies, although those were often limited to commuting trips, or concentrated on multiple-worker households (Giuliano and Small, 1993; Raney *et al.*, 2000; Raux and Andan, 1997; Weber, 2003). Our research contributes to this literature by showing that the modest role of transport-related factors is not limited to commuting time and multiple-worker households but also pertains to non-work travel and households with one or no workers.

The study results can also be viewed from a land use and transport policy perspective. Elsewhere we have argued that one of the dangers of reducing car travel by building compact, high-density developments is that travel times may rise (Schwanen *et al.*, 2004). This was deemed undesirable, because it may undermine the effectiveness of those policies. The results presented in this chapter suggest that single workers and two-worker couples are somewhat less sensitive to urban form than the retired and one-worker couples (at least as far as travel time is concerned). Building compact developments may therefore provide individuals in the former household types with better conditions for modifying their travel behaviour. Conversely, single workers and two-worker couples are *ceteris paribus* the most frequent users of public transport (Schwanen *et al.*, 2002), so the gains in terms of modal shift may be limited. One solution to the apparent contradiction between certain land use policies may be to develop policies targeting specific household types instead of generic national policies. Such policies could be based on the variation in both travel time and trip frequency. Regarding the latter, we assume that a higher trip frequency is indicative of a higher level of social participation and hence beneficial to the individual. On the basis of the study results, we recommend that the building of residences in high-rise buildings near public transport facilities in larger cities play a prominent role in policies for single workers and two-worker couples, whereas concentrating new developments in relatively compact suburban locations may be a better strategy for one-worker couples or retired households.

References

Alonso, W. (1964) *Location and Land Use*, Harvard University Press, Cambridge, MA.

Bhat, C.R. (2000) 'Duration Modelling', in D.A. Hensher and K.J. Button (eds), *Handbook of Transport Modelling*, Elsevier Science Ltd., Amsterdam, pp. 91-111.

Bhat, C.R. and Guo, J. (2004) 'A Mixed Spatially Correlated Logit Model: Formulation and Application to Residential Choice Modelling', *Transportation Research B*, vol. 38, pp. 147-168.

Brun, J. and Fagnani, J. (1994) 'Lifestyles and Locational Choices. Trade-offs and Compromises: A Case Study of Middle Class Couples Living in the Ile-de-France Region', *Urban Studies*, vol. 31, pp. 921-934.

Champion, T. (2001) 'A Changing Demographic Regime and Evolving Polycentric Urban Regions: Consequences for the Size, Composition and Distribution of City Populations', *Urban Studies*, vol. 38, pp. 657-677.

Chapin, F.S. and Hightower, H.C. (1965) 'Household Activity Patterns and Land Use', *American Institute of Planners Journal*, vol. 31, pp. 222-231.

Clark, W.A.V. (2000) 'Monocentric to Polycentric: New Urban Forms and Old Paradigms', in S. Bridge and S. Watson (eds), *A Companion to the City*, Blackwell Publishers, Oxford, pp. 141-154.

Clark, W.A.V. and Dieleman, F.M. (1996) *Households and Housing: Choice and Outcomes in the Housing Market*, Center for Urban Policy Research, Rutgers University, New Brunswick, NJ.

Dieleman, F.M., Dijst, M. and Burghouwt, G. (2002) 'Urban Form and Travel Behaviour: Micro-level Household Attributes and Residential Context', *Urban Studies*, vol. 39, pp. 507-527.

Dijst, M., De Jong, T. and Ritsema van Eck, J. (2002) 'Opportunities for Transport Mode Change: An Exploration of a Disaggregated Approach', *Environment and Planning B*, vol. 29, pp. 413-430.

Giuliano, G. and Small, K.A. (1993) 'Is the Journey to Work Explained by Urban Structure?', *Urban Studies*, vol. 30, pp. 1485-1500.

Handy, S.L. (1996) 'Understanding the Link between Urban Form and Nonwork Travel Behavior', *Journal of Planning Education and Research*, vol. 15, pp. 183-198.

Hanson, S. and Schwab, M. (1987) 'Accessibility and Intra-urban Travel', *Environment and Planning A*, vol. 19, pp. 735-748.

Herz, R. (1982) 'The Influence of Environmental Factors on Daily Behaviour', *Environment and Planning A*, vol. 14, pp. 1175-1193.

Kitamura, R. (1983) 'Serve Passengers Trips as a Determinant of Travel Behavior', in S. Carpenter and P. Jones (eds), *Recent Advances in Travel Demand Analysis*, Gower, Aldershot, pp. 137-162.

Kwan, M.P. (2000) 'Gender, the Home-Work Link and Space-Time Patterns of Non-employment Activities', *Economic Geography*, vol. 76, pp. 370-394.

Levinson, D.M. and Kumar, A. (1997) 'Density and the Journey to Work', *Growth and Change*, vol. 28, pp. 147-172.

McLafferty, S. and Preston, V. (1997) 'Gender, Race, and the Determinants of Commuting: New York in 1990', *Urban Geography*, vol. 18, pp. 192-212.

Meurs, H. and Haaijer, R. (2001) 'Spatial Structure and Mobility', *Transportation Research D*, vol. 6, pp. 429-446.

Misra, R. and Bhat, C. (2000) 'Activity-Travel Patterns of Non-workers in the San Francisco Bay Area: An Exploratory Analysis', *Transportation Research Record*, vol. 1718, pp. 43-51.

Raney, E.A., Mokhtarian, P.L. and Salomon, I. (2000) 'Modelling Individuals' Consideration of Strategies to Cope with Congestion', *Transportation Research F*, vol. 3, pp. 141-165.

Raux, C. and Andan, O. (1997) 'Residential Mobility and Daily Mobility: What are the Ties?', in P. Stopher and M. Lee-Gosselin (eds), *Understanding Travel Behaviour in an Era of Change*, Pergamon, New York, pp. 29-52.

Schwanen, T., Dieleman, F.M. and Dijst, M. (2001a) 'Travel Behaviour in Dutch Monocentric and Polycentric Urban Systems', *Journal of Transport Geography*, vol. 9, pp. 173-186.

Schwanen, T., Dieleman, F.M. and Dijst, M. (2003) 'Car Use in Netherlands Daily Urban Systems: Does Polycentrism Result in Lower Commute Times?', *Urban Geography*, vol. 24, pp. 410-430.

Schwanen, T., Dijst, M. and Dieleman, F.M. (2001b) 'Leisure Trips of Senior Citizens: Determinants of Modal Choice', *Tijdschrift voor Economische en Sociale Geografie*, vol. 92, pp. 347-360.

Schwanen, T., Dijst, M. and Dieleman, F.M. (2002) 'A Microlevel Analysis of Residential Context and Travel Time', *Environment and Planning A*, vol. 34, pp. 1487-1507.

Schwanen, T., Dijst, M. and Dieleman, F.M. (2004) 'Policies for Urban Form and Their Impact on Travel: The Netherlands Experience', *Urban Studies*, vol. 41, pp. 579-603.

Schwanen, T. and Mokhtarian, P.L. (2003) 'Does Dissonance Between Desired and Actual Neighbourhood Type Affect Individual Travel Behaviour? An Empirical Assessment from the San Francisco Bay Area', *Proceedings, European Transport Conference*, 8-10 October 2003, Strasbourg.

Snellen, D. (2001) *Urban Form and Activity-Travel Patterns: An Activity-Based Approach to Travel in a Spatial Context*, PhD Thesis, Urban Planning Group, Eindhoven University of Technology, Eindhoven.

Statistics Netherlands (2002) *Onderzoek Verplaatsingsgedrag 2001: Documentatie voor Tape Gebruikers*, Statistics Netherlands, The Hague/Heerlen.

Stead, D. (2001) 'Relationships Between Land Use, Socio-economic Factors, and Travel Patterns in Britain', *Environment and Planning B*, vol. 28, pp. 499-528.

Sun, X., Wilmot, C.S. and Kasturi, T. (1998) 'Household Travel, Household Characteristics, and Land Use', *Transportation Research Record*, vol. 1617, pp. 10-17.

Turner, T. and Niemeier, D. (1997) 'Travel to Work and Household Responsibility: New Evidence', *Transportation*, vol. 24, pp. 397-419.

Van de Vijvere, Y., Oppewal, H. and Timmermans, H. (1998) 'The Validity of Hierarchical Information Integration Choice Experiments to Model Residential Preference and Choice', *Geographical Analysis*, vol. 30, pp. 254-272.

Weber, J. (2003) 'Individual Accessibility and Distance from Major Employment Centers: An Examination Using Space-Time Measures', *Journal of Geographical Systems*, vol. 5, pp. 51-70.

Weisbrod, G.E., Lerman, S.R. and Ben-Akiva, M. (1980) 'Trade-offs in Residential Location Decisions: Transportation Versus other Factors', *Transport Policy and Decision Making*, vol. 1, pp. 13-26.

Wyly, E.K. (1998) 'Containment and Mismatch: Gender Differences in Commuting in Metropolitan Labor Markets', *Urban Geography*, vol. 19, pp. 395-430.

Chapter 3

A Lifestyles Approach to Investigating Residential Mobility and Travel Behaviour

Joachim Scheiner and Birgit Kasper

Introduction

Today, spatial research and planning are confronted with complex contextual conditions which have changed substantially in the past decades. Two phenomena need to be considered. These are:

- an increasing socio-cultural differentiation or even fragmentation of society (individualisation, differentiation and pluralisation of lifestyles);
- a dynamic development of spatial structures and time regimes, including increasingly complex forms of mobility on different levels (e.g. housing mobility and travel behaviour as basic forms of spatial mobility).

The main aim of this chapter is to investigate both phenomena through research. For spatial and mobility research, this requires a sophisticated understanding of social and spatial structures. At the same time, new conclusions have to be drawn for current planning strategies in the context of the development of urban neighbourhoods.

Basic Principles

Lifestyles

In German sociology, lifestyle research has developed since the late 1980s. The starting point was Beck's thesis about increasing individualisation: traditional structures of social inequality are losing their relevance because 'old' vertical inequality is being supplemented by new horizontal inequalities, 'beyond classes and strata' (Beck, 1986, p. 121). The clear pattern of social strata is, it is claimed, being scattered in a mosaic of bits and pieces, which remain dynamically connected by social mobility. The 'dream' of never-ending prosperity (Lutz, 1984) in the post-war decades facilitated an unexpected liberation from traditional patterns, including the disappearance of linear, predictable courses of life, better chances for education for all sectors of the population, longer duration of adolescence, changes in gender relations (including growing female labour market participation), smaller households, diversification and flexibility of employment and the dissolution of traditional time regimes. With regard to mobility, motorisation in the 1960s and 1970s increased at rates that consistently defied forecasts (Scheiner, 2002).

For lifestyle research, these structural developments are the background rather than the subject of the research subject itself. Lifestyle is defined as 'regular patterns of behaviour, that represent structural situations as well as habitual behaviour and social affinities' (Lüdtke, 1996, p. 140). An abundant field of research for self-stylisation concerns leisure time and thus it is investigated intensively. At the theoretical level, voluntaristic concepts have to be distinguished from structuralistic concepts. In German sociology, voluntaristic concepts tend to disconnect lifestyles from social stratums (Schulze, 1992; Lüdtke, 1995). However, the interdependence between lifestyle and social status cannot be neglected. Empirical results show that classical stratum variables (income, professional status) have become less important than age and education, and partly gender (Schulze, 1992; Spellerberg, 1996; Schneider and Spellerberg, 1999; Klee, 2001). This indicates the persistence of the connection between education and promotion to the economic elite with parents' education and profession (Schimpl-Neimanns, 2000). This concept points to a structural perception of lifestyles (Bourdieu, 1982).

Mobility

A common thesis is that certain lifestyle groups have specific forms of mobility. But 'mobility' has several meanings. It can mean social and spatial mobility: short-term (travel), or long-term mobility (housing mobility, choice of location). Moreover, it is a term used for actual movement (relocation, travel behaviour, moving up or down socially) as well as for potential and opportunity. The latter influence motion, but are also themselves derived from the accessibility of destinations as a 'supply' (Topp, 1994). Finally, spatial mobility is often used as a synonym for physical motion, but it includes the use of media as well ('virtual mobility'), through both individualised use (e.g. internet, fax and phone) and traditional mass media (e.g. television, radio, newspaper and magazines). These differentiations are of great relevance for analyses of lifestyles and mobility.

The concept of the (partial) dissolving of lifestyles from socio-structural frameworks implies increased spatial opportunities. The analogy seems to be true for the spatial level: because of loosening structural conditions, spatial considerations are less of a restriction for individual lifestyles. Furthermore, spatial affiliation to the neighbourhood could decline (because of motorisation and increasing use of cars, virtual mobility, and so on).

Secondly, individualisation and pluralisation of lifestyles will imply a changing dynamic in social and spatial mobility. For example, mobility considerations after a change of job have changed: the decision between long-distance commuting and moving closer to the place of work which often has to be made after a professional change increasingly favour commuting, which is facilitated by the availability of a car, and promoted by homeownership, which increases connections with the home location (Kalter, 1994). Modern forms of professional development (double-income households) and frequent changes of job often restrict a short-distance choice of location anyway.

Thirdly, the increasing 'mediatisation' of society and the partial replacement of face-to-face interaction by virtual communication increase the extension of spatial opportunities. Subsequently, physical interrelations change (Scheiner, 2001). It is unclear how this change will evolve. The central question is whether physical mobility will be replaced by tele-communication or whether both forms reinforce themselves mutually (see Vogt, 2000). In conclusion, processes of mobility are interrelated on different levels (housing and daily mobility, physical and virtual mobility) and in a social and economic context.

Connections

Lifestyles and Travel Behaviour

In the 1990s, mobility research translated the concept of lifestyles into 'mobility styles'. A differentiated understanding of travel demand was created, connecting lifestyles with travel behaviour (Götz *et al.* 1997; Scheiner, 1997; Wulfhorst *et al.* 2000). So far, it is normally limited to modal choice (Götz *et al.* 1997).

Scheiner (1997) typifies the population of different research areas in Stuttgart, Germany by the spatial orientation of activity spaces. He distinguishes groups with a concentration on a few destinations, and groups with dispersed orientations. Significant differences between distances and modal choice resulted in the characterisation of different 'mobility styles'. In recent studies, the concept of mobility styles has found application. Partly, the aim of this research is to describe typical forms of mobility behaviour (Lanzendorf, 2001), but it also attempts to develop theoretical models to explain mobility behaviour (Hunecke, 1999).

However, some central questions remain unanswered: the relevance of lifestyles in mobility research is still unclear. Generally, typologies of lifestyles are treated as independent variables and therefore as autonomously emerging styles. The question remains how they are structurally influenced by non-lifestyle-specific resources or restrictions: what is 'behind' lifestyles is unclear. The question is well grounded by the strong correlation between lifestyles and socio-demographic issues (e.g. age) as well as by theoretical considerations about the resource dependence of lifestyles.

Secondly, mobility research still focuses mainly on modal choice. Further aspects, such as distances travelled, activity participation, or time spent on activities are neglected. Nevertheless, these aspects remain important from an analytical as well as from an applied point of view with respect to sustainable transport planning. As examples, the distances travelled are connected to the consumption of resources and to transport emissions, and opportunities to participate in activities are highly relevant for different sectors of the population, such as older or mobility-restricted people (Kasper and Scheiner, Chapter 5, this volume).

Lifestyles and Residential Mobility

Living a certain lifestyle puts individuals in a context with respect to their spatial environment. The relationship may be direct, when activities rely on 'scenes', like discos, pubs, sports facilities or other meeting points (Schulze, 1992). However, domestic as well as 'non-spatial' lifestyles (e.g. media-oriented, net surfing) also imply a 'statement' about space. It may indicate 'just' a concentration on the private sphere, or a focus on global contacts where individuals 'don't just dissolve in the internet and live on in cyberspace' (Rhode-Jüchtern, 1998, p. 7) because of their material existence.

Concerning the internal infrastructure of the home and the neighbourhood, and housing location, these differentiated designs of daily life are a challenge (e.g. Klee, 2001). While some need shopping malls, sport facilities and an entertainment district close to home, for others, internet access and delivery services are suitable. Most recently, these phenomena have been discussed in connection with lifestyles and residential mobility, particularly choice of housing location.

Within sociology, discussions about spatial planning and lifestyles emerged from segregation research. The pluralisation of lifestyles is associated with young urban élites (so-called 'Yuppies', 'Dinks' etc.) with economically and culturally dominating lifestyles, who cover urban space symbolically and functionally and who displace other population groups by invading new neighbourhoods (gentrification). In contrast, other groups like older people are often excluded from lifestyle research (e.g. Spellerberg, 1996; Klee, 2001). Dangschat (1996) concludes that the idea of social de-structuration and pluralisation of lifestyles describes just one part of society: 'the sunny side of modernisation winners' (*ibid*, p. 127), because freedom from structural constraints is not available to all.

Housing location as a spatial distribution of social groups has to be distinguished from housing mobility as an indicator for the development of housing biographies and locational choice. The housing unit (type, size, standard) is the linking variable, since the unequal spatial distribution of housing types influences the choice of housing location. Schneider and Spellerberg (1999) state that lifestyles still differ significantly between urban and rural environments. Spatial differentiation is also 'visible' within cities (see Klee, 2001 for Nuremberg, Wulfhorst *et al.* 2000 for Cologne). Beside the locations, the extent of housing mobility differs significantly across lifestyles (Schneider and Spellerberg, 1999).

After a critical review of space-related lifestyle research, two points have to be considered. First, the general focus lies on high-density centres of urban areas: extremely differentiated lifestyles are expected to concentrate in such places because of socio-cultural heterogeneity and economic polarisation (Dangschat and Blasius, 1994). This narrow perspective conflicts with claims for the universal validity of lifestyle research (e.g. Schulze, 1992). Moreover, lifestyles are normally regarded as independent. Their relative explanatory value in comparison with social structures remains unanswered.

Residential Mobility and Travel Behaviour

Residential mobility and travel behaviour are not only two dependent variables for the investigation of lifestyles, they are connected to each other. This connection has not yet adequately been analysed, although it was discussed in the 1970s in Anglo-American urban research (Chapin, 1974), and sporadically in German social geography (Troxler, 1986). Only recently has the connection between housing mobility and daily travel been recognised and put to use in applied urban planning. Geier *et al.* (2000) compared the spatial orientation of the old-established population and newcomers in suburban Berlin. They found that the 'neo-suburbanites' maintain their orientation towards the central city in the medium term, resulting in relatively long daily travel distances. Scheiner (2002) noted differences in Berlin regarding spatial orientation in relation to spatial origin. While West-Berliners tend to undertake their activities in the Western part of the city, East-Berliners living in the same neighbourhood tend to choose their activities in the Eastern part. Changes in travel behaviour as a consequence of residential relocation to suburban areas, such as the increase of distances travelled or the purchase of a second car in a household, are reported by several authors. On the other hand, however, the first car in a household is the precondition for moving to the suburbs: households without a car usually do not move to suburbia (Herfert, 1997). From this point of view, there is no clear causality between residential mobility and travel behaviour. Instead, extensive mutual influences have to be expected. Households without a car might choose their housing location more in terms of the availability of public transport and supply of infrastructure at the neighbourhood scale than households with a car.

Not only relocation of housing, but also maintenance of housing locations has an impact on travel behaviour. Kalter (1994) analyses the context of migration and commuting. His results show an increasing percentage of long-distance commuting (from 2.6 per cent of commuting in 1985 to 6.6 per cent in 1997, in Vogt *et al.* 2001) and a tendency to maintain housing location. He concludes that commuting increasingly replaces moving home. For some commuters, commuting is the 'precursor' to moving or a short-term solution until a change of job occurs, but for 46 per cent of the long-distance commuters the 'housing and job' combination remains stable for at least ten years (Kalter, 1994).

The Development of the Research Concept

Figure 3.1 integrates the interdependencies discussed above into a research concept for the project entitled 'StadtLeben' (or 'CityLife'), which is the subject of this chapter. The focus is on residential mobility and travel behaviour as well as the mutual context and relationship with social structures. Decisions on mobility behaviour are reached within the context of certain space-time structures. These do not determine human activities, rather they have to be understood as dynamic and permeable resources. Space-time structures are macro-structures that consist of global and national spatial and time regulations (e.g. spatial division of labour, EU regional planning policy, high-speed transport infrastructure) as well as settlement structures and time-regimes on the scale of cities and neighbourhoods, such as land use, quality of life in local communities, small-scale time regimes (e.g. opening hours and working time agreements), and location in the urban context. Interpretations have to be made with regard to economic, social, political and technical conditions (e.g. real estate market, fiscal housing grants, mobility-related taxes). Neither lifestyles nor mobility can be separated from macro-structural frameworks.

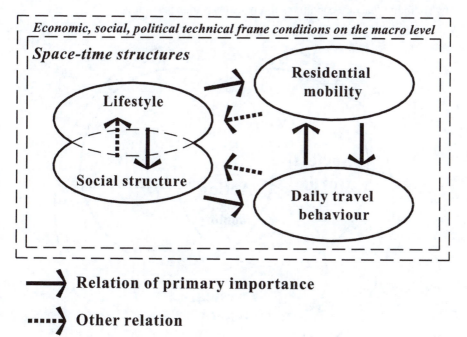

➜ **Relation of primary importance**

┅➜ **Other relation**

Figure 3.1   Research structure

Source: Scheiner, adapted from Hesse and Trostorff (2002)

Social structures and social positions on the one hand, and lifestyles on the other, must be seen in relation to each other, though lifestyles have a stronger dependence on social status than *vice versa*. The term 'lifestyle' must not be seen voluntaristically in this context. 'Chosen' lifestyles are affected by structural conditions that might restrict or widen further options.

If lifestyles partly depend on social positions, they are not adequate as exclusive explanations for mobility research. The value of the concept of lifestyles for mobility research lies primarily in the differentiation of social structures by subjective patterns of explanation, aims of activity, value orientation, preferences and (sub)cultural affiliations. Because neither spatial nor social structures are able to steer mobility behaviour, lifestyle research can establish differentiated explanations for target groups, in contrast to current explanations on the basis solely of socio-economic and demographic factors.

On the one hand, realised mobility is the expression of social behaviour and results from aims and individual values: on the other it is embedded in a social and spatial context (Figure 3.2). It is precisely in confrontation with this context that the margins emerge within which mobility is possible. However, these margins are not structurally fixed, but may be changed at the individual level, for instance, by mobility itself. Therefore it is important to note that the contexts, while not chosen by the individual, are conditions for, not causes of, behaviour.

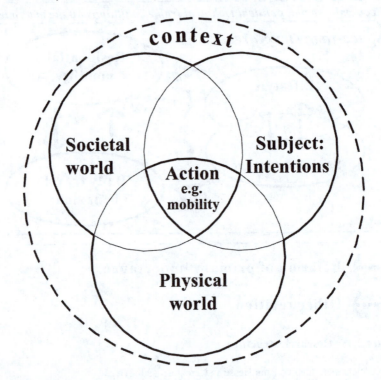

Figure 3.2   Context for action

As already stated, the basic thesis is that different lifestyle groups are characterised by specific forms of mobility. Thus, in methodological terms, housing mobility as well as travel behaviour are seen as dependent variables. Housing mobility could be analysed in terms of the extent of mobility or of stability (occupancy, number of relocations in a specific time, distances), and of choice of location. The reasons for housing mobility are relevant as well, since they correspond to spatial patterns. Whereas local and regional mobility tends to relate to dissatisfaction with one's housing situation or to personal circumstances (e.g. birth of a child or marriage), long-distance mobility is dominated by job changes (for the case of Frankfurt/Main, see Dobroschke, 1999).

Key aspects of travel behaviour are: type of travel, quantity and timing of activities, choice of destinations and spatial orientation (activity spaces), distances, and modal choice. An analysis of these aspects exceeds current studies concerning lifestyle-specific travel behaviour, which focus on modal choice. Residential mobility and travel behaviour are regarded as interwoven, with the priority being the impact of residential mobility on travel behaviour: residential mobility is a long-term decision that dominates travel behaviour and, in effect, intervenes between lifestyle and travel behaviour. Conversely, there is no doubt about the influence of certain forms of travel behaviour on housing mobility.

So, what is the benefit of this approach? In the following sections, we give an example of how these rather theoretical considerations might be empirically investigated by quantitative and qualitative methods at the neighbourhood level, and show how the results could be transferred to solutions for sustainable mobility and urban planning.

From Research Concept to Empirical Analyses and Implications for Planning

A central question in applied research is how built environments will meet the new demands resulting from less predictable ways of life, pluralisation and socio-spatial differentiation of lifestyles. Increasing resistance to the development of major projects or area-wide rehabilitation of urban neighbourhoods in the 1980s resulted in comprehensive or participatory planning methods. Despite the tendencies of globalisation and large-scale development, these approaches remain valid, especially at the neighbourhood level where lifestyles find their spatial setting. Moreover, neighbourhoods are the places in which specific lifestyles might create communities. Therefore, the spatial focus in the 'StadtLeben' project is the neighbourhood.

The Case Studies

As the spatial context, three neighbourhoods in the City of Cologne, Germany, were chosen with certain criteria in mind. They had to differ from each other, but at the same time each had to be a typical example of one kind of neighbourhood. The differences lie in:

- the distance to the city centre and the availability of public transport (accessibility);
- the social and demographic structure (age, size of household, income);
- the dynamics of development (including urban development and housing mobility);
- the deficits, with respect to the built environment to opportunities for different activities (retail, workplaces and so on).

The areas were the focus of a pilot study carried out in spring 2002 to test the methodological approach. At the time of writing, the main survey was being carried out in another seven neighbourhoods in the city and region of Cologne. The chosen neighbourhoods for the pilot were:

- Ehrenfeld, an inner-city sub centre (in the Wilhelminian style), built at the end of the 19th century;
- Stammheim, a settlement in the first peripheral ring (of modern functionalism) with flats in three- or four-storey terraced housing, built in the 1960s;
- Esch, a suburb with its origin as a rural village (suburbia), which has steadily expanded since the 1950s with single-family terraced houses or semi-detached and detached single occupancy houses.

Methods of Empirical Research

Because of the interdisciplinary project approach, several empirical methods were used. First, a standardised survey with 180 face-to-face interviews in each neighbourhood examined topics such as residential mobility, housing satisfaction, travel behaviour, lifestyles, social networks, use of information and communication technology, availability of means of travel, and socio-demographic information. Secondly, 20 qualitative face-to-face interviews with residents and experts were made in each neighbourhood. 'Experts' are individuals who work in the neighbourhood with or for specific groups of residents and who know the community, the problems and the dynamics of the place very well (e.g. a pastor, alderman, school director, police officer and executive of the housing corporation). In general, the aim of these interviews was to understand the common and the subjective significance of attitudes and settings in the neighbourhood. Concerning opportunities for the neighbourhoods, the interviews focused on the different lifestyles or communities that exist side-by-side or conflict with each other. There are diverse interests in each neighbourhood, which result in social and spatial opportunities, in the desire for changes, and in a requirement for new developmental strategies.

In the following sections, three sets of key findings are presented: first, findings on the spatial distribution of lifestyles over the study areas; second, results of two multiple regression analyses, which investigate the relevance of lifestyles as an explanatory factor for residential mobility; and third, results from the expert interviews in the three neighbourhoods. While the regression analyses are primarily of analytical interest, the other findings give an insight into the character of the study areas, and are more planning-oriented.

Lifestyles and Space

Construction of Lifestyles The lifestyles identified in this project are based on leisure preferences, cultural tastes (e.g. television viewing and reading habits), values, life aims, and density of the social network. By means of a factor analysis, eight dimensions of lifestyles were found. Two dimensions relate to leisure: out-of-home-oriented (e.g. cinema, concerts and educational courses) and home-and-family-oriented (e.g. playing with children and gardening). Two more dimensions relate to life aims: traditional values (e.g. thriftiness, security and unselfishness) and self-realisation (e.g. leading an exciting life, achieving a leading position and political engagement). The other four dimensions are based on cultural taste and relate to aesthetic categories: 'trivial', 'tension', 'high-culture' (television) and 'high-culture' (reading). The trivial category is related to watching quiz shows and soap operas on television, and reading light novels. The tension category is linked to action movies, horror movies, and reading comics. The two high-culture categories are related to watching documentaries, political and cultural programmes, and to reading classical literature, novels, poems, specialised books and biographies. The categories correlate closely to those found by Schulze (1992). Two more variables relate to the social network: frequency of private e-mail or telephone conversations with friends, colleagues and neighbours, and frequency of private meetings with these groups. Six lifestyle groups were identified and were characterised by the following dominating factors:

1. traditional: trivial category, traditional values, little self-realisation, little out-of-home leisure;
2. homely culturally-interested: high-culture television, low frequency of private meetings;
3. event-oriented: tension category, sparse high-culture reading;
4. out-of-home convivial: self-realisation values, out-of-home leisure, high frequency of private meetings, high frequency of private e-mails and phone calls;
5. reserved: no factors occur positively, particularly no traditional values, no trivial category, no high-culture television, low frequency of private meetings;
6. convivial, family-oriented: home-and-family-oriented leisure, high frequency of private meetings, high frequency of private e-mails and phone calls.

Results Each study area has its own specific combination of lifestyles (Figure 3.3). While in suburban Esch homely lifestyles are dominant (homely culturally-interested, convivial family-oriented), in Ehrenfeld out-of-home convivials are predominant. In both areas, the dominating lifestyles match the spatial context perfectly: while Esch is a neighbourhood that has hardly any opportunities for out-of-home leisure activities (except activities such as walking or cycling), Ehrenfeld is characterised by a wide range of leisure opportunities including pubs, restaurants, cultural facilities and so on. Both locations seem to be chosen by their residents with respect to their preferred lifestyles.

In Stammheim, things are different. Traditional as well as event-oriented lifestyles appear more frequently than on average. This combination leads to conflicts between the traditionals, who want a quiet, pleasant neighbourhood (as was seen to have existed in Stammheim in the sixties and seventies), and the event-oriented, who are mainly young adults with a 'street-life'-oriented culture of meeting in gangs, music and fun. However, neither of these groups chose

Stammheim because it fitted their lifestyle needs. The traditionals came when housing supply was still very limited in the post-war decades. The event-oriented, on the other hand, arrived either as young parents or as children with their parents who were assigned public housing.

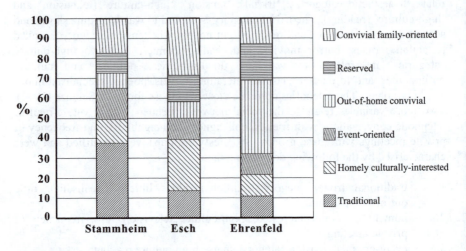

Figure 3.3   Lifestyles in the study areas

Source: StadtLeben household survey

Do Lifestyles Play a Role in Residential Mobility? Results From Multiple Regression Analyses

Regression Methods   As lifestyles are more or less closely related to socio-economic and demographic structures, the influence of these structures has to be held constant for a thorough examination of the additional influence of lifestyles on mobility. Therefore, as described above, lifestyles are analysed independently from such structures, while the latter have to be controlled. The following variables were included in the analyses as explanatory factors: age, household size, presence of children in the household, living in a partnership, employment, job position, educational level, income per capita in the household, nationality, and the eight lifestyle dimensions mentioned above. (Gender is excluded, because residential mobility is realised by households, not by individuals.) Some variables are constructed by decomposing ordinal into binary variables. Table 3.1 shows the results. The standardised coefficients 'B' are decisive for the interpretation of the strength of influence. The dependent variables investigated are the 'extent of residential mobility' (number of relocations since 1989), and 'spatial bonds' (length of residence in the neighbourhood). Linear regressions are appropriate, as both of these variables are metric.

Results According to Table 3.1, certain lifestyle dimensions seem to have some explanatory power for residential mobility, even when socio-demographic structures are controlled. This is true for the number of relocations as well as the length of residence in a certain neighbourhood. In both models, the overall model fit (explained variance) is good, particularly as one has to note that the models are limited to social attributes of individuals, while the macro level (property market) is excluded.

Table 3.1   Results of multiple regression analyses of residential mobility

Variable	Number of relocations since 1989		Length of residence in the neighbourhood	
	Unstd. B	Standard. B	Unstd. B	Standard. B
(Constant)	3.81		-7.65	
Age	-0.05	-0.46	0.50	0.57
Employment	n.s.		-4.01	-0.12
Household size (number of persons)	-0.51	-0.27	2.57	0.17
Child in household	1.05	0.20	-7.27	-0.17
Living in partnership	0.39	0.08	-3.37	-0.09
Leading job position	0.62	0.12	n.s.	
Nationality	n.s.		5.39	0.08
Per-capita-income	n.s.		0.00	0.08
University grade	0.58	0.12	-2.84	-0.07
Home-and-family-oriented leisure	-0.28	-0.14	1.77	0.11
Aesthetic category: high culture (reading)	0.22	0.11	n.s.	
Aesthetic category: trivial	n.s.		1.39	0.08
Explained variance (R^2_{corr})	0.36		0.50	

Source: StadtLeben (2002)
P: 0.05
n.s: not significant.

According to the first model (number of relocations), the following population groups are particularly mobile: individuals in leading job positions and with a university degree, young people, individuals living in households with children, households made up of partners, and/or living in small households. Moreover, high-cultural leisure preferences are connected to higher mobility, while home-and-family-oriented leisure preferences are linked to lower mobility. Two of these results seem to contradict each other: higher residential mobility in households with children *and* in smaller households. Apparently, singles (young singles, not retired people) as well as families, tend to move more often than an average person. One has to note that two relocations since 1989 are already above average. Because individuals in households with children are generally young, most of them moved at least once since 1989 when the household was formed. Many of them moved a second time because of the birth of their children. Age, household size and presence of children in the household are (in descending order of importance) the most important predictor variables for the extent of mobility.

According to the second model (columns on the right hand side), the following population groups tend to live in their neighbourhood for a comparatively long time: older people, people in households without children, not in paid work, with German nationality, without a university degree, in large households, and with home-and-family-oriented leisure preferences and a tendency towards the trivial aesthetic category. Once again, two lifestyle dimensions prove to be important influences for residential mobility. Again, by far the most important predictor variable is age.

The hypotheses for the StadtLeben project were that lifestyles are highly relevant for the explanation of residential mobility, and that lifestyles should complement, but not replace 'traditional' explanation patterns. Both these hypotheses are confirmed by the analyses. Lifestyle plays an important, but complementary, role for the explanation of the investigated indicators of residential mobility. More important are demographic factors, particularly age and household structure.

The analyses, however, have highlighted only a small part of the complex study approach. The relationship between residential mobility and travel behaviour and between social structures, lifestyles and travel behaviour will be investigated in the research project as well. Moreover, important indicators of residential mobility remain to be studied, such as spatial aspects of moving (e.g. moving to a suburb or to an inner city quarter), relocation distances, and reasons for moving. In the further course of the project, in-depth analyses on the basis of a larger sample are necessary, for instance because of the spatially unequal distribution of lifestyles. This calls for separate, comparative analyses in a larger number of study areas to prove systematic influences of lifestyles over various area types.

Results from Expert and Household Interviews in the Case Studies

The qualitative interviews complement the quantitative survey. They are characterised by the search for connections between lifestyles and motives or explanations for residential mobility and travel behaviour. The experts interviewed gave a good insight into the connection between neighbourhoods and the (different) predominant lifestyles. Ehrenfeld is a neighbourhood with a 'live and let live' attitude. Different ethnic and social groups live in a functionally and structurally diverse setting. The experts claim that this variety of groups make life and work in Ehrenfeld appealing. Because of the nature of the community, conflicts tend to be solved actively. The 'out-of-home convivial' lifestyle is simultaneously constituting and reinforcing this context.

In contrast, for the experts working in Stammheim the composition of lifestyles is seen as a 'challenge'. Stammheim has to deal with stigmatisation and a lack of positive identity. This is the motivation for commitment: helping to fight stigmatisation and disadvantages. Stammheim is characterised by a significant degree of separation between different groups of the population. These are the 'native' people from Old-Stammheim, the first inhabitants of New-Stammheim who have now evolved from families to senior households, and the various waves of immigrants who were placed in public housing units. Between old-established and in-coming groups, there are latent, and partly even manifest conflicts. They are generally caused by newcomers' children playing in the streets, older children forming gangs and meeting in public places, and generally different cultural backgrounds. For newly arrived low-income inhabitants the choice of location was always limited at the large- and small-scale. One expert's interpretation is that, because of lack of choice, it was difficult for people to approach each other which created (besides social and economic problems) internal conflicts. Others see the conflicts as exaggerated and believe that Stammheim is still 'a pretty normal neighbourhood'. Without doubt, one major disadvantage of Stammheim is the rigid spatial and organisational structure. Since the construction of the neighbourhood, it was nearly impossible to customise the buildings or the open space to the changing or competing needs of the traditional and the convivial inhabitants.

In Esch, the experts explain that the neighbourhood is close to ideal. It is an atmosphere of exclusivity and distance from urbanity. There is an impetus for residents to contribute at least to some extent to the community and to benefit from mutual support. Compared with the other two neighbourhoods there is a strong uniformity of lifestyles and the motivation to 'arrive' in a community. Problems emerge when the built environment does not match the needs (e.g. of event-oriented inhabitants) or the lifestyle changes over time from family and home orientation, to out-of-home convivial. Using the example of Esch, an explanation for the existing distribution of lifestyles and the choice of housing location is given below.

Spatial Development of Esch and Reasons to Locate There   In the eighties, a successful marketing campaign with the slogan 'living in Esch: like being on holiday' was used to attract young families who wanted to acquire property in one of the large development areas. The permanent growth of the new quarters not only provided new housing for young households who wanted to stay in the neighbourhood because of family ties or good experiences with Esch, but also new families looking for a specific type of housing. Altogether, the reasons for locating in Esch were:

- a purposeful return to the house or community where the person grew up, because of family ties or positive experiences with the neighbourhood;
- 'co-incidental' moving-in, because a sought-after home was offered in a well respected neighbourhood, where a suburban life seemed possible;
- deliberate desire to stay in the neighbourhood, especially for children moving out of their parents' home into a flat or a house of their own.

Purposeful Return   For a specific way of living, Esch is an appropriate neighbourhood. Whether detached or not, the single family home with a garden gives parents the aspired space that is not obviously available in inner city areas. The example of Mrs M shows that the specific type of housing is appealing for her. Positive experiences of suburban life brought her back to Esch:

> When I was 21 years old, in 1970, I moved out and in 1977 I came back here. In Cologne, it was easier to study and to date. Then I got my first daughter and I thought, a child and a garden is better than a child and big avenue. And pretty soon, my daughter will move in to her own flat, needless to say in Cologne. You have to experience that, to be right in the middle of events, but when the 'storm and stress' is over, you can find your peace here (Mrs M, 54, single-parent, two daughters, convivial family-oriented).

This woman is expressing the fact that lifestyles change over time and that specific spatial structures support or restrict lifestyles. She is sure that the 'storm and stress' times, which can be denoted as an event-oriented lifestyle, can be realised in an inner city neighbourhood, whereas the suburbs seem to be unsuitable for that lifestyle.

'Co-incidental' Moving-in   The motivation for moving in to a newly built development area mostly lies in the desire for enough living space for children in a peaceful and idyllic environment. The search for a suitable location is mostly driven by economic circumstances. Most of those interviewed, who 'co-incidentally' moved in, argued that they were searching both around, and in, Esch, and they were able to find a house at an affordable price. Concerning lifestyles, the question is whether the demographic and economic characteristics of the people moving in work as a filter, and lead to the dominance of one or two lifestyles. This homogenisation simplifies finding new friends in a neighbourhood, and this was seen as a good thing by the respondents. Of minor importance is the fact that the new neighbourhood is attached to the village of Esch. Any references to the locality, taking on public responsibilities or commitments to the community are minimal. The result is a shortage of new people in local associations and cultural events. With the village as 'scenery', the marketing campaign 'living in Esch: like being on holiday' was successful in attracting one type of lifestyle, but it did not result in the steady growth of the village.

Deliberate Desire to Stay in Esch   There are important reasons to feel connected to Esch and to stay there. A close-knit family or neighbourhood is the basis for those who describe Esch as their home and who feel the social bonds as an important anchor in their life. It is important to be able to evolve in the social network of community. For example Mr L found a flat near his parents' house and recently his wife moved in too. However, he found that '… it is too small for both of us. We are looking for a house, but most definitely in Esch, because you can't find another neighbourhood like that anywhere in Cologne' (Mr L, 27, married, event-oriented). A similar view is given by Mrs K. For her, Esch 'is not the most awesome place', but she lives close to her family and especially to her sister, so 'frequently, she takes care of our kids'. This close relationship prevents her from moving away (Mrs K, 34, married, two children, convivial family-oriented). This connectedness is not only important for young families, but also for elderly people. Mrs. S. is 80 years old and out-of-home convivial. Because of her health she was not able to live in her split-level house any longer and had to move to an apartment in Esch. She can stay embedded in the tight grid of mutual support and maintain her out-of-home convivial lifestyle.

These examples explain why in every type of spatial development most of the lifestyles can be found. There are reasons for moving or staying which are more important than finding the perfect built structure for an existing lifestyle. The spatial closeness to relatives or friends superimposes other decision-making criteria for a different choice of housing location, or a new way of life. In reverse this means for the spatial development that, to strengthen the supportive function of families, friends or neighbourhoods, all the space and infrastructure should be in compliance with the requirements not only of one, but of all the different lifestyles.

Next Steps in the Research

Comparative interpretations of lifestyles, neighbourhoods, communities and spatial mobility will be concluded and integrated in planning designs for housing and mobility. The designs will serve as a bridge between pure research and applied urban planning. But it is important to think of 'design' not only in a two-dimensional way. Planning strategies in this context are conceivable as spatial, organisational, structural or even political designs.

It is important to note that, although the project focus is the neighbourhood level, the strategies that will be developed will have to take the regional level into account too. This is because mobility is the key factor for individuals and households to overcome spatial restrictions and enhance their activity opportunities. Thus, small-scale neighbourhoods must not be treated as independent units, but be seen in their regional context. For instance, an improved retail supply in one neighbourhood might lead to shorter distances for the inhabitants, but at the same time it might attract inhabitants of other quarters. Therefore the overall sum of distances travelled, and the negative impact of traffic on the environment and the city, might increase. The designs will be discussed, tested and proposed for implementation. It will be the responsibility of the neighbourhood whether new patterns of community or accessibility will be developed.

Future Developments

The development of mobility in connection with individualisation and pluralisation of lifestyles is increasingly resistant to planning regulations. We can see this in growing dispersal in spatial development, which opposes land-use policy and regional planning programmes, and in the limited success of supply-oriented transport planning. There is a particular deficit concerning the perception of spatial mobility as a long-term process, consisting of housing mobility and daily activities. The research concept outlined here is designed precisely to address this deficit by connecting mobility behaviour, lifestyle, social structure, and spatial structure. With a view to more sustainable development of mobility and spatial structures, such an approach is indispensable: mobility research and transport planning cannot carry on using the assumption that space and mobility have a straightforward causal relationship.

For urban planning, the challenge is to combine the differentiation of lifestyles with traditional requirements. Despite extensive prognoses of increasing use of information and communication services, the neighbourhood remains the focal point of human life, and the backdrop for lifestyles. As needs become more diverse, the design and organisation of the local environment as well as housing mobility and choice of location have major impacts on travel behaviour and access to daily destinations.

Assuming that spatial behaviour is increasingly disconnected from (infra)structural conditions, planning also has to disengage from such conditions. This would give an opportunity to develop a broader concept of planning that is more individualised and demand-oriented with a broad array of organisational, infrastructural, constructive, legal, financial and informative measures. Then the phrase 'integrated planning' would be truly justified.

Note

This chapter is based on research from the interdisciplinary project 'StadtLeben' (CityLife). This is a collaborative project involving transport researchers, urban planners, geographers and psychologists from the following institutions: RWTH Aachen, Institute for City Building, Construction and Transport (co-ordination); Free University, Berlin, Institute for Geographical Sciences, Department of Urban Research; Ruhr University, Bochum, Cognition and Environmental Psychology Unit; University of Dortmund, Faculty of Transport and Transport Planning. The project is supported by the German Federal Ministry of Education and Research under the 'Building and Housing' research programme.

Many of the publications listed below are available only in German. Translated titles are given.

References

Beck, U. (1986) *World Risk Society*, Suhrkamp, Frankfurt.
Bourdieu, P. (1982) *Die Feinen Unterschiede (Distinction)*, Suhrkamp, Frankfurt.
Chapin, Jr., F.S. (1974) *Human Activity Patterns in the City: Things People Do in Time and in Space*, Wiley and Sons, New York.
Dangschat, J. (1996) 'Space as a Dimension of Social Distinction and Place as a Stage for Lifestyles?', in O.G. Schwenk (ed.), *Lifestyles Between Analysis of Social Structure and Cultural Science*, Leske and Budrich, Opladen, pp. 99-135.

Dangschat, J.S. and Blasius, J. (1994) *Lifestyles in Cities*, Leske and Budrich, Opladen.

Dobroschke, W. (1999) *Frankfurt Out-Migration Survey 1998*, Statistical Reports of Frankfurt, 2-3/99.

Geier, S., Holz-Rau, C. and Krafft-Neuhäuser, H. (2000) 'Suburbanisation and Transport', *International Transport*, vol. 53, pp. 22-26.

Götz, K., Jahn, T. and Schultz, I. (1997) *Mobility Styles: A Socio-Ecological Study Approach. Research Report 'Urban Sustainable Mobility'*, ISOE, Frankfurt.

Herfert, G. (1997) 'Residential Suburbanisation in the New Länder: Structures and Regional Disparities', in G. Meyer (ed.), *From Centrally Planned to Free-Market Economy: Economic and Socio-Geographic Development in the New Länder*, Contact Studies of Geography 3, Mainz. pp. 93-107.

Hesse, M. and Trostorff, B. (2002) 'Residential Milieux, Lifestyles and Spatial Mobility in East German Urban Landscapes', in A. Mayr, M. Meurer and J. Vogt (eds) *City and Region – Dynamics of the Living Environment*, Report of the Conference and Scientific Contributions of the 53rd German Geographers' Conference in Leipzig, 29 September–5 October 2001, German Society for Geography, Leipzig.

Hunecke, M. (1999) 'Lifestyles, Mobility Styles and Mobility-Related Models of Action', in The Research Institute for Regional and Urban Development of the Federal State of North Rhine-Westphalia (ILS) (ed.), *U-MOVE: Youth and Mobility*, ILS-Reports 150, ILS, Dortmund, pp. 30-39.

Kalter, F. (1994) 'Commuting Instead of Migrating? The Choice and Stability of the Combinations of Residence and Workplace Location', *Journal of Sociology*, vol. 23, pp. 460-476.

Kasper, B. and Scheiner, J. (2005) *Spatial Development and Leisure Mobility in an Ageing Society*, Chapter 5, this Volume.

Klee, A. (2001) 'The Spatial Reference of Lifestyles in the City', *Munich Geographic Journals*, vol. 83, L.I.S., Passau.

Lanzendorf, M. (2001) *Leisure Transport. On the Road to Socio-Ecological Mobility Research*, Publications of Geography of Tourism 56, University of Trier, Trier.

Lüdtke, H. (1995) *Time Use and Lifestyles. Empirical Analyses on Leisure Behaviour, Expressive Inequality and Quality of Life in West Germany*, Marburg Contributions to Sociological Research 5, University of Marburg, Marburg.

Lüdtke, H. (1996) 'Methodological Problems in Lifestyle Research', in O.G. Schwenk (ed.), *Lifestyles Between Analysis of Social Structure and Cultural Science*, Leske and Budrich, Opladen. pp. 139-163.

Lutz, B. (1984) *The Short Dream of Perpetual Prosperity*, Campus, Frankfurt.

Rhode-Jüchtern, T. (1998) 'Space of "Reality" and Space of "Possibility": Attempts to Escape "Container-Thinking"', *Geography*, vol. 52, pp. 1-13.

Scheiner, J. (1997) *Individualisation of Activity Spaces: Contribution to a Geography of Everyday Life* (unpublished Diploma Thesis), Geographical Institute of the Free University of Berlin, Berlin.

Scheiner, J. (2001) 'Spatial Mobility in the Media Society', *Spatial Planning*, vol. 97, pp. 196-201.

Scheiner, J. (2002) 'Daily Mobility in Berlin: On Inner Unity and the Explanation of Travel Demand', in M. Gather, A. Kagermeier and M. Lanzendorf (eds), *Transport Development in the New Länder*, Erfurt Geographic Studies 10, University of Erfurt, Erfurt, pp. 37-59.

Schimpl-Neimanns, B. (2000) *Did Educational Expansion Lead to a Decrease in Social Inequality in the Participation in Education? Methodological Considerations and Results of Multinomial Logit Models for the Period 1950-1989*, Centre for Surveys, Methods and Analyses (ZUMA) Working Report No. 2000/02, ZUMA, Mannheim.

Schneider, N. and Spellerberg, A. (1999) *Lifestyles, Housing Needs, and Spatial Mobility*, Leske and Budrich, Opladen.

Schulze, G. (1992) *The Experience Society*, Campus, Frankfurt.

Spellerberg, A. (1996) *Social Differentiation by Lifestyles: An Empirical Study of Quality of Life in West and East Germany*, Edition Sigma, Berlin.

StadtLeben (2002) *Final Milestone Report*, RWTH Aachen, Aachen, Berlin, Bochum and Dortmund, http://www.isb.rwth-aachen.de/stadtleben.

Topp, H. (1994) 'Less Traffic But Same Mobility?', *International Transport*, vol. 46, pp. 486-493.

Troxler, J.M. (1986) *Residential Mobility and Commuting in Suburbia: Theoretical Concept and Empirical Study in the South-Western Agglomeration of Zurich*, Lang, Bern.

Vogt, W. (2000) 'The Impact of Teleworking and Telecommerce on Transport', in Bonn Road and Transportation Research Association (FGSV) (ed.), *Sustainable Mobility in Cities and Regions*, FGSV-Colloquium, 31 May and 1 June 1999, Bonn, FGSV, Köln.

Vogt, W., Lenz, M., Kalter, F., Dobeschinsky, H. and Breuer, P. (2001) *The Role of Daily Long Distance Commuting for Generated Traffic*, Reports of the Federal Highway Research Institute (BAST), Transport Engineering V 88, BAST, Bergisch Gladbach.

Wulfhorst, G., Beckmann, K.J., Hunecke, M. and Heinze, M. (2000) 'Land Use and Travel Behaviour: Mutual Influences Between Urban Development, Lifestyle and Travel Demand', in M. Hunecke (ed.) *Options for Structuring Sustainable Mobility*, Workshop Report of the Secretary of Future Studies (SfZ) 27, Secretary of Future Studies, Gelsenkirchen, pp. 5-48.

Chapter 4

Spatial Analysis and Modelling Based on Activities: A Pilot Study for Antwerpen and Gent, Belgium

Hans Tindemans, Dries Van Hofstraeten,
Ann Verhetsel and Frank Witlox

Introduction

This chapter is an introduction to the research project 'SAMBA' (Spatial Analysis and Modelling Based on Activities) undertaken by teams at four Belgian universities: Antwerpen, Gent, Louvain-La-Neuve and Namur. The main objective of the SAMBA project was to obtain an estimate of the demand for mobility in Belgium, based on 'chains of activity'. These activity chains are drawn from data collected during the first Belgian national survey on household mobility (known as 'MOBEL') and from data at the regional and local level (known as 'OVG'). This chapter explores the data from the OVG household surveys in the metropolitan areas of Antwerpen and Gent. The main goal is to formulate a number of hypotheses on the socio-demographic and activity-related characteristics of the trips, using a descriptive statistical analysis.

The chapter has the following structure. First a brief overview of the activity-based approach, with special attention to the dimension of space, is presented. Second, the project's aims are set out. Third, an introduction to the data is given. Fourth, different data errors are stated, and fifth the analysis of the main variables in the data set is presented. The objective is to find out which variables in the surveys can be used to explain 'spatial' behaviour of the respondents. Trip distance, trip duration, trip purpose, means of transport, hour of departure and hour of return, together with socio-demographic data are considered. Formulating hypotheses on the spatial characteristics is the first step in modelling the spatial dimension in an activity-based context. Finally, the chapter ends with some conclusions.

Towards a Spatial, Activity-Based Approach

In the field of travel demand research, various methods have been developed to predict travel decisions subject to certain constraints (e.g. costs, demographic composition of the population, external changes). In general, two dominant methods can be defined: the trip-based approach and the activity-based approach. However, in the last two decades, the realisation that personal travel is derived from the need to participate in different activities in different locations has lead to a shift from the trip-based to the activity-based approach (Kitamura, 1988).

A general definition of the activity-based approach is given by Jones *et al.* (1990), where they state that 'the activity-based approach shares a common philosophical perspective whereby the conventional approach to the study of travel behaviour […] is replaced by a richer, more holistic, framework in which travel is analysed as daily or multi-day patterns of behaviour, related to and derived from differences in lifestyles and activity participation among the population' (*ibid*, p. 34). A more developed definition, by Ettema and Timmermans (1997a), states that:

> … activity-based approaches describe which activities people pursue, at what locations, at what times and how these activities are scheduled, given the locations and attributes of potential destinations, the state of the transportation network, aspects of the institutional context, and their personal and household characteristics. (*ibid*, p. xv)

The main idea is that one first needs to understand activity behaviour before one can analyse travel behaviour; and that travel is generally not undertaken for its own sake, but follows from taking part in activities at locations that are not the person's current location (Pas, 1996). Many researchers have recognised that it is time to study the underlying processes of travel and related behaviour (Doherty, 2002). Trip-based models do not reflect this underlying behaviour, and treat activity attributes as travel attributes. A series of applications of activity-based approaches have been developed in the past: 'CARLA' and 'STARCHILD' are two examples of simulation-based activity-based approach models (Jones *et al.*, 1983). Gärling *et al.* (1994) developed 'SCHEDULER' to produce activity schedules from long- and short-term calendars (McNally, 2000). Ettema and Timmermans (1997b) developed 'SMASH', a tool that generates activity patterns. Another example of an activity-based application, focussing on econometrics, is 'TRANSIMS' (Bowman and Ben-Akiva, 1997).

Travel demand analysis is intrinsically spatial yet in travel modelling spatial analysis is seldom recognised (Bhat and Zhao, 2002). When the spatial dimension is part of the modelling approach, the planning area consists of several zones, each of which represents an aggregate spatial unit from where trips are produced and to where trips are attracted. Bhat and Zhao (2002) highlight the need to accommodate spatial issues in travel modelling.

Bates (2000) pointed out that spatial separation is the essence of travel demand. It is clear that there is a variation in transport demand over time, but there are also spatial implications. Yet little research has been conducted on the geographical dimension of travel demand. In a recent overview of space-time approaches to travel behaviour, Timmermans *et al.* (2002) stated that spatial variables have not been examined in studies on activity duration and time allocation. There is still no definitive conclusion about whether spatial characteristics are influencing time used in travel and activity patterns. In research on trip chaining and stop-pattern formation, Kumar and Levinson (1995) found that trip chaining was significantly related to a spatial variable, i.e. location within the metropolitan region. In other words, residents who live close to the city centre are less likely to link work and non-work activities when compared to those who live in outer suburbs. But still it seems that many activity-based models need better spatial representation. Timmermans *et al.* (2002) encourage geographers to jump on the bandwagon. Bhat and Koppelman (1999) also point out that studying interactions between space and time needs more attention in the future, as much research on temporal aspects of activity participation leaves the spatial dimension unexamined.

Spatial Analysis and Modelling Based on Activities (SAMBA)

In the SAMBA study of mobility demand in Belgium, activity chains, and especially their spatial dimension, are considered. The purpose of SAMBA is to build a synthetic population that can be used to create better origin and destination matrices. The synthetic population needs to be, statistically speaking, representative of the mobility behaviour of the actual population. Nowadays in Flanders, most travel demand models are trip-based, four-step models (Verhetsel, 1998). Only recently have policy makers invested in surveys that can serve as a base for activity-based analysis. In fact, the Flemish Mobility Departments want to use the results of an activity-based analysis to modify the functions for trip generation, trip distribution, modal split and assignment in the conventional models.

The main goals of SAMBA are:

- spatialisation of travel survey data;
- spatio-temporal modelling of activity chains; and
- construction of a synthetic population (Figure 4.1).

The first step is to enrich the databases with a spatial dimension. Within the surveys, the addresses of the locations where the activities have taken place were collected. One of the largest tasks was to geocode the trips recorded in the surveys. Given the recent evolutions in Geographical Information Systems (GIS) this could largely be automated. The spatial data in the surveys of Antwerpen and Gent are already corrected and geocoded by use of ArcView and MapInfo. Prior to geocoding, errors in names of streets, post codes, and so on were detected and corrected (see below).

In the second stage of the project a description of the space-time chaining of the households' activities was made. To obtain a space-time representation of the activity chains a space dimension had to be added because, until now, this approach focused on the time dimension only (e.g. Cirillo and Toint, 2001). To our knowledge, the determining elements of a space-time analysis are localisation, distance, time taken, purpose and household structures (and there may be other elements). From the analysis, hypotheses were formulated and tested on the spatial characteristics of trips. The significant results will be used in the spatial activity-based modelling approach.

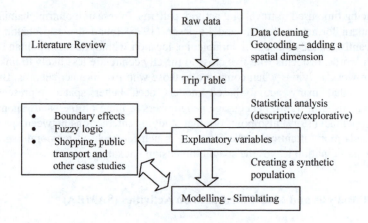

Figure 4.1　SAMBA project research structure

From this spatial model, a synthetic model for population mobility was constructed. The purpose of this phase was to move from the sample to the population. Based on the model developed with information from surveyed households, a synthetic population was created which was statistically representative of the mobility behaviours of the actual population. If we know the way in which households organise their activities (in space and time), the trips associated with these activities and their characteristics can be deduced. This tells us the mobility demand.

Description of the Data

Although the SAMBA project includes different surveys of different levels, this chapter discusses data from Travel Behaviour Research surveys (OVG, 1999-2001) in two major urban regions in Flanders: Antwerpen and Gent. Both data sets contain an extensive description of socio-demographic characteristics of the households and of each individual, as well as a two-day consecutive travel diary filled in by everyone in the household over the age of five. Hence, the collected data can be grouped into three broad categories (Cirillo and Toint, 2001):

1.　background information on the household (e.g. household structure, household location, household resources, including means of transport and their use);
2.　background information on individuals (e.g. year of birth, gender, education level and whether or not they have a driving licence); and
3.　description of each trip, including information on the associated activities (e.g. street name, post code, hour of departure and arrival, distance, length of trip, means of transport, and purpose of trip).

The data set for Antwerpen includes 2,527 households or 5,613 people who performed 29,778 trips. In the Gent region we used a data set of 2,995 households, 6,785 people and 35,878 trips (see Table 4.1). In our activity-based approach, the individual trip was considered as the basic element of the entire travel and activity pattern of that individual. Therefore we combined the trips in chains of each individual. In our study we define:

- a 'trip' as a movement of a household member from an origin to a (different) destination (Cirillo and Toint, 2001); and
- a 'chain' as a sequence of trips starting and ending at the base location (in fact the starting point during that day).

Table 4.1   An overview of data, Antwerpen and Gent (from OVG Travel Behaviour Research, 1999-2001)

Urban district	Antwerpen (Antwerp)	Gent (Ghent)
Year of survey	1999	2000
Number of households	2,527	2,995
Number of people	5,613	6,785
Number of trips	29,778	35,878

As the SAMBA project has a spatial focus, locating trips on a digital reference map was one of the most important steps. Since we wanted to combine the data with other geographical layers, e.g. transportation networks or land use, the first step was to check the address (street name and post code) and the activity for each trip for errors and inconsistencies. The large number of different errors appearing in the address files made complete automated correction impossible. Instead, manual correction was needed. For 25 per cent of the cases in Antwerpen, and for 35 per cent of the cases in Gent, the addresses or purposes were adjusted or corrected. Often the spelling of street names or the post codes were incorrect or descriptions of the destinations were flawed. These errors could be adjusted by using search engines on the Internet. Inconsistencies appeared, for example, when the purpose 'going home' was related to an address which was not the home address. Data was also missing for street names, post codes or purpose of trip. All addresses abroad (outside Belgium) were omitted from this study. An overview of the frequencies of errors is given in Table 4.2.

The second step in the process was the geocoding of the correct address data. Geocoding means that the data was linked to its corresponding geographical co-ordinates on a digital reference map by means of GIS software. As the reference map for this study, the digital map of Flanders provided by OC-GIS Vlaanderen was used. In both districts about 85 per cent of all trips could be geocoded, and hence used in our spatial analyses. The remaining 15 per cent that could not be located were not completely lost as they still contain a lot of useful information.

Table 4.2　　Frequencies of errors in the data

Code	Antwerpen N = 29,778		Gent N = 35,878	
Correct data	60.1%	Geocoded:	48.3%	Geocoded:
Corrected or adjusted data	25.0%	85%	34.9%	83%
Description (e.g. shop 'X', firm 'Y'), but no street. Purpose and post code correct.	1.9%		9.6%	
Post code and/or street not locatable or missing. Purpose correct.	6.6%		3.4%	
Purpose not correct, but post code or street correct.	0.3%	Not geocoded: 15%	0.4%	Not geocoded: 17%
Locatable, but purpose missing.	0.8%		0.7%	
Too much data missing.	3.3%		0.4%	
Purpose 'going home' is inconsistent with indicated address.	1.6%		1.4%	
Abroad	0.4%		1.0%	

Tracing and eliminating errors and inconsistencies early in the modelling process was an important task in obtaining good quality results. In addition to the difficulties related to geocoding, at least three other sources of errors were found: trip chaining errors; fatigue-errors; and rounding-up or down of reported times and distances.

Analysis

In this chapter, the emphasis is on activities (the purpose of trips) and activity chains because travel, and therefore trips, are caused by the need to participate in activities. Since different activities are located in specific places, a spatial aspect is always involved. In this section, we consider which variables are most likely to both explain activities causing trips and the spatial characteristics of the trip. We examine:

- the frequency of trips for each socio-demographic group (who?);
- the activity chain (what?);
- the activity or trip purpose (why?);
- trip duration and trip distance (where? when?); and
- the means of transport (how?).

Because the figures for Antwerpen and Gent are very similar, the Tables and Figures in this section contain data for just one of the metropolitan areas. In those cases where it is relevant, the results are given for both data sets.

Table 4.3 Frequencies of trips and chains (Antwerpen)

	% of all trips N= 29,778	% of all chains N= 12,262	# different combinations N=1,373
One-trip chains	**2.8**	**6.7**	**23**
Two-trip chains	**53.8**	**65.3**	**143**
H-shopping-H	11.1	13.4	
H-work-H	10.9	13.2	
H-entertainment-H	7.3	8.7	
H-school-H	5.2	6.3	
H-visit someone-H	5.0	6.1	
H-bring/get someone-H	3.3	4.0	
H-services (doctor, bank)-H	2.3	2.8	
H-walk/drive/cycle-H	0.8	1.0	
H-business visit-H	0.6	0.6	
Other two-trip chains	7.2	8.7	
Three-trip chains	**19.2**	**15.6**	**275**
H-shopping-shopping-H	2.0	1.6	
H-entertainment-entertainment-H	0.9	0.8	
H-work-shopping-H	0.8	0.7	
H-shopping-visit someone-H	0.8	0.6	
H-bring/get-shopping-H	0.5	0.4	
H-work-work-H	0.5	0.4	
H-services-shopping-H	0.4	0.3	
H-bring/get-work-H	0.4	0.3	
Other three-trip chains	12.3	9.9	
Four-trip chains	**12.0**	**7.2**	**359**
H-work-work-work-H	0.4	0.3	
H-bring/get-work-bring/get-H	0.4	0.3	
H-shopping-shopping-shopping-H	0.4	0.2	
H-work-shopping-work-H	0.3	0.2	
H-work-entertainment-work-H	0.3	0.2	
Other four-trip chains	10.1	6.0	
Five-trip chains	**6.0**	**2.9**	**268**
Six-trip chains	**2.9**	**1.2**	**128**
Seven-trip chains	**1.5**	**0.5**	**59**
More than seven-trip chains	**1.9**	**0.5**	**118**

H: Home

Mobility of Different Socio-Demographic Groups

The first analysis is of the distribution of trips by different socio-demographic groups. To gain an insight into the frequency of travel by specific groups, we have to compare the travel data with the demographic data. The findings do not differ much between Antwerpen and Gent. We concluded that in both urban areas age, profession and education are important elements with respect to activity-levels. People aged between 25 and 45, the more educated, employees and executives are most active, resulting in a relatively larger proportion of trips by these groups. Conversely, retired, less educated and unemployed people clearly do fewer activities outside the home.

Trip Chain and Trip Type

From the Antwerpen travel behaviour survey, it can be deduced that less than half of the activities that take place outside the home are combined in a chain (Table 4.3). Defining a chain as a sequence of trips starting and ending at the base location (home), more than 65 per cent of all chains are two-trip chains.

More than 20 per cent of the trips are either 'home-shopping-home' or 'home-work-home' chains. If activities are combined, they usually occur in three or four trip chains. A sequence of more than five activities is very rare. However, it is important to take into account when analysing trip chains, the high number of different activity combinations, particularly for three-, four- and five-trip chains.

Purpose of the Trip (Activity)

In Figure 4.2, the frequency of the purpose of trips are presented. Since 'home' is the base location where most people start and end their journey, it is by far the most frequent end location. Because this research focuses on out-of-home activities, in the rest of the analysis the trips returning to home will not be included. Actually, shopping is the most important out-of-home activity, followed by work, then 'entertainment, sport, culture or leisure', visiting someone, bringing or collecting someone, and school.

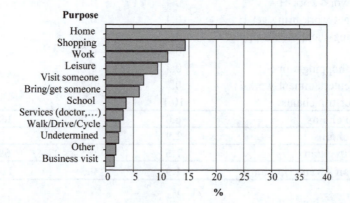

Figure 4.2   Purpose of trip (Antwerpen)

If activities are combined (as in Table 4.3), the two main activities, i.e. shopping and work, were often found in combination (e.g. 'home-work-shopping-home'). Commonly, work locations have a fixed spatial dimension and they are clustered in the same spatial zones. Consequently, from a spatial analytical viewpoint it is interesting to examine whether shopping, when linked to work, is also associated to fixed locations. Attending school was a third important purpose for a trip that can be examined for respondents under 20. 'Entertainment, sport and culture' are activities with a high frequency, but are difficult to study because: they have a wide distribution in time and space; are person-related; and are three very broad categories covering vastly different activities.

Figure 4.3, depicts the variation in certain activities during weekdays and at the weekend. If the importance of an activity can change over time, this will have an impact in space as well. For instance, when trips are concentrated in time congestion might occur and people might change their travel pattern to search for alternative roads and/or modes. First, the number of trips varies over time: people do most trips on a Friday and the fewest on a Sunday (Figure 4.4). Saturday is the second busiest travel day. Second, the occurrence of activities varies over time. A difference can be found between weekday and weekend activities: school, work and business visits are typical weekday activities, while shopping, 'entertainment, sport and culture', 'walking or driving around' and visiting someone are more frequent during the weekends. Most shopping trips occur on Saturdays (more or less 30 per cent) but during weekdays it is also a common activity (20 per cent). Leisure activities and personal visits are most popular during weekends. The number of those trips is almost equal over Saturdays and Sundays, but because fewer trips are made in total on Sundays, they are a higher proportion of Sunday travel.

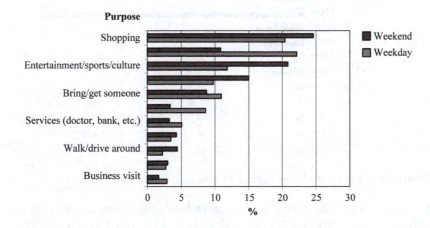

Figure 4.3   Purpose of trip on weekdays and weekends (Gent)

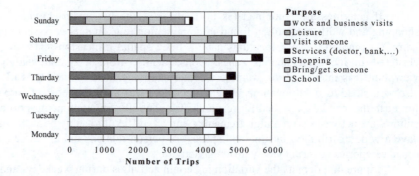

Figure 4.4   Purpose of trip by day of the week (Gent)

Figure 4.5 presents an overview of the purposes of trips that are typical during morning and evening commuting times. When leaving home between 6 a.m. and 9 a.m., 43 per cent of people go to work, 19 per cent to school and 11 per cent give lifts to someone. When people make trips between 4 p.m. and 7 p.m., more than half of the trips are back to the home (e.g. work-home and school-home trips), 10 per cent go shopping and 9 per cent visit someone. So there is a clear difference in purpose between morning and evening travel.

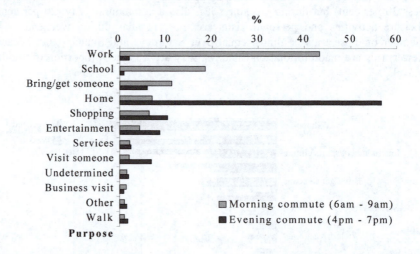

Figure 4.5   Purpose of trip during commuting times (Antwerpen)

The triangular graph in Figure 4.6 depicts the hour of departure and the three main activity groups: shopping, 'work and school' and 'entertainment, sport and culture'. In the morning, most people go to work or school. After 9 a.m., shopping trips appear frequently, and work and school trips only sporadically. 'Entertainment, sport and culture' trips occur generally after 6 p.m. and during the night.

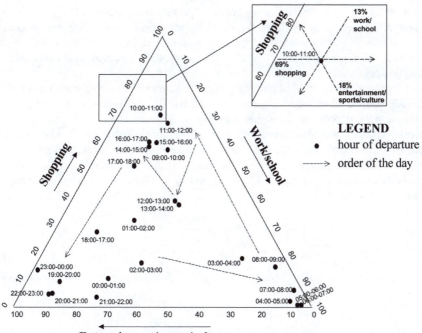

Figure 4.6 **Triangular graph showing hour of departure for trips for 'shopping', 'work and school' and 'entertainment, sports, and culture' (Antwerpen)**

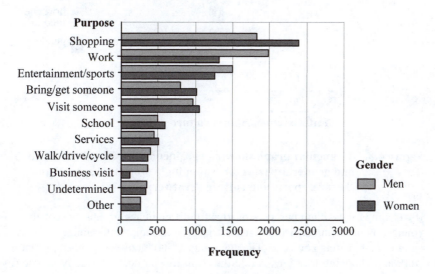

Figure 4.7 **Purpose of trip by gender (Antwerpen)**

Figure 4.7 shows the relationship between gender and purpose of trip. There is a clear difference to be noticed: typically, women make more trips for shopping, giving lifts (we assume most of the time to their children), visiting someone and services. Men generally do more trips for work, 'entertainment, sport and culture' and business visits.

Since, in most families, male household members usually earn more than female household members do, there is a similar link between income and purpose (Figure 4.8). People with a higher monthly income are likely to do more trips for work, business and 'entertainment, sport and culture'. Respondents who earn less each month travel more for activities such as going for a 'walk, drive or cycle', visiting someone, shopping or giving someone a lift. Many retired people have low monthly incomes so, in Figure 4.8, those on low incomes and elderly people appear close to each other.

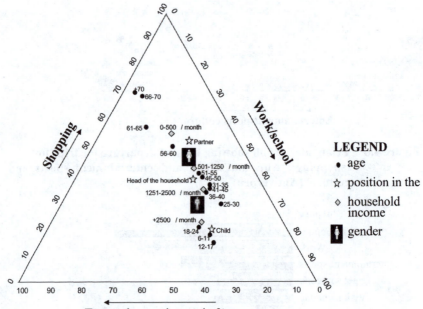

Figure 4.8   Triangular graph showing age, income, position in the household and gender, by trips for 'shopping', 'work and school' and 'leisure, sports and culture' (Antwerpen)

If we compare the main purposes of trips for different age groups, we conclude that younger people (under 18) do more trips for school, 'entertainment, sport and culture' and visiting someone. The age group 18-60 (active respondents) visit more work and shopping locations, while the main trip purpose of elderly people (over 60) is shopping, followed by 'entertainment, sport and culture' and visiting someone. Older people have less work or school duties and have more time for 'entertainment, sport and culture' trips and a very high percentage of their trips are for shopping (see also Figure 4.8).

We already stated that men, people with high incomes and middle-aged people do more work, business and 'entertainment, sport and culture' trips. Similar results hold for the position in the household: the head of the household (usually a man, middle-aged, higher earning) does more business, work and 'entertainment, sport and culture' trips (see also Figure 4.8). He also takes trips to 'walk, drive or cycle' for recreation, and to go to service centres (e.g. to the bank). Partners of the head of household do more shopping and giving lifts. Obviously, children make almost 90 per cent of the school trips.

Figure 4.9 shows that the car is the most frequently used mode of transport. Giving lifts is generally done by car (as a driver), sometimes by bicycle or on foot. Business visits and work trips are also mostly by car (as a driver). For 'entertainment, sport and culture' many trips are made by car as a passenger. Public transport, bicycle and train are means of transport that are often used by respondents making school trips. For trips with the purpose of services and shopping, cars (as a driver) and bicycles are frequently used. To walk, drive or cycle around, respondents logically choose to go on foot, use the car or use their bicycle.

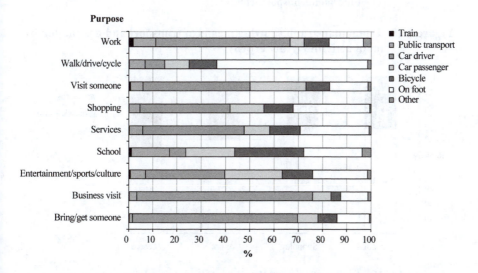

Figure 4.9   Trip purpose by means of transport (Antwerpen)

In Figure 4.10 an alternative way of presenting our findings is used. The triangular graph also points out the hierarchy of the destination: for shopping trips for instance we notice that respondents visit suburbs, and to a lesser degree Antwerp city centre. Only 7 per cent of the respondents shop outside the Antwerp urban area. Work locations usually are situated outside the Antwerp urban area (see also Figure 4.11) and entertainment, sport and culture can be found outside the city centre. For school trips, 90 per cent have their destination either in the city centre or the suburbs.

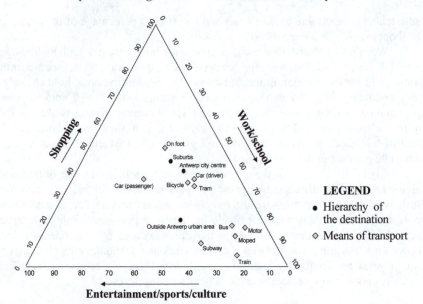

Figure 4.10 Triangular graph showing means of transport and destination by main activities (Antwerpen)

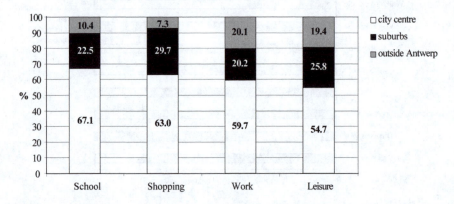

Figure 4.11 Hierarchy of trip destinations for main activities (Antwerpen)

An interesting link is the relationship between trip distance and the purpose of the trip. Respondents cover fewer kilometres for school, shopping and services trips (an average of 4km). Most of the time, these amenities can be found close to the place of residence. Furthermore, we can expect that people combine school, shopping and services with each other or with other activities. So in cities where these activity locations are available in a small area, we can assume that fewer kilometres have to be covered to reach these locations. It can be noticed that business visits and work trips generally have longer distances (13km on average). 'Entertainment, sport and culture' and 'visiting someone' trips also usually have longer distances (an average of 10km). Almost 3 per cent of the 'entertainment, sport, culture' trips have a distance of more than 100 kilometres. The same pattern can be seen for trip duration, but there is a larger spread due to the use of different means of transport, each with a specific speed, ranging from very slow (walking) to very fast (car).

Taking a look at the average trip duration (in minutes) for different trip purposes, the results vary between 14 minutes on average for services, bringing or getting someone, school and shopping, and an average of 22-23 minutes for business trips, 'entertainment, sport and culture', work and visiting someone. The activities 'walking, driving or cycling around' or just strolling around are exceptions. The average duration of these activities is almost an hour, which might be explained by the fact that respondents often take a whole day cycling around without stopping at an activity location. Both trip duration and trip distance are shown in the triangular graph (Figure 4.12).

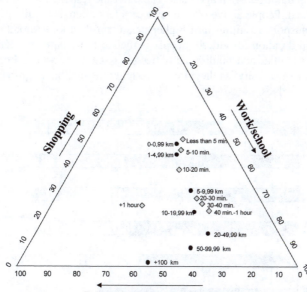

Figure 4.12 Triangular graph showing trip distance and trip duration for trips for 'shopping', 'work and school' and 'entertainment, sports and culture' (Antwerpen)

Trip Distance and Duration

From the previous section we now see that most trips are rather local, since mean trip distance and duration are short. Yet, there are some differences according to gender. Women often take more shopping, services and other short distance trips, while men take more longer distance trips, e.g. for work and business.

The relationship between income and trip duration/trip distance is also clear. The higher the monthly income, the longer respondents travel to their activities: ranging from 20 minutes for the lowest incomes (less than 500 Euro per month) to almost 26 minutes on average for the highest income group (more than 2,500 Euro per month). But, the difference is more obvious for the average trip distance: almost an average of 20 kilometres for respondents in the highest income group, compared with 9 kilometres for the lowest earners.

With respect to age and trip distance it was deduced that both in Antwerpen and Gent the highest average distances were travelled by 40 to 50 year olds. Above the age of 50, the mean trip distance decreases. Children cover short mean trip distances, due to their limited choice of transport mode and their simple activity pattern during weekdays: mainly home-school related trips (knowing that schools are usually chosen close to the place of residence).

When analysing age and trip duration there is an almost continuous increase in trip duration when age rises. The older the respondent, the longer she or he is on the road. People above 60 use their cars less often, but walk, go by bike or use public transport, resulting in a higher mean trip duration. Another reason for the higher trip duration for elderly people is their activity patterns. Retired people often have no regular and binding activities (e.g. school or work). For them trips are not always a necessity, as they are for younger people, but are often seen as an activity in themselves.

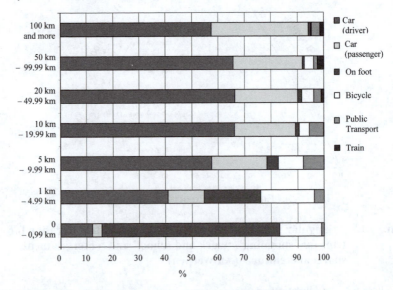

Figure 4.13 Trip distance by means of transport (Antwerpen)

The link between trip distance and the means of transport is shown in Figure 4.13. Trips of less than 1 kilometre are mainly made on foot or by bicycle. For trips between 1 and 5 kilometres, respondents choose their car (as a driver), their bicycle or go on foot. When trips are longer than 5 kilometres, nearly no trips are made on foot and only 10 per cent by bicycle. Trains only appear as a means of transport for trips over 20 kilometres. Public transport is most popular for trips between 1 and 20 kilometres.

Mode of Transport

The last variable to be studied is the transport mode used to reach the activity location (see Figures 4.14 and 4.15). The car is by far the most popular means of transport in Antwerpen. Almost 55 per cent of all trips were made by car: 40 per cent as the driver and 15 per cent as a passenger. Walking counts for more than 20 per cent and cycling for 12 per cent. Public transport is at first sight only of minimal use. The data for Gent are very similar, except that there is a relatively higher car use (43 per cent as the driver and 16 per cent as a passenger), and slightly fewer trips are made on foot (17 per cent).

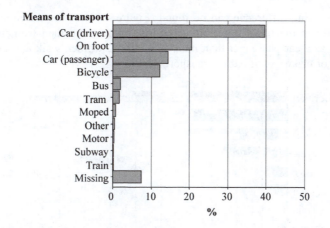

Figure 4.14 Means of transport (first trip stage) (Antwerpen)

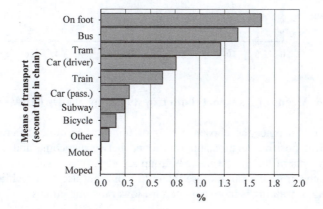

Figure 4.15 Means of transport (second trip stage) (Antwerpen)

In order to get a good idea of the use of the different means of transport, the trips were split into consecutive stages. A trip stage can be defined as a part of the trip made with or without a vehicle. Often a respondent first goes on foot to the train station (first stage), then takes the train (second stage) and finally takes the bus to his or her work (third stage). Yet, in our data sets, more than 90 per cent of all trips were made by only one means of transport. This is probably not a realistic figure. We believe it is due to inaccurate reporting. Car (as the driver) is frequently used as a means of transport, mainly in the first stage: of course being the driver is more common than being a passenger. This implies that more respondents drive alone to their activities. Walking is the second most important mode of travel in the first stage, but it is the main mode in the second stage. Cycling is important in the first stage, but disappears almost completely in the second. Public transport is very popular in the second stage, especially buses and trams and to a smaller degree trains and subways, because preceding trips are needed to reach public transport stops.

A striking difference can be found (Figure 4.16) in the different genders' use of different means of transport: men drive more often than women, who do more trips as a car passenger than men. In addition, women walk and cycle more frequently or make use of public transport.

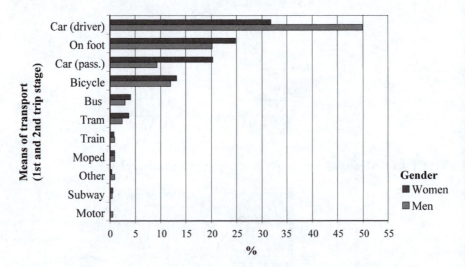

Figure 4.16 Means of transport (both trip stages) by gender (Antwerpen)

Dependent on income, the chosen means of transport is quite different (Figure 4.17). A clear positive relationship was found between income and car driving. Few respondents of the lowest income group are car drivers. The so-called higher income groups drive the car and use the train more, but use local public transport less. Cycling or walking is more common for lower income groups.

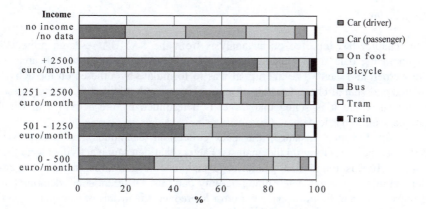

Figure 4.17 Income by means of transport (first stage in trip) (Antwerpen)

In Figure 4.18, the means of transport is plotted against age group. Younger people are more likely to make trips as a car passenger, on foot or by bicycle. Respondents under the age of 12 make more trips as car passengers, between 12 and 18 they do more trips by bicycle. The group between 18 and 25 is a transitional group. From the age of 18 people are allowed to drive a car, which implies that for those young people car driving appears, although walking and cycling are still important. For the age groups between 25 and 65 (the active population), car driving is by far the most frequently used means of transport. The frequency of driving a car decreases with rising age and is absorbed by walking and car passenger trips. The other means of transport are of minimal importance, except train and public transport for youngsters between 12 and 25, and bus and tram for elderly people.

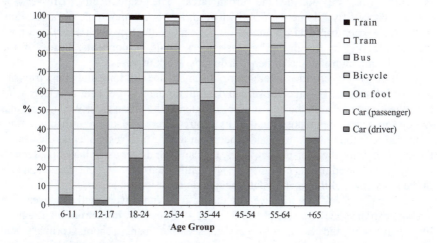

**Figure 4.18 Means of transport (first and second stage in trip) by age group
(Antwerpen)**

Conclusions

This chapter has reported on an analysis from the SAMBA research project. It explored the data from Flemish household surveys in the metropolitan areas of Antwerpen and Gent. The main goal was to formulate hypotheses on the activity related and spatial characteristics of trips. The research adopted the activity-based approach where it is stated that travel is determined by the activities in which people want to participate.

In the first instance, the data collection techniques and errors were described before setting up the analysis. Factors that determine activities were then studied. It was found that gender, age and income are three important socio-demographic variables determining activity patterns. Different socio-demographic groups have specific time-space patterns. Moreover, the means of transport used to reach their activities is very different for each group.

The activities that appear most frequently in the data sets of Antwerpen and Gent are related to shopping, work, 'entertainment, sport and culture' or school. These four activity groups mainly determine the activity pattern of most respondents. Often they are the central activities around which other activities are organised. During weekdays, school and work are the main activities, but on Saturday and Sunday when shopping and leisure activities become more important, no main activity can be identified.

Most shopping trips are rather short (less than 5 kilometres). Yet, many respondents choose to use their cars, probably because it is easy to carry shopping. Women and low-income earners are more likely to do shopping trips than men and high-income earners. It is striking that elderly people are such devoted shoppers.

The second most frequent activity is work. Respondents often cover long distances (about 13 kilometres on average). This is because in Antwerp 20 per cent of work trips are outside the urban area. The capital city, Brussels, is approximately fifty kilometres from Antwerp, and is an important work location. In the Antwerpen trip data set almost 60 per cent of the trips with a work purpose were made by car (as driver or passenger). Male respondents, heads of the household and high-income earners, made most work trips.

For leisure activities, average trip distances are still long and many trips are over 10 kilometres. For the Antwerpen data, more than 40 per cent of leisure trips have their destination in the city suburbs or outside the urban area. We suggest that some sport cannot be practised in the city centre. There is also a significant number of tourist or holiday trips to outside the urban area. Since respondents often leave the city centre for their leisure activities, the car (as a driver as well as a passenger) is a frequently used means of transport. Generally men, high-income earners, heads of the household, children and young people do most leisure trips.

Finally, for school trips we saw that respondents cover small distances. The average trip distance of a school trip is about 4 kilometres. In metropolitan regions like Antwerpen and Gent, it is easy to see that many schools (primary and secondary schools as well as universities and colleges) can be found in a relatively small area. For Antwerp more than 65 per cent of the school trips have their destination in the city centre. So respondents seldom have to leave the city to participate in these activities. Most of the time students have no car and are obliged to use other means of transport, e.g. public transport (18 per cent) or cars as a passenger (19 per cent). But in most cases, they cycle (28 per cent) or walk (25 per cent).

This analysis must be seen as an initial stage in the research as it has resulted in some fundamental travel characteristics on which the spatial modelling can be built. Further research focuses on spatial dimensions of activity chains by means of discrete choice models (see Ben-Akiva and Lerman, 1985). A synthetic population will be created in order to construct new origin-destination matrices. These will be used in the existing transport models. In addition, a study of boundary effects, rough set analysis and detailed case studies will provide a better insight into the spatial dimensions of activity chains.

Acknowledgements

The research was undertaken as part of the Second Scientific Support Plan for a Sustainable Development Policy (SPSD II), for the Belgian State, Prime Minister's Office, Federal Office for Scientific, Technical and Cultural Affairs. The authors would like to thank the Flemish Government, namely Eddy Peetermans for assistance with GIS applications, and Wilfried Goossens for providing the data.

References

Bates, J. (2000) 'History of Demand Modelling', in D.A. Hensher and K.J. Button, (eds), *Handbook of Transport Modelling*, Pergamon, Oxford, pp. 11-33.

Ben-Akiva, M. and Lerman, S.R. (1985) *Discrete Choice Analysis: Theory and Applications to Travel Demand*, MIT Press, Cambridge, M.A. and London.

Bhat, C. and Koppelman, F. (1999) 'Activity-Based Modelling of Travel Demand', in R.W. Hall (ed.) *Handbook of Transportation*, Science Kluwer, The Netherlands, pp. 35-61.

Bhat, C. and Zhao, H. (2002) 'The Spatial Analysis of Activity Stop Generation', *Transportation Research B*, vol. 36, pp. 557-575.

Bowman, J. and Ben-Akiva, M. (1997) 'Activity-Based Travel Forecasting', in U.S. Department of Transportation (DoT), *Activity-Based Travel Forecasting Conference*, *Report DOT-97-17*, US DoT, Washington D.C.

Cirillo, C. and Toint, Ph. (2001) *An Activity-Based Approach to the Belgian National Travel Survey*, Groupe de Recherce sur les Transport, FUNDP, Namur.

Doherty, S. (2002) *Conceptual Frameworks for Understanding Activities and Travel*, Social Sciences and Human Research Council of Canada, http://www.wlu.ca/~sdoherty/mcri/detailed.html.

Ettema, D. and Timmermans, H. (1997a) 'Activity-Based Approaches: An Introduction', in D.F. Ettema and H.J.P. Timmermans (eds), *Activity-Based Approaches to Travel Analysis*, Pergamon, Oxford, pp. xv-xx.

Ettema, D. and Timmermans, H. (1997b) 'Theories and Models of Activity Patterns', in D.F. Ettema and H.J.P. Timmermans (eds), *Activity-Based Approaches to Travel Analysis*, Pergamon, Oxford, pp. 1-36.

Gärling, T., Kwan, M.P. and Golledge, R. (1994) 'Computational Process Modelling of Household Activity Scheduling', *Transportation Research B*, vol. 28, pp. 355-364.

Jones, P.M., Dix, M.C., Clarke, M.I. and Heggie, I.G. (1983) *Understanding Travel Behaviour*, Gower, Aldershot.

Jones, P.M., Koppelman, F. and Orfeuil, J.P. (1990) 'Activity Analysis: State-of-the-Art and Future Decisions', in P.M. Jones (ed.) *Developments in Dynamic and Activity-Based Approaches to Travel Analysis*, Gower, Aldershot.

Kitamura, R. (1988) 'An Evaluation of Activity-Based Travel Analysis', *Transportation*, vol. 15, pp. 9-34.

Kumar, A. and Levinson, D.M. (1995) 'Chained Trips in Montgomery County, Maryland', *Institute of Traffic Engineers Journal*, vol. 65(5), pp. 27-32.

McNally, M. (2000) 'The Activity-Based Approach', in D.A. Hensher and K.J. Button (eds), *Handbook of Transport Modelling*, Pergamon, Oxford, pp. 53-69.

Pas, E. (1996) 'Recent Advances in Activity-Based Travel Demand Modelling', *Activity-Based Travel Forecasting Conference Proceedings*, June 2-5, 1996, Texas Transportation Institute, Arlington, Texas.

Timmermans, H.J.P., Arentze, T.A. and Joh, C.H. (2002) 'Analysing Space-Time Behaviour: New Approaches to Old Problems', *Progress in Human Geography*, vol. 26(2), pp. 175-190.

Verhetsel, A. (1998) 'The Impact of Spatial Versus Economic Measures in an Urban Transportation Plan', *Computers, Environment and Urban Systems*, vol. 22(6), pp. 541-555.

Chapter 5

Spatial Development and Leisure Mobility in an Ageing Society

Birgit Kasper and Joachim Scheiner

Introduction

Transport requirements in Germany, as in other western countries, will be characterised in the future, far more than today, by the needs of elderly people. The percentage of people over 60 is likely to increase from 24 per cent in 2001 to 37 per cent in 2050 (Federal Statistical Office Germany, 2003). Hence, transport demands will also change significantly. First, because of fewer business trips, a growing share of leisure travel, both in terms of trips and distances is expected. Second, the increasing availability of driving licenses and cars among seniors will go along with continuing individualisation in choice of transport mode. The share of people with a driving license among 61-80 year olds increased from 37 to 56 per cent between 1991 and 1998. In particular, the share of women in this category grew from 21 to 37 per cent (men from 67 to 82 per cent, Federal Ministry of Transport, Building and Housing, 2000). Currently, this gender differentiation is accelerating. Hence, the demands for leisure mobility demand from elderly people will increase, and there will be changes in demand in the future as well. Several other factors contribute to this:

- increasing age span after retirement, and the longer lasting health that goes with longer life expectancy;
- the comparatively high level of affluence, e.g. because of the high portion of people who own property, which is often already paid for;
- the increasing differentiation of wants and activity patterns that goes along with the individualisation of lifestyles, which are only partly altered by age because of cohort specific elements (Wahl, 2001).

At the present time, however, the mobility of elderly people is regarded as limited in comparison to other age groups. The percentage of people who leave their home on any given day clearly declines by age. The space for external activities for mobile seniors are comparatively limited to their residential area, and the modal share of walking is much higher than among younger people (based on the authors' analysis of KONTIV, 2002). There are multiple causes for these facts, including: the high portion of non-motorised households, the absence of job trips, strong ties to the residential district, and physical impairment among seniors. The share of severely disabled and immobile people strongly rises by age, from 1.6 per cent among children under 14 to 26.1 per cent among the over 65s (Federal Statistical Office Germany, 2000).

Strong bonds to the neighbourhood are accompanied by distinct location requirements. They can be summarised by two terms: safety and micro-spatial accessibility (Scheiner and Holz-Rau, 2002). Safety is related to 'security' (from crime, as well as familiarity with the residential area) and 'road safety' (as achieved, perhaps, by safe design of footpaths, traffic management, slow traffic speeds and so on). Accessibility concerns access to local amenities such as daily shopping facilities, medical supplies (doctors, pharmacies), churches, green areas, and meeting places (see Mollenkopf *et al.*, 1998). Meeting places do not only mean leisure facilities such as cafés, clubs or meeting centres. They can also be spaces for opportunities for informal, casual meetings, such as benches, mail boxes, playgrounds, squares, promenades etc. Micro-spatially distributed shopping facilities also permit social contact 'by the way' and encourage older people to leave their homes. Thus, there are not merely functional, but also social qualities in facilities such as weekly markets.

However, the development of settlement and spatial population structures has been characterised by tendencies that mitigate against these requirements. The micro-spatial accessibility of supply and leisure facilities has continually decreased since mass motorisation in the 1960s. The main reasons for this are the ongoing concentration of retail and other services in ever bigger units and, quite recently, the 'ageing of the periphery', i.e. the relative shift of the elderly population in favour of urban outskirts and suburban regions (one-family house areas and satellite towns), but also rural low-density regions, mainly in East Germany. While in suburbia this corresponds with an era of construction, the over-ageing of East German rural regions is due to demographically selective migration.

In conclusion, the increasing mobility chances of many elderly people are countered by decreasing accessibility for the less mobile. Regarding leisure mobility, a significant differentiation between elderly people can be seen first, for the chances of access to leisure options, and second for leisure aspirations and types of leisure mobility.

Aims and Methods of the 'FRAME' Project

Project Aims

Given the aforementioned considerations, the 'FRAME' research project investigates types and conditions as well as individual decisions underlying seniors' leisure mobility (FRAME is an acronym for 'Freizeitmobilität aelterer Manschen' or 'Leisure Mobility of Senior Citizens'). The aim of the project is to generate knowledge to help develop environmentally friendly, socially balanced and economically solid mobility options for leisure activities for elderly people. Featuring the term leisure *mobility* in the project name emphasises that the research interest lies not only in the realised forms of spatial behaviour: but also the *chances* of elderly people to participate in travel and thus in public life. These chances are partly limited, despite the 'young elderly' and 'new elderly' (Opaschowski, 1998), which are observed (or propagandised) in lifestyle and market research.

Strategically, the 'pillars' of sustainable transport planning (reduction of travel demand and distances, modal shift away from the car, optimisation of traffic flows) have to be complemented by 'mobility maintenance'. For the highly mobile elderly, the same standards of assessment as for the younger population have to be applied. Regarding mobility restricted people (ill, frail, infirm or lonely), the maintenance or promotion of appropriate mobility options has to be considered.

Project Structure and Methods

The FRAME project is broadly organised into three steps (Figure 5.1). At the beginning, a structure analysis was developed where seniors' requirements, in terms of transport and leisure, were investigated. The results were concretised at the local level of the study areas. As a consequence of the frequently non age-specific supply and demand, the supply analysis was broadly conceived and not limited to (seemingly) age-typical options.

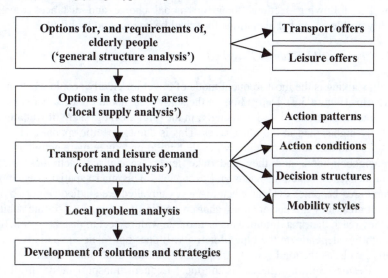

Figure 5.1   Project structure and main fields of analysis

The next step was an investigation of seniors' transport and leisure demands in three study areas, based on a standardised household survey, which was carried out between November 2001 and July 2002. The study areas were Bonn, a city of roughly 300,000 inhabitants and the former capital of Germany, parts of its suburbs on the west side of the Rhine, and parts of the Eifel, a rural area west of Bonn. Thus, three spatial categories were distinguished (city, suburban and rural). In total, 4,500 face-to-face interviews with people aged 60 or over were carried out.

As a third step, the results of the household survey and the structure analyses were discussed in a workshop with local experts, such as spatial planners, transport planners, transport providers, representatives of leisure facilities, social facilities, senior housing facilities and so forth. Interviews with experts as representatives of the 'supply side' also played a central role in this step. The focus was a local problem analysis and the development of suggestions for good practice solutions.

Leisure Mobility of Elderly People: The Results of the Household Survey

In the following sections, selected results from the household survey are presented. The sample includes 58.5 per cent women and 41.5 per cent men. Between the three areas there are no noteworthy differences in the subjective ratings of individual health, satisfaction with health, or individual mobility levels, although there are significantly more 'very old' people in the Bonn sample (in Bonn 20 per cent are over 80, in the suburban area, 12 per cent, and in the rural area, 15 per cent). The following sections focus on modal choice and distances travelled, mobility problems, and explanations for travel behaviour and mobility.

Modal Choice and Distances Travelled

Overall, walking is the most frequent mode of travel for elderly people when making leisure trips (Figure 5.2). Depending on the study area, about 60 to 70 per cent of all trips are undertaken on foot. Surprisingly, in the rural area, the share of walking trips is notably higher than in the other areas. This is due to specific spatial and activity behaviours: in the rural area, elderly people tend to undertake more activities within their neighbourhood, and they undertake fewer 'specialised' activities, such as cultural activities, restaurant visits and excursions. This micro-spatial orientation in the rural area becomes evident when distances travelled are studied (Figure 5.3). In the rural area, they are considerably shorter than in the other areas. In the suburban area, they reach their maximum. This is also true with respect to distance per activity, although this depends on the type of activity. It does not relate to spatially varying activity levels, as the total activity frequency is similar in all study areas.

Besides walking, the car is the most frequent transport mode in all study areas, particularly for long-distance trips. While only roughly a quarter of all trips are undertaken by car, the car is used for seven out of every ten kilometres travelled. The use of transport modes differs significantly between the areas. While in Bonn, the frequency of use of all public transport (taxi, bus, tram, underground and local train) is considerably higher than in the suburban and rural areas, in the suburban area the private car is used disproportionately often. Bicycles are used quite regularly in Bonn and in the suburban area.

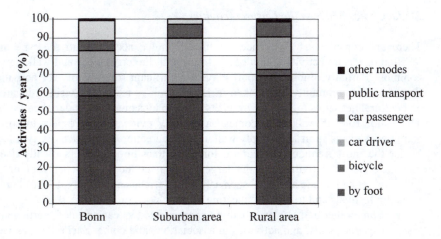

Figure 5.2   Transport mode choice of older people for leisure trips

Source: FRAME Household Survey

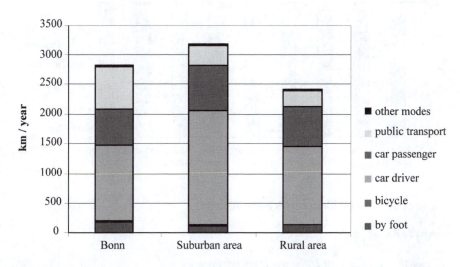

Figure 5.3   Annual distances travelled for leisure by older people, by modal choice

All distances were calculated as one-way 'linear' distances with a detour factor of 1.2.
Source: FRAME Household Survey

Modal Choice and Specific Leisure Activities

There are conspicuous differences in modal choice according to the type and location of leisure activity (Figure 5.4). In general, the private car and walking are common. Partially, public transport plays a significant role, mainly for activities that are most commonly undertaken in Bonn, such as restaurant visits, education and cultural activities (e.g. museum visits). Excursions are often undertaken by bus. The major role of walking becomes particularly evident with respect to social activities, such as sport and simply walking for recreation. These activity types are by far the most frequent, accounting for more than three quarters of all leisure activities. Social activities are the largest group, containing 36 per cent of all activities. They include activities such as visits to friends and family, to the church, to public festivals and to seniors' meetings.

Some other activity types can be characterised as car-oriented, particularly visits to sports events, and activities in associations and clubs. Excursions, as well as educational and cultural activities, also have a high share of car trips, but also a high share of public transport, therefore they can be characterised as typical 'motorised' activities rather than as specifically car-oriented.

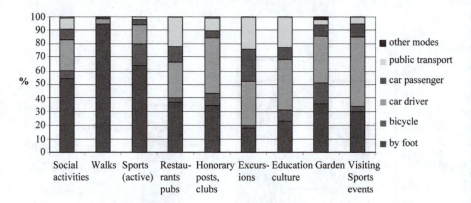

Figure 5.4   Modal choice by leisure activity

Source: FRAME Household Survey

Rating the 'Comfort' of Different Transport Modes

The dominance of the car is evident when transport modes are rated for comfort (Figure 5.5). Sixty five per cent of respondents judged the car the most comfortable means of transport. Seven per cent decided in favour of public transport, 24 per cent in favour of the train (multiple responses were possible). In an open question in the questionnaire, 'comfort' proved to be the most important criterion for mode choice. However, the least used transport modes are still regarded as comfortable to some. People, who frequently use a specific means of transport, tend to consider it more comfortable than others.

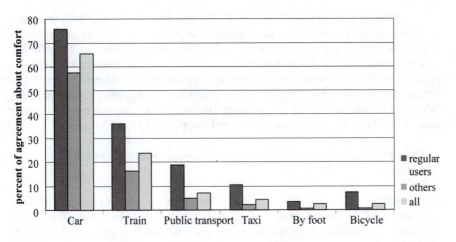

Figure 5.5   Most comfortable transport mode and modal choice

Multiple responses possible
Source: FRAME Household Survey

Unfulfilled Desires to Take Part in Leisure Activities

The research interest in FRAME lies not only in actual travel behaviour, but also in the chances of seniors to participate in leisure activities. In this sense, a measure for mobility could be whether a person is able to realise his or her wishes to take part in an activity.

Table 5.1   Unfulfilled desires to take part in leisure activities (per cent)

	% of respondents
No unfulfilled activity wishes	51.4
Some unfulfilled activity wishes	48.6
Most significant unfulfilled wishes	
Holidays	9.5
Culture (theatre, concert, opera, museum, exhibitions)	8.7
Sports activities	7.5
Walking, hiking, bicycle tour	7.0
Excursions	4.4
Dancing, festivals, courses	2.8
Restaurants, pubs, cafés	1.2
Meeting relatives, friends, acquaintances	0.9
Visiting sport events	0.8
Shopping	0.8
Other	2.6

Source: FRAME Household Survey

Table 5.1 shows that chances for elderly people to take part in leisure activities are partly restricted, despite increasing motorisation and better health. Half of all interviewees (48.6 per cent) had at least one unfulfilled wish to take part in a particular activity. Most frequently cited were holidays and cultural activities (visiting the theatre, concert, opera, museum or exhibition), followed by sports and 'intrinsic trips', where the trip itself is the activity (walking, hiking, cycling tours). When excursions are added to the latter, 'intrinsic trips' are the most frequently cited. This shows how important it is for elderly people to just 'get around'.

Mobility Problems: Explaining Unfulfilled Desires to Take Part in Leisure Activities

Taking part in a few activities outside of the home does not necessarily indicate poor mobility, in the sense of potential, but unfulfilled desire to take part in activities may indicate restricted mobility. So what are the reasons? We have to distinguish between reasons that are quoted by the interviewees themselves and causes which can be deduced by researchers from external conditions. For instance, gerontological mobility researchers claim that the absence of a private car is responsible for inferior mobility and poor life quality (Rothe, 1993), and even that giving up driving is a risk factor for the onset of depression (Federal Ministry for Family Affairs, Senior Citizens, Women and Youth, 2001).

In the FRAME project, the most frequently stated reasons for not taking part in activities were being alone, health problems and problems with public transport (Table 5.2). As specific deficits of public transport, intricacy of timetables and ticket machines and generally insufficient public transport connections are most frequently quoted, followed by fear of crime. The frequent mention of problems with public transport is a clear reference to a demand for improvement.

Beyond the obstacles stated by the interviewees themselves, connections between unfulfilled wishes and assumed external constraints can be examined. In doing so, it becomes evident that neither car availability nor living alone, as opposed to being in a partnership, have a big impact on the existence of unfulfilled activity wishes (Table 5.3). People with a driving license and a car in the household state unfulfilled wishes just as often as people living in households without a car. Hence, it is not the car that guarantees satisfaction, rather, that car owners among seniors are the more out-going ones, with multiple activity wishes occasionally staying unsatisfied. This interpretation is supported by the fact that interviewees living in a partnership (who are on average much younger than solitary people and who probably still 'expect more from life') claim unfulfilled activity wishes slightly more frequently. Between the three study areas, no noteworthy differences in unfulfilled wishes occur.

Table 5.2   Interviewees' reasons for unfulfilled desires to undertake leisure activities (per cent)

Reasons for unfulfilled participation in leisure activities	%
Do not want to do this alone	47.0
Health reasons	41.2
Public transport (unfavourable location of stations, generally insufficient connections, entrance/exit, intricate timetables/ticket machines, fear of exposure to crime)	40.8
Partner (partner's health; has got no time, different interests, is against it)	35.4
Lack of time	34.7
Do not like to go out in the dark	34.3
Supply of leisure facilities (none in the vicinity, unfavourable daytime of events, poorly equipped facilities)	30.1
Weather conditions	27.4
Do not have the chance to use a car	27.3
among those without a car in their household	*13.7*
Social aspects of leisure supply (too many people; there are only young people or only old people)	21.6
Personal condition (difficulties of organisation, feel too old)	20.1
Financial situation	15.5
Insufficient parking spaces	14.3
Other important reasons	23.2

Multiple responses possible
Source: FRAME Household Survey

Age has a impact on unfulfilled wishes, but it is contrary to most expectations of gerontological mobility research. It is not the older, less mobile, who most frequently state unfulfilled wishes, but the 'young seniors'. In contrast, bad health conditions have, as expected, a heavily constraining influence: the less satisfied people are with their own health, the more often they have unfulfilled wishes. This relationship turns out to be even stronger when unfulfilled wishes by 'health judgement' are analysed within different age categories. However, because of the expected high correlation between the mentioned and other assumed factors, additional multivariate analyses seem appropriate. These are presented in the following section.

Table 5.3   Unfulfilled desires to undertake leisure activities by assumed key determinants (per cent)

	Unfulfilled activity wishes? (%)	
	Yes	No
Car availability		
Driving license and car in household	49.6	50.4
No driving license, but car in household	33.2	66.8
No car in household	49.6	50.4
Partnership		
Yes	50.3	49.7
No	45.4	54.6
Age category		
60 to 64	53.3	46.7
65 to 69	50.1	49.9
70 to 74	44.6	55.4
75 to 79	46.3	53.7
80 to 89	46.6	53.4
90 +	42.4	57.6
Satisfaction with own health		
Very unsatisfied	61.2	38.8
Unsatisfied	59.8	40.2
Satisfied	48.0	52.0
Very satisfied	42.3	57.7
Study area		
Bonn	48.8	51.2
Suburban area	46.9	53.1
Rural area	50.0	50.0

Source: FRAME Household Survey

Determinants of Travel Behaviour and Mobility Problems

As mentioned above, it is frequently stated that the private car plays a major role in the mobility and satisfaction of senior citizens. However, car availability itself is closely related to personal life circumstances. It is often the more healthy and better-off, and therefore more satisfied and more mobile seniors, who own a car. According to this, the influence of the car might be overestimated if other variables are not being controlled.

Table 5.4 shows the results of four logistic regression models. This method was chosen because the indicators of actual mobility show very high variations. This is reflected in the very low variance explanation rate in many an analysis. Therefore, the indicators were transformed into ordinal scales with three equally large groups of interviewees. Then, the 'upper' and the 'lower' third of the interviewees were compared: in other words, the 'highly mobile' with the 'least mobile'. Thus, we get binary variables ('highly mobile', yes or no). The middle third is excluded from the analysis. Comparing the extremes gives a more accentuated picture of the determinants of mobility, and a comparatively high share of explained variance can be achieved.

The indicator 'satisfaction with out-of-home leisure activities' has a very skewed distribution. Sixty per cent of the interviewees are 'very satisfied', another 37 per cent 'rather satisfied'. Only 3 per cent are 'rather unsatisfied' or 'very unsatisfied'. Therefore, a distinction was only made between 'very satisfied' and 'rather or very unsatisfied'. Again, the 'midfield' ('rather satisfied') was excluded. Some key results are:

- The model fit in two of the four models might be regarded as good to very good (activity diversity: $R^2=0.39$, leisure distance: $R^2=0.33$). The activity frequency model ($R^2=0.12$) lies in the average of microscopic transport analyses. The leisure satisfaction model ($R^2=0.09$) is below average.
- In general, the most important influencing factors are the respondents' mobility, the strength of the social network and general health conditions. Healthy elderly people with a strong social network undertake more and a bigger variety of activities, cover longer distances, and they are more satisfied with their leisure.
- Younger seniors also undertake more diverse activities and cover longer distances. But they are not necessarily more active or more satisfied than older seniors.
- Car availability has a strong effect on two of the four variables investigated. People living in households with a car undertake a higher variety of activities than people without car, and they cover longer distances. However, both effects must not be interpreted as an 'impact' of the car because similar results are found for those who have a season ticket for public transport. So the ownership of the car or the purchase of the ticket can be seen as an effect of individual attributes of a person, which are not expressed sufficiently in the other variables. These 'unexplained' attributes distinguish people with diverse leisure interests from other people. These preferences for a big variety of (possibly highly specialised) leisure activities foster the purchase of a car or a season ticket. The availability of a car or season ticket is therefore rather a consequence than the cause for a certain way of life. Anyway, according to the activity frequency and the leisure satisfaction model, people with a car are no more active or satisfied than people without a car.
- Settlement structures do not seem to be relevant for any of the variables investigated. Neither the type of area (urban, suburban, rural) nor the level of leisure facilities in the place of residence have a significant impact. This

is even more so with regard to the contrasting selection of study areas. In other words, if there are no differences between the areas studied here, it is highly unlikely for such differences to be found between less distinctive areas. This surprising result was confirmed by detailed spatial analyses that are documented in Scheiner (2004).

- Socio-economic factors (income, education) play a role in activity diversity and distances covered, but the effects are of minor relevance, compared to demographic and health-related factors, and the social network.
- While in many cases, the 'medium' category of an explanatory variable (e.g. medium mobility level, medium sized social network) has a minor (although significant) effect, the extreme, or 'worst', category causes a near complete cessation of out-of-home activity level or diversity. This means that people in the 'medium' category (e.g. with distinct mobility or health restrictions) are still active outside of home.
- Health and socio-demographic factors can explain activity diversity more precisely than activity frequency. This calls into question the classic image of frail, lonely and therefore immobile seniors in very old age. The said factors strongly influence the diversity, but only slightly the frequency of activities undertaken. Consequently, seniors with serious health restrictions and a weak social network are active, but not in such a diverse way as more healthy, younger people with a strong social network. Finally, the standardised effects of health and ability confirm these results, because their effects on activity diversity are much stronger than on activity frequency.

(For a detailed discussion of methods and results see Scheiner, 2004.)

Table 5.4   Factors influencing leisure mobility of elderly people: results of four logistic regressions

Variable	Activity frequency B	Std. B	Activity diversity B	Std. B	Annual leisure distance B	Std. B	Leisure satisfaction B	Std. B
Age (reference category: 60-69 years)								
70-84 years	n.s.		1.154	0.811	0.938	0.660	n.s.	
85 years or more	n.s.		2.306	1.320	1.775	1.016	n.s.	
Gender male (reference category: female)	0.409	-0.289	n.s.		n.s.		n.s.	
Income above average	n.s.		0.529	0.374	0.706	0.499	n.s.	
Employed	n.s.		n.s.		n.s.		n.s.	
Education (reference: elementary school or no graduation)								
Education: intermediate high school	n.s.		n.s.		1.018	0.655	n.s.	
Education: high school	n.s.		0.596	0.410	0.558	0.384	n.s.	

	Activity frequency		Activity diversity		Annual leisure distance		Leisure satisfaction	
Health condition (reference: good)								
Bad health condition	0.834	-0.506	1.211	0.734	0.981	0.595	1.669	1.012
Medium health condition	0.399	-0.280	n.s.		n.s.		n.s.	
Mobility (reference: good)								
Bad ability to move	3.006	-1.192	n.s.		1.900	0.753	n.s.	
Medium ability to move	0.801	-0.466	1.675	0.975	n.s.		n.s.	
Social network (reference: strong network)								
Weak social network	1.215	-0.831	1.908	1.306	1.112	0.761	0.843	0.577
Medium social network	0.497	-0.342	0.562	0.387	0.591	0.406	n.s.	
Living in partnership	n.s.		n.s.		0.617	0.426	0.759	0.524
Availability of transport means								
Car in household	n.s.		1.288	0.882	1.332	0.912	n.s.	
Season ticket for			0.754	0.490				
public transport	n.s.				1.028	0.668	n.s.	
Study area	n.s.		n.s.		n.s.		n.s.	
Leisure supply at			n.s.					
place of residence	n.s.				n.s.		n.s.	
High neighbourhood			0.486	0.344				
satisfaction	n.s.				n.s.		n.s.	
Interaction terms								
Living in partnership (70-84 years)	0.660	-0.430	n.s.		n.s.		n.s.	
Living in partnership (84 years or older)	1.107	-0.463	n.s.		n.s.		n.s.	
Constant	1.291		0.197		0.635		3.662	
R² (goodness-to-fit)	0.123		0.389		0.333		0.092	

Notes: Table 5.4 shows the un-standardised and the standardised regression coefficients B (logit coefficients) of the significant explaining variables ($\alpha=0.01$). The standardised coefficients are independent from the measured scale of the respective variables and therefore decisive for the interpretation of the strength of influence. The algebraic sign indicates the direction of the connection. All analyses are undertaken with unweighted data to avoid distortions of significance.

R^2 (McFadden) is calculated by comparing the log-likelihood-function of the complete model with the log-likelihood-function of the constant model. It works as a measure for the explained variance of the dependent variable. Values of 0.2 to 0.4 are regarded as a good model fit (Urban, 1993).

n.s.: not significant.

Interaction terms were included if the correlation coefficient between two variables exceeded r>0,4 resp. r<-0,4. Only the interaction terms included in the table were significant.

Source: FRAME Household Survey

Providing Leisure and Transport Facilities: Potentials and Problems, Results from Interviews with Experts

Besides the household survey, the opinions of experts who provide leisure facilities and leisure transport, and who know about seniors' decision making were sought, via interviews. The selection criterion was the expert's ability to judge the potential for, and problems of, leisure options for elderly people. Such options include:

- spatial options, e.g. meeting-places, cafés and excursion destinations;
- activity specific options, e.g. clubs or sports facilities;
- time specific options, e.g. 'seniors' days';
- financial options e.g. seniors' tickets;
- information options e.g. help with self-help, education and advice; and
- organisational options, e.g. care, or transfers.

Interview topics included leisure options, mobility wishes and mobility problems to assess seniors' demands, as well as planning and recommending improvements. Qualitative methods were chosen to evaluate the experts' opinions. In so doing, we tried to investigate the decision structures that transform conditions and individual or institutional aims into actions.

Experts' Views on Mobility Problems

Transport Providers and Transport Authorities   Thirty individuals participated in the survey of transport providers and transport authorities. The results indicate that the specific needs of elderly people are frequently taken into consideration. This is not only the result of a self evaluation by the interviewees, but also proved by evidence of their actions in practice.

Realised, or at least scheduled, construction, technical, organisational and co-operative measures are, for example, low-floor vehicles, seniors' tickets and barrier-free design. However, the transport providers and authorities have mixed views on these measures. Low-floor vehicles, barrier-free construction, senior tickets, safety concepts, and the new design of timetables and ticket machines are almost unanimously judged positively. However, other measures like 'tempting offers' for seniors (e.g. handing out a senior ticket in exchange for a driving license) are rated more negatively.

Correlating these statements with general constraints, which inhibit the achievement of more 'senior-friendly' public transport (e.g. lack of demand, financial problems, lack of problem awareness), we can form some preliminary recommendations: co-operation and communication strategies are necessary to connect providers' solutions with customers' interests. Furthermore, it is evident that the problems go beyond transport problems in a narrow sense. Hence, classic transport system solutions alone will not be successful.

Providers of General Leisure Facilities (i.e. Those not Specifically for Seniors)
The staff in general leisure facilities are not particularly interested in leisure

activities and mobility of elderly people, even if their share of senior visitors is above average (e.g. golf clubs, thermal baths and river trips). Only in a few cases did the interviewees take the needs of elderly people explicitly into consideration. Valuations of mobility problems or possibilities to improve the mobility of seniors hardly exist. One reason for this is that the relevance of mobility problems is not discernible for the interviewees. For the large number of car-using seniors, a sufficient number of parking spaces are available, therefore, accessibility seems to be guaranteed. In the bus travel sector, the interviewees were aware of seniors' needs and wishes, as well as of their potential physical impairments. They do not, though, turn their attention to attracting new customers. In a few cases only, were the experts interested in technical or infrastructure improvements.

Providers of Leisure Facilities for Older People In contrast to the providers of general leisure facilities, the staff in leisure facilities for elderly people had a good understanding of their patrons' needs. These facilities are usually available for everyday leisure activities, and are often a destination and a starting point for further activities. Programmes include coffee and games afternoons, dance and fitness, lectures and educational courses. Staff in several facilities complained about the decreasing numbers of visitors. The reasons they stated were changing requirements and leisure interests, longer lasting health and the changing self-perception of seniors. Because it is doubtful whether these facilities will be able to stay competitive among the 'mobile seniors', even if they provide new activities, it may be necessary to offer decentralised leisure facilities to the less mobile, highly aged seniors in the future.

With respect to everyday leisure mobility, there are distinct differences in accessibility, depending on the leisure facility's catchment areas. In the suburban and rural area, with poorer public transport, a central location of facilities is important to ensure accessibility within walking distance. Otherwise, individual co-ordination activities are necessary to participate in leisure. Few facilities in the suburban and rural areas assure accessibility by themselves, so minibuses driven by volunteers are often provided. The usually better public transport in the city not only promotes accessibility, but also allows a choice between various facilities. Thus, seniors from neighbourhoods on the east side of the Rhine come to the west's senior leisure facilities and accept travel times of more than 30 minutes.

Experts in Seniors' Housing Facilities Interviews with experts in senior housing facilities (i.e. residential homes and seniors' residences) were particularly useful in identifying ways to promote elderly people's leisure mobility. They indicated mobility problems arising from age specific disability though. In the last years of life, people increasingly move to such a facility, so the portion of people with age-specific mobility problems is high.

The facilities surveyed ranged between 20 and 130 inhabitants. The leisure activities were on a regular basis around various topics, and were organised by social-cultural or therapeutic services. This is explained by the residents' wants: they expect a certain routine, otherwise they become overstrained. About 50 to 80 per cent of residents are able to leave the homes alone. The activities they undertake vary significantly, from leaving the home for a stroll, to taking a short journey alone or in a small group. But mobility constraints are not related only to physical or psychological impairment. There are other constraints too, as discussed below.

Key Mobility Constraints for Elderly People

In relation to mobility constraints, the experts surveyed identified the following areas where the needs of elderly people have to be taken into account.

Spatial and Temporal Accessibility As expected, public transport connections vary greatly between and within the three case study areas. In areas with insufficient connections, the experts judged this as a central, but rarely as an easily solvable, problem. In some cases improvements, like the installation of a bus stop in front of the seniors' home, had already been provided.

Mobility problems were not seen as too important, so long as a town centre is within walking distance. The location of the centre is seen as useful to give residents a daily aim. Beyond the removal of obvious barriers (particularly steps), the experts point at less obvious barriers, e.g. lack of seats or inaccessible lavatories, which restrict mobility. If topography and spatial structure allow the use of infrastructure for the slightly physically impaired (e.g. incontinent), securing the mobility of elderly people still requires spaces for immobility: places to rest and opportunities for repose.

Concerning the spatial integration of senior housing facilities into the settlement context, a causal relationship with mobility cannot be found. Sufficient spatial integration does not necessarily lead to contentment with, and use of, leisure facilities in the same way that insufficient integration does not necessarily lead to immobility.

Spatial conditions are not the only determining factor for the leisure mobility of older people. The impact of routines and habits in maintaining a high quality of life is evident with respect to activities as well as to modal choice. The expansion or limitation of options alone does not inevitably lead to changes in behaviour, though it supports the potential to change.

Perceptions of Safety and Security Without doubt, objective and subjective danger might restrict the use of public spaces, such as green areas or train stations. The experts shared the opinion that subjective security plays a major role in the self-dependent use of public space and public transport. Transport providers have reacted by installing SOS-telephones, cameras and security guards. Some interviewees also refereed to a successful 'security training' programme run by the police in Bonn. This involves male and female seniors being instructed in a four-day course on topics like fear, communication, help, trip planning and prevention. These seniors are now working as 'multipliers', undertaking security talks in senior facilities and encouraging other seniors to live a more active life. The responses are positive: freedom to move around has improved, knowledge about police activities has calmed anxieties, and improved self-awareness has been beneficial.

Ease of Use and Quality of Public Transport The complexity of regulations and operating procedures on public transport has an ever more restricting effect with increasing age, but also with a lack of routine and experience. However, contact people who give information or advice are seen as very useful. For example, the experts claim that having conductors in regional trains is helpful, because otherwise people have no certainty that they are on the right train. This problem affects railways in particular, because in buses the drivers can give information.

The experts felt that older people valued help from neighbours and people who accompany them on trips. They are considered as a way of helping overcome physical or spatial limitations. Some residential homes have promoted contact with relatives, friends and acquaintances, as well as access to volunteers, for this reason.

With respect to the quality of public transport, many experts in the survey praised improvements in standards in trains, trams and buses, as well as construction measures at stations and bus stops. With lifts, low-level buses, spaces for wheel chairs in buses and other technical modifications, the use of public transport has been greatly improved for seniors. Therefore, most of the interviewees' suggestions referred to improvements in services or timetables.

The experts viewed the seniors' complaints about public transport differently. Partly, they agreed with the same shortcomings and supported the calls for improvements; but they also considered some points as marginal, and did not see any need for action. An important issue here is how seniors can participate in developing concrete suggestions for improvement. Existing co-ordination and co-operation measures may need to be scrutinised.

Conclusions and Prospects for the Future

Leisure mobility of elderly people is diverse, and opportunities to take part in leisure activities have specific limitations and constraints. In non age-specific leisure facilities, there is little awareness about seniors' needs. Transport providers and transport authorities do not pay much attention to providing new options for older people, although considerable improvements have been made in transport infrastructure. Elderly people often regard public transport as a reason for abandoning leisure pursuits. In total, roughly half of the elderly people interviewed had unsatisfied desires to take part in leisure activities.

Leisure activity spaces for seniors are remarkably neighbourhood-oriented. The majority of trips are undertaken on foot. However, most of the motorised leisure trips are undertaken by car. On the one hand, the increasing car use of the more sophisticated 'active seniors' for leisure activities provides extended access. But, in addition to the negative environmental impacts, this is a social problem when it leads to the 'thinning out' of local leisure facilities. This process causes mobility limitations as soon as people are unable to drive or have access to a car. Besides the accessibility of leisure facilities and urban design, the 'social design' of paths and trips (accompaniment, spaces where people do not feel safe etc.) are highly important. Sustainable transport planning needs to apply the same standards of assessment to highly mobile elderly people as it does to the younger population.

With respect to people with mobility restrictions, the maintenance or promotion of appropriate travel participation has to be taken seriously.

The development of sustainable, i.e. environmentally friendly, socially balanced and economically sound, mobility options has to be adjusted to the respective spatial and social conditions. The results from the household survey and the expert interviews point out that transport planning measures are not the only, and maybe not even the primary, way to improve leisure mobility for elderly people. Sustainable leisure mobility is also a matter of spatial structures (micro-spatial accessibility to facilities) and a matter of transport management, such as providing good services and ensuring security. Hence, the development of more sustainable leisure mobility patterns for senior citizens is an integrated task for a wide variety of professionals including transport planners, spatial planners, city administrators, leisure facilities managers and providers, housing developers and many more.

Note

The FRAME project is funded by the German Federal Ministry of Education and Research. Project participants are: the Centre of Evaluation and Methods, University of Bonn (project co-ordination), the Geographical Institute (Department of Urban and Regional Research), the University of Bonn, and the Department of Transport Planning, Faculty of Spatial Planning, University of Dortmund.

Many of the publications listed below are available only in German. Translated titles are given.

References

Federal Ministry for Family Affairs, Senior Citizens, Women and Youth (2001) *3rd Report on the Situation of the Aged Generation in Germany: Age and Society*, Federal Ministry for Family Affairs, Senior Citizens, Women and Youth, Berlin.

Federal Ministry of Transport, Building and Housing (2000) *Transport Statistics 2000*, Deutscher Verkehrs-Verlag, Hamburg.

Federal Statistical Office Germany (2000) *Statistics of the Severly Disabled 1999*, Federal Statistical Office Germany, Wiesbaden.

Federal Statistical Office Germany (2003) *The Population of Germany Until 2050*, Federal Statistical Office Germany, Wiesbaden.

Kasper, B. and Scheiner, J. (2003) *Regional Public Transport Planning for the Elderly*, Space and Mobility: Papers of the Department of Transport Planning and Research 5, University of Dortmund, Dortmund.

Mollenkopf, H., Flaschenträger, P. and Werner, S. (1998) 'Housing and Mobility of the Elderly', in German Centre of Gerontology (ed.), *Regional Distinctions of Ageing and Mobility of the Elderly*, Campus, Frankfurt, pp. 264-350.

Opaschowski, H.W. (1998) 'What Is New About the "New Elderly"? The Aged Generation: Yesterday, Today, Tomorrow', *Marketing Journal*, vol. 3, pp. 164-166.

Rothe, J.P. (1993) 'No More Car Driving: A Critical Incident in Life', *Journal for Road Safety*, vol. 39, pp. 12-16.

Scheiner, J. (2004) 'Mobility, Satisfaction, and the Motorcar: Multivariate Analyses of Leisure Mobility', in R. Grotz, C. Holz-Rau and G. Rudinger (eds) *Leisure Mobility of the Elderly*, Blue Series Transport, University of Dortmund, Dortmund.

Scheiner, J. and Holz-Rau, C. (2002) 'Senior Friendly Settlement Structures', in B. Schlag and K. Megel (eds), *Mobility and Social Participation of the Elderly*, Kohlhammer, Stuttgart, pp. 198-221.

Urban, D. (1993) *Logit Analysis*, Fischer, Stuttgart.

Wahl, A. (2001) *Lifestyles and the Influence of Generation, Biography and Zeitgeist*, Technical University Berlin, Berlin.

Chapter 6

Reducing Travel by Design:
What About Change Over Time?

Robin Hickman and David Banister

Introduction

The search for sustainable urban form and sustainable transport systems has its origins all the way back to the earliest settlements. 'Proto-urbanisation', the earliest form of development, was found at sites such as Jericho, Abu Hureya, Mureybat and Çatal Hüyük more than 10,000 years ago. And true city form is thought to have developed on the alluvial plains of the Tigris and Euphrates, in the area known as Sumeria, sometime between 4000 and 3000 BC (see Soja, 2000).

Ever since these early days, attempts have been made to improve the quality of life in, and ultimately the sustainability of, towns and cities. Over the last 120 years, urban planning theory and practice has developed rapidly; the key contextual references are numerous with a rich, varied and international literature field including Howard (1898), Geddes (1915), Lynch (1960), Jacobs (1961) and Hall (1988 and 1998) amongst many, many others.

Most recently, transportation problems have come to the fore in discussions concerning 'efficient' urban form. Integrated land use and transport planning is overly used as a phrase by practitioners, often with little idea of what this means. Meanwhile, air pollution, energy consumption and traffic congestion continue to rise in our towns and cities, and getting people to reduce the impact of their car-dependent lifestyles remains extremely difficult: according to Boarnet and Crane (1999) this is the ultimate planning brick wall.

This chapter considers the topic of integrated land use and transport planning, particularly the scope for using land use planning in reducing travel by the private car. The questions underlying our thinking are as follows:

- To what extent does the built environment affect how often and how far people walk, cycle, use the bus or train or drive the car?
- Does the land use and transport interaction relationship change over time, with travel behaviour modifying itself as households and workplaces co-locate?
- And, finally, can land use policy and planning be strategically and locally applied to reduce car use?

Deconstruction of the Literature Field: Where are the Knowledge Gaps?

The literature investigating the potential for land use planning and urban form to influence travel behaviour continues to expand rapidly. The underlying theme of much of the research is to evaluate the potential contribution of land use planning in reducing car-based travel. Within this, there are at least three important sub-themes: locating a mix of uses in close proximity to each other, thereby making multiple trip chaining possible; reducing journey distances; and encouraging a modal shift to public transport, walking and cycling. The need to reduce car-based travel is itself rooted in the search for sustainability, and in particular the reduction of energy consumption.

An additional dimension is that of land use change over time: land use change is typically in the region of 1-2 per cent per annum, which is potentially insignificant in the short term, but of greater importance incrementally over time. Also, locally, major developments, such as new housing or employment developments, or a new health or leisure centre, may have a disproportionate impact on travel behaviour patterns from one time period to another.

A number of areas have received considerable coverage in the literature, such as: the influence of population size, density, the provision and mix of local facilities, local urban form, the location of development, balance of jobs and housing and also wider socio-economic variables, for example, the influence of income and household composition. Stead (1999) has brought a number of these issues together using regression analysis. For example, he suggests that socio-economic variables explain between 19-24 per cent of the variation in distance travelled, and land use variables up to 3 per cent at the individual level of analysis. At an area-wide level these variables increase: socio-economic variables explain between 23-55 per cent of the variation in distance travelled and land use variables up to 27 per cent.

Conflicting messages however arise from the wider research field. Debate remains as to the relative contribution of each urban form and socio-economic variable in terms of influencing travel behaviour. There remains considerable disagreement in the literature. Any attempt to categorise the thinking is in danger of over-simplifying the views, however, Schwanen *et al.* (2001) have usefully identified two broad camps, and these are detailed, and slightly amended, below.

- The 'interventionists' who assert that urban form can and does impact on travel behaviour, and, critically, can be used to positively design more sustainable towns and cities (work drawing on empirical evidence mostly from compact city examples in Europe and Australia, e.g. Newman and Kenworthy, 1989 and 1999; and Curtis and Headicar, 1995).
- The 'sceptics' who query the usefulness of planning interventions, and suggest that the efficiency of 'invisible hand' market mechanisms leads naturally to a 'co-location' of residential and employment locations. They believe that adjustments occur over time, unrelated to planning interventions, which bring workplaces and homes closer together and hence reduce commuting costs and distances (much of this work is based on research from suburban Los Angeles, e.g. Gordon and Richardson, 1989 and 1997).

In addition to the different nuances in argument and interpretation, and despite the large amount of research carried out in the land use and transport interaction field, there still remains a large number of research questions. Table 6.1 (A and B) highlights a number of these, first by examining the existing contradictory knowledge and then by noting a number of the less researched areas. Research findings from the literature field are organised by topic and author.

Table 6.1   The knowledge gaps

A. Existing (contradictory) knowledge

Resident population size: dispute as to whether population size impacts on modal choice, travel distance and energy consumption.

- No correlation between urban population size and modal choice in the U.S.A. (Gordon *et al.*, 1989).
- The largest settlements (>250,000 population) display lower travel distances and less travel by car (ECOTEC, 1993).
- The most energy efficient settlement in terms of transport is one with a resident population of 25-100k or >250k (Williams, 1997).

Resident population density: dispute as to whether increasing density impacts on modal choice, travel distance and energy consumption. Various views as to optimum urban form in reducing car travel; ranging from compact cities to 'decentralised concentration' and even low density suburban spread.

- Increasing densities reduces energy consumption by transport (Newman and Kenworthy, 1989).
- There is no clear relationship between the proportion of car trips and population density in the U.S.A. (Gordon *et al.*, 1989).
- As densities increase, modal split moves towards greater use of rail and bus (Wood *et al.*, 1994).
- Compact cities may not necessarily be the answer to reducing energy consumption, due to effects of congestion, also decentralisation may reduce trip length (Breheny and Rockwood, 1993; and Gordon and Richardson, 1995).
- 'Decentralised concentration' is the most efficient urban form in reducing car travel (Jenks *et al.*, 1996).
- Density is the most important physical variable in determining transport energy consumption (Banister, 1997).
- Higher densities may provide a necessary, but not sufficient condition for less travel (Owens, 1998).
- As people move from big dense cities to small, less dense, towns they travel more by car, but the distances may be shorter (Hall, in Banister, 1998).

Provision and mix of services: dispute as to whether local provision of services and facilities impacts on modal choice, travel distance and energy consumption.

- Local provision does not determine modal choice, personal and household characteristics are the determinants (Farthing *et al.*, 1996).
- Diversity of services and facilities in close proximity reduces distance travelled, alters modal split and people are prepared to travel further for higher order services and facilities (Banister, 1996).

Location: dispute as to impact of location – in terms of distance from urban centre, strategic transport network and influence of green belt – on modal choice, travel distance and energy consumption.

- Location of new housing development outside existing urban areas, or close to strategic transport network, or as free-standing development, increases travel and influences mode split (Curtis and Headicar, 1995).
- Location is an important determinant of energy consumption and car dependency (Banister, 1997).
- Development close to existing urban areas reduces self-containment and access to non-car owners (Headicar, 1997).

Socio-economic: dispute as to impact of personal and household characteristics on modal choice, travel distance and energy consumption. Also as to whether personal and household characteristics are more important determinants of travel than land use characteristics.

- Trip frequency increases with household size, income and car ownership (Hanson, 1982).
- Travel distance, proportion of car journeys and transport energy consumption increase with car ownership (Naess, 1993 and Naess and Sandberg, 1996).

B. Less well researched areas

'Temporal dimension'

- Effect of change over time: some anecdotal evidence of 'co-location' of households and employment over time in California, USA. But, little systematic tracking of the impact of time on travel behaviour.

Further land use variables

- Urban design quality: some anecdotal evidence in the USA, particularly from the new urbanist authors and commentators (see, for example, Calthorpe, 1993), showing the differential impacts of neo-traditional grid networks versus cul-de-sac route networks on travel behaviour. Some initial evidence in the UK from Marshall (2000).

Further socio-economic variables

- Dual-income households: assessment of how the choice of new housing location is influenced by the location of two workplaces, extent of 'excess travel' and reasons behind it, role of travel factor in choice of location of new home. Little known assessment in the UK.
- Surrounding mobility levels: impact of the surrounding level of mobility on travel behaviour in terms of mode choice, journey to work length and energy consumption. Some anecdotal evidence in the USA. Little known assessment in the UK.
- Attitude: some research in California, USA as to the impact on travel behaviour. Little known assessment in the UK.

As we can see, the literature has real depth, yet there are many contradictions in the research results, even in the well-researched areas. The reasons for this may be related to definitions, e.g. different measures of variables (such as density) used in studies; or analytical, e.g. different research techniques used; or indeed locational, where, geographically, variables have varying influence on travel patterns.

The main research gaps are based around these contradictions. For example, a number of key issues are evident: how can we gain a clear picture and quantify the strength and significance of known land use variables, and what are the ranges of influence? How does travel behaviour change over time and by location? Does 'co-location' of households and employment occur? Will efforts to improve physical proximity be less successful in achieving travel reduction in certain areas, perhaps where levels of mobility are high? Likewise, proximity to the strategic transport network, the existence of public transport corridors or green belt designations; what is the likely impact of these influences on travel behaviour?

A Focus for the Research

We have highlighted a broad-ranging topic, and unfortunately one that is much too wide for this single chapter. And so, here, we examine just one of these issues – perhaps the most important of the research gaps identified in the literature review: the impact of *time* on the land use and transport interaction relationship. Figure 6.1 provides a 'mind map' of our research structure, showing its place in relation to earlier and potential future work.

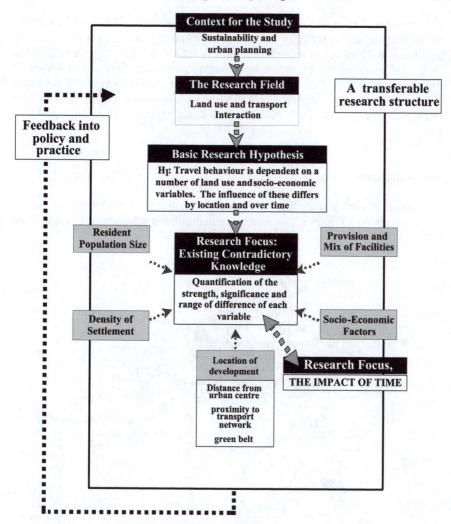

Figure 6.1   The land use and transport relationship, and the influence of time

Very little research in the transport and land use interaction field has directly examined the impact of time on travel behaviour. Traditionally, time has been treated as a framework within which social activities are carried out (Giddens, 1979): time and space are perceived to exist independently. Harvey has developed this thinking, considering interdependence and the nexus of geography and history, developing a theory of spatio-temporality (2000). It is from these thoughts that we draw inspiration here, testing our study data for spatio-temporality effects.

Within the land use and transport interaction literature, Gordon and Richardson's work (1989 and 1997) is perhaps the most interesting in terms of considering the temporal angle. They speculate that co-location may occur in polycentric and even low-density suburban areas, whereby firms and households periodically re-adjust spatially to achieve balanced average commuting distances and duration. However, it appears that there is little empirical evidence behind this thesis and, as far as we are aware, no systematic tracking of individual household travel behaviour over time. Much of the other research (Newman and Kenworthy, 1989 and Curtis and Headicar, 1995) is based on a snapshot in time, with analysis usually confined to one year's data, and little thought given to changing trends over time.

The Study Laboratory

The empirical survey work that lies behind the analysis in this chapter was carried out in Surrey (see Figure 6.2) a county located to the south-west of London in the UK.

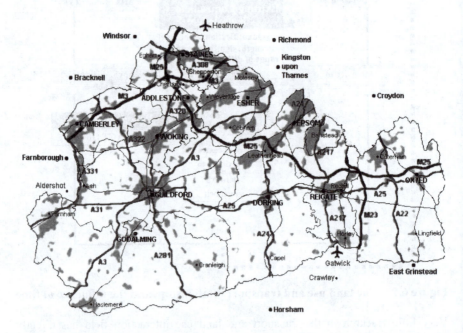

Figure 6.2   The county of Surrey

Using Surrey as the study area has some distinct advantages: the county is one of the most affluent areas in the UK, has high income levels, car ownership rates and personal mobility. Hence, Surrey is potentially one of most difficult areas to work in, in terms of reducing car dependence, in the UK.

Below, in Figure 6.3, we show how the main urban areas have developed in Surrey over the last century; the impact on travel behaviour patterns has been enormous, but is little understood. Clearly future growth is likely to have a great impact on travel behaviour patterns in and around the county.

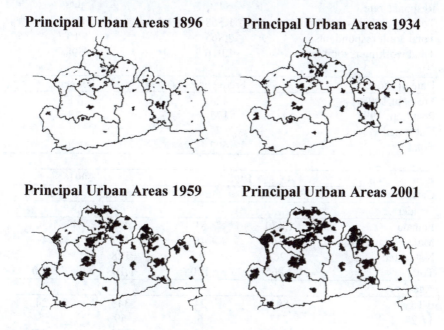

Principal Urban Areas 1896   **Principal Urban Areas 1934**

Principal Urban Areas 1959   **Principal Urban Areas 2001**

Figure 6.3   Urban development in Surrey 1898-2001

Source: Jim Storrar, Surrey County Council (2004). Urban areas as defined in Local Plans and using historical mapping.

Empirical Research: Household Surveys

The main phase of empirical research used two household surveys of new houses in Surrey. Two rounds of surveys were sent out: the first to occupiers of new households in 1998; and a follow up, to the same households, in 2001. Key descriptive data is shown below in Table 6.2 (A and B).

Table 6.2   The household surveys, key descriptive data

A.	1998	2001
Number of surveys	2,920	1,568
Response rate	54%	39%
Total households returned	1,568	607
Total adult respondents	2,865	1,103
Total working respondents	1,916	698

Date of move	Frequency	Per cent
Pre-Sept 1998	428	71
Post-Sept 1998	172	28
Not stated	7	1
Total	607	100

B.	1998		2001	
Category	Frequency	Per cent	Frequency	Per cent
Gender				
Female	1,470	51	498	50
Male	1,369	48	477	49
Not stated	26	1	128	1
Total	2,865	100	1,103	100
Age				
0-16	893	24	345	24
17-24	237	6	69	5
25-44	1,531	41	510	35
45-retirement	678	18	310	21
Over retirement	402	11	214	15
Not stated	17	0	0	0
Total (discounting under 16s)	2,865	76	1,103	76
Total	3,758	100	1,448	100
Occupation				
Employed: full time	1,499	52	511	46
Retired	443	15	227	21
Looking after home or family	307	11	119	11
Self employed	222	8	76	7
Employed: part time	195	7	111	10
Student	105	4	36	3
Unemployed	43	2	12	1
Other	51	2	5	0
Not stated	0	0	6	1
Total	2,865	100	1,103	100

Research Analysis: The Critical Impact of Time

The results are interesting in showing the change in travel behaviour over time; people do appear to co-locate, but only to a marginal degree (Figure 6.4). Below we summarise how new house occupiers in Surrey modify their travel behaviour over time, using measures of journey distance, time and energy consumption (a combination of journey distance and mode share).

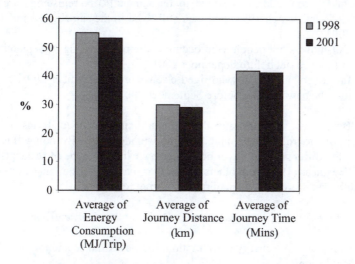

Figure 6.4   Changing travel behaviour over time in Surrey

Average energy consumption (MJ/Trip) reduces by 2 per cent, journey distance (km) by 3 per cent and journey time (minutes) by 2 per cent from 1998 to 2001. Car mode share reduces by 4 per cent over the same time period. Although this is quite a marginal change, we should remember that the three year study time period is quite short.

Looking in more detail at the data, we can see that the key co-locating groups are those that travel from Surrey to Outer London for work (a reduction in energy consumption of 21 per cent), those that travel from households in rural areas to the main towns in Surrey (-29 per cent energy consumption), and households in the lowest house value band, <£200,000 (-16 per cent energy consumption). What does this tell us? Possibly that those who are most likely to co-locate are those that make rural to urban trips, of an orbital nature, and are in the lowest income bands, i.e. an intuitive story: people are likely to change their commuting patterns if they are currently making difficult and lengthy journeys in congested areas and find it financially difficult to continually make these costly journeys.

The Impact of Time by Type of Resident

A further way of examining the change in travel behaviour over time is to disaggregate the dataset into three groupings: 'stayers', 'out-movers' and 'in-movers'. The disaggregations used are defined as follows:

- Stayers are people who occupied the new housing in September 1998 (taken from addresses added to the Council Tax register between April 1997 and March 1998) and who still lived in the same house in September 2001.
- Out-movers are people who occupied the new housing in September 1998, but moved out before September 2001.
- In-movers are people who lived elsewhere in September 1998, but moved into the new housing before September 2001.

Below we demonstrate the temporal influence in terms of energy consumption, journey length and time, and mode share. By doing this we can examine the differences in travel behaviour over time by type of resident. Cervero (1996), Headicar (1997) and others, remember, have suggested that in-movers are likely to have different travel patterns to existing residents.

Impact on Energy Consumption, Journey Distance and Journey Time

Figure 6.5 shows how energy consumption, journey distance and journey time vary by resident grouping.

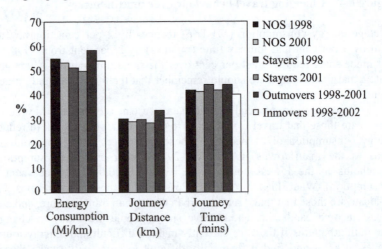

Figure 6.5   Energy consumption, journey distance and journey time by type of resident

Note: NOS – New Occupiers Survey total

As we can see, there are a number of important trends:

- The stayers are clearly the least energy consuming in their travel behaviour patterns. Energy consumption reduces by 3 per cent, journey distance by 5 per cent, and journey time by 5 per cent from 1998-2001.
- The out-movers represent the most mobile grouping; accounting for 17 per cent more in energy consumption, an 18 per cent greater journey distance and 5 per cent more in journey time than the stayers in 2001.
- The in-movers are more mobile than the stayers, but less mobile than those moving out; accounting for 7 per cent less in energy consumption, 10 per cent reduced journey distance and 9 per cent reduced journey time, compared with the out-movers.

The Impact on Mode Share

Interestingly, there are key differences in mode share between the different types of resident groupings (see Table 6.3). The out-movers are the most car dependent, with a car mode share of 73 per cent in 1998. The in-movers have a car mode share of 66 per cent in 2001. Over time the stayers reduce their car dependency from 71 per cent to 68 per cent.

Table 6.3   Mode share by type of resident

Mode	NOS 1998	NOS 2001	Stayers 1998		Stayers 2001		Out-movers 1998-2001		In-movers 1998-2001	
			Total	%	Total	%	Total	%	Total	%
Car driver	72	68	319	71	272	68	167	73	132	66
Train or Underground	17	16	86	19	70	18	45	20	28	14
Other	11	15	45	10	56	14	18	8	39	21
Total	100	100	450	100	398	100	230	100	199	100

Data: Surrey New Occupiers Survey 1998 and 2001, Surrey County Council (1998) and Hickman and Surrey County Council (2001).
New Occupiers Survey (NOS) 2001: stayers 2001 + in-movers 1998-2001

Time and the Land Use and Transport Relationship

As we have seen, much of the previous research that has concentrated on the impact of land use variables, such as population size, density and location, and wider socio-economic factors on travel behaviour, has, mainly for data reasons, not covered the temporal effect. Below we show the importance of the effect of time and how it impacts on these variables in Surrey.

Density

Trends in Surrey broadly reflect those in the UK as a whole (Banister, 1997): as the density of development increases, average energy consumption and journey distance decrease. Looking at the stayers we can see how the change over time affects the different density ranges: the 20-35 residents per hectare range modify their behaviour by quite large margins (a 16 per cent reduction in energy consumption and 19 per cent reduction in journey distance, Table 6.4).

Table 6.4   The stayers: energy consumption and journey distance by density

Residential population density	1998 Total	2001 Total	1998-2001 (%)	1998 Total	2001 Total	1998-2001 (%)
	Energy consumption (MJ/jtw)			Journey distance (km)		
0-1	55.5	57.9	4	36.4	32.9	-10
1-10	52.3	53.5	2	30.2	29.6	-2
10-20	50.4	49.4	-2	28.7	28.8	0
20-35	51.7	43.4	-16	30.6	24.9	-19
>35	42.8	43.1	1	26.9	26.4	-2
Total	51.2	49.9	-3	29.9	28.4	-5

Data: Surrey New Occupiers Survey 1998 and 2001
Residential population density is measured by ward density, residents per hectare

Figure 6.6 highlights further how density is related to energy consumption, but this time split by the different types of resident grouping. The out-movers are nearly always the highest energy consumers, with the exception of the really low (<1 residents per hectare) and higher (over 35 residents per hectare) density ranges.

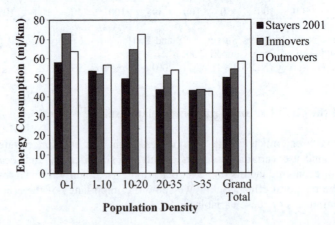

Figure 6.6   Density by type of resident

Population Size

Settlement size can also be a key determinant of travel patterns. In the UK, we tend to find the larger the population size, the shorter the trips, with the exception of urban areas of between 25,000 and 50,000, which show lower travel distances and energy consumption. This is not altogether the case in Surrey: there is no general increase in travel by population size. This perhaps reflects the fact that 'rural' areas in Surrey are not very remote and not long distances away from other settlements, relative to other parts of the UK. Interestingly, again the 25,000-50,000 size range does show low energy consumption.

Over time we again see interesting trends. Individuals appear to modify their behaviour, reducing their energy consumption and travel distances (Table 6.5). This is with the important exception of the 25,000-50,000 size range, which increases energy consumption over time. This is a difficult trend to explain and one that requires further examination.

Table 6.5 The stayers: energy consumption and journey distance by population range

Residential population size	1998 Total	2001 Total	1998-2001 (%)	1998 Total	2001 Total	1998-2001 (%)
	Energy consumption (MJ/km)			Journey distance (km)		
Rural	50.7	50.9	0	29.5	29.1	-2
1,000-10,000	44.2	43.6	-1	26.7	23.7	-12
10,000-25,000	51.2	48.2	-6	30.2	27.2	-10
25,000-50,000	45.5	51.8	14	24.2	27.4	13
>50,000	55.0	52.1	-5	31.8	31.0	-2
Total	51.2	49.9	-3	29.9	28.4	-5

Data: Surrey New Occupiers Survey 1998 and 2001.

Figure 6.7 highlights further how population size is related to energy consumption, this time split by the different types of resident grouping. The out-movers are again nearly always the highest energy consumers, with the exception of the 25,000-50,000 size range, where the in-movers dominate.

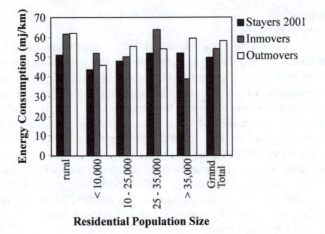

Residential Population Size

Figure 6.7   Population range by type of resident

Household Location

Analysis of household location, using three categories of town centre, rest of urban area and rural, also provides an insight into travel behaviour and change over time. Town centre locations appear to be related to low average energy consumption patterns, with the rest of the urban area exhibiting higher consumption patterns, and rural areas higher still. Journey length is less markedly affected, suggesting that mode share is the key driver here, although rural areas have longer travel distances.

Over time, the rest of urban area and rural area locations modify their behaviour with reduced energy consumption and reduced journey lengths. Town centre locations increase their energy consumption over time, mainly by becoming more car dependent (Table 6.6).

Table 6.6   The stayers: energy consumption and journey distance by household location

Household location	1998	2001	1998-2001 (%)	1998	2001	1998-2001 (%)
	Energy consumption (MJ/km)			Journey length (km)		
Town centre	47.6	51.6	8	29.2	29.1	0
Rest of urban area	50.4	48.5	-4	29.2	27.8	-4
Rural	55.2	53.0	-4	32.3	29.7	-8
Total	51.2	49.9	-3	29.9	28.4	-5

Data: Surrey New Occupiers Survey 1998 and 2001.

Final Thoughts

So what have we learnt? Firstly, that the world is a complicated place, and any attempt to simplify the land use and transport relationship into a series of statistical relationships is, to some extent, an exercise in aporia, i.e. an unpassable path or 'a route to nowhere'. The many, and increasingly sophisticated attempts, to analyse land use and transport interactions have led to numerous different conclusions and, although there is a general consensus that land use is related to travel behaviour, there is certainly little agreement as to the extent of influence or causality. However, what is clear is that there is a critical need for further research in this area: we know surprisingly little about the interaction of urban form variables (e.g. density, settlement size and location) with socio-economic variables (e.g. house value, household income and attitudes to travel) and travel behaviour. A simple transfer of results from one place to another would be useful for policy makers and practitioners, yet it appears that this cannot be done with any confidence without an improved understanding of the key determinants of travel behaviour.

In this chapter, we have identified another dimension to the complexity of the land use and transport relationship: that of time. The temporal effect appears to be very important, even over a short time span such as three years, and even where the time variability has been controlled for by concentrating on the stayers.

We started our commentary with a brief look at the history of urban development, and saw that for 10,000 years humankind has been seeking to develop and improve the quality of life in our towns and cities. It is perhaps no surprise that assessments that fail to incorporate the impact of time are missing a vital piece of the jigsaw. And it appears that Harvey's concept of spatio-temporality (2000), as usually applied to geographical literature, is well worth considering and pursuing when considering the land use and transport relationship. The nexus of geography and history is important: analysis without this dimension, is, to a certain extent, flawed.

Over the years, land use impacts on travel behaviour have not been sufficiently understood and hence have not been given sufficient weight in the search for, what is now, the holy grail of reduced car dependence. The continuing change in the land use and transport relationship adds yet further complexity. And, not surprisingly, missing such a critical part of the story means that efforts to improve the sustainability of our towns and cities are not always working to the degree we would expect.

References

Banister, D. (1995) 'Reducing the Need to Travel: The Research Evidence', in J.H. Earp, P. Headicar, D. Banister and C. Curtis *Reducing the Need to Travel: Some Thoughts on PPG13*, Oxford Planning Monographs, vol. 1(2), Oxford.

Banister, D. (1996) 'Energy, Quality of Life and The Environment: The Role of Transport', *Transport Review*, vol. 16(1) pp. 23-35.

Banister, D. (1997) 'The Theory Behind the Integration of Land Use and Transport Planning', *Proceedings, Waterfront Conference*, 5-9 April, London.

Banister, D. (1998) *Transport Policy and the Environment*, Routledge, London.

Boarnet, M.G. and Crane, R. (1999) *Travel by Design: The Influence of Urban Form on Travel*, Oxford University Press, New York.

Breheny, M. and Rockwood, R. (1993) 'Planning the Sustainable City Region', in A. Blowers (ed.), *Planning for a Sustainable Environment*, Earthscan, London.

Calthorpe, P. (1993) *The Next American Metropolis: Ecology Community and the American Dream*, Princeton Architectural Press, New York.

Cervero, R. (1996) 'Jobs-Housing Balancing Revisited', *Journal of the American Planning Association*, vol. 62(4), pp. 492-511.

Curtis, C. and Headicar, P. (1995) 'Reducing the Need to Travel: Strategic Housing Location and Travel Behaviour', in J.H. Earp, P. Headicar, D. Banister and C. Curtis, *Reducing the Need to Travel: Some Thoughts on PPG13*, Oxford Planning Monographs, vol. 1(2), pp. 29-47.

ECOTEC (1993) *Reducing Transport Emissions Through Planning*, A Report for the Department of the Environment, Transport and the Regions, Her Majesty's Stationery Office, London.

Farthing, S., Winter, J. and Coombes, T. (1996) 'Travel Behaviour and Local Accessibility to Services and Facilities', in M. Jenks, E. Burton and K. Williams (eds), *The Compact City: A Sustainable Urban Form?* E and FN Spon, London.

Geddes, P. (1915) *Cities in Evolution*, Williams and Norgate, London.

Giddens, A. (1979) *Central Problems in Social Theory*, MacMillan, London.

Gordon, P. and Richardson, H.W. (1989) 'Gasoline Consumption and Cities: A Reply', *Journal of American Planning Association*, vol. 55, pp. 342-355.

Gordon, P. and Richardson, H.W (1995) 'Sustainable Congestion', in J. Brotchie (ed.), *Cities in Competition*, Longman, London.

Gordon, P. and Richardson, H.W. (1997) 'Are Compact Cities a Desirable Planning Goal?', *Journal of the American Planning Association*, vol. 63(1), pp. 95-106.

Hall, P. (1988) *Cities of Tomorrow: An Intellectual History of Urban Planning and Design in the Twentieth Century*, Blackwell, Oxford.

Hall, P. (1998) *Cities in Civilisation*, Pantheon, New York.

Hanson, S. (1982) 'The Determinants of Daily Travel Activity Patterns: Relative Locations and Socio-Demographic Factors', *Urban Geography*, vol. 3(3) pp. 179-202.

Harvey, D. (2000) *Spaces of Hope*, University of California Press, CA.

Headicar, P. (1997) 'Spatial Development and Travel Planning, Implications for Planning', *Proceedings, Waterfront Conference*, 5-9 April, London.

Hickman, R. and Surrey County Council (2001) *Surrey New Occupiers Survey Reviewed*, Surrey County Council, Surrey.

Howard, E. (1898) *Garden Cities of To-morrow*, Swan and Sonnenschein, London.

Jacobs, J. (1961) *The Death and Life of Great American Cities*, Vintage, New York.

Jenks, M., Burton, E. and Williams, K. (1997) *The Compact City: A Sustainable Urban Form?*, E and FN Spon, London.

Lynch, K. (1960) *The Image of the City*, MIT, Cambridge.

Marshall, S. (2000) *Transport and Urban Design*, unpublished PhD Thesis, University College London, London.

Naess, P. (1993) 'Transportation Energy in Swedish Towns and Regions', *Scandinavian Housing and Planning Research*, vol. 10, pp. 187-206.

Naess, P. and Sandberg, S.L. (1996) 'Workplace Location, Modal Split and Transportation Energy in Thirty Residential Areas in Oslo', *Journal of Environmental Planning and Management*, vol. 38(3), pp. 349-370.

Newman, P.W.G. and Kenworthy, J.R. (1989) *Cities and Automobile Dependence: An International Sourcebook*, Gower Technical, Aldershot.

Newman, P.W.G. and Kenworthy, J.R. (1999) *Sustainability and Cities*, Island Press, Washington.

Owens, S. (1998) 'Urban Transport and Land Use Policies in East and West: Learning from Experience?', *International Journal of Environment and Pollution*, vol. 10(1), pp. 104-125.

Schwanen, T., Dieleman, F.M. and Dijst, M. (2001) 'Travel Behaviour in Dutch Monocentric and Polycentric Urban Systems', *Journal of Transport Geography*, vol. 9, pp. 173-186.

Stead, D. (1999) *Identifying land Use Characteristics Associated with More Sustainable Travel Patterns*, unpublished PhD Thesis, University College London, London.

Surrey County Council (1998) *Surrey New Occupiers Survey*, Surrey County Council, Surrey.

Williams, J. (1997) *The Relationship Between Settlement Size and Travel Patterns in the UK*, unpublished University College London Working Paper, London.

Wood, C. Watson, S. and Banister, D. (1994) 'A Framework for Assessing the Impact of Urban Form on Passenger Transport Energy Use', *Proceedings, Planning, Transport Research and Computation Conference*, 5 October, Manchester.

Part B:
The Relationship between Different Aspects of Urban Form and Sustainable Transport

Chapter 7

The Effects of Proximity to Infrastructure on Employment Development: Preliminary Evidence from the Netherlands

Kees Maat and Dominic Stead

Introduction

Transport infrastructure plays a fundamental part in the development of cities and regions. Important transport routes generate substantial development pressure. In the past, city centres had the strongest effect on the location of activities but more recently there is the view that accessibility to the motorway system is more important for some employment location decisions. Various types of employment sectors can now be found in clusters, often close to transport infrastructure, despite technological developments that theoretically make proximity less important (see for example Forkenbrock and Foster, 1996; Krugman, 1991; Quigley, 1998; Scott, 1998).

Although many new employment developments are still within urban and metropolitan regions, transport axes between urban regions are often a preferred location. This phenomenon, often termed 'corridor development' in the literature (see for example Hall, 1996; Priemus, 2001) has been discussed for some time in the scientific and planning literature, but empirical evidence for the increased importance of transport corridors for employment remains elusive.

To fill this gap, this chapter seeks to identify empirical evidence of the location of employment along transport corridors. The study area is the transport corridor along the A12 motorway in The Netherlands, between The Hague (to the west) and the German border (to the east). Empirical analyses of employment growth along transport infrastructure were performed to test the hypothesis that corridor development is occurring. These analyses include testing the variation of employment development according to various proximity indicators. Statistical analysis and geographical information technology were used to do this. The data were derived from detailed digital land use maps and automated registers, including employment data from 1991 and 1997. The results suggest that employment has grown faster near to transport infrastructure and motorway exits.

The chapter examines recent spatial patterns of employment change in relation to transport infrastructure. It does not, however, look at the issue of cause and effect: whether (or how) proximity to infrastructure causes employment growth. The chapter is divided into five main sections. First, the hypotheses for the research are identified. Next, the state of the art is reviewed. Third, the case study area, variables, and research methods are described, followed by presentation of the research results. Finally, conclusions are drawn, and the implications are discussed.

Corridors and Employment Development

Defining the Concept

The concept of the 'corridor' is used in different ways (see for example Ministry of Economic Affairs, 1997; Priemus 2001; Trip *et al.*, 2001). In a physical sense, a corridor is a bundle of linear infrastructure, and the infrastructure is the backbone of the corridor. In addition to the linear infrastructure, the transport system has nodes, which are the exchange points, such as motorway exits and railway stations. A corridor, however, would be no more than its infrastructure if there were no development along the axis. Thus, a corridor also has an economic dimension, which in turn provides an important basis for urbanisation (Garreau, 1991).

In terms of spatial planning, a corridor offers important advantages, such as opportunities for clustering transport and other development (see, for example, Priemus, 2001). Transportation axes can also have major economic development opportunities (see for example Ministry of Economic Affairs, 1997). It is evident that the characteristics, or even the existence of a corridor, depends on its scale. At the level of (urban) regions, corridors are concentrations of urbanisation, growing along the arterial roads of cities (VROM-Raad, 1999). National corridors cover the national transport axes, connecting urban nodes. 'Megacorridors' are wide zones of urban networks along international transport axes. The case study area examined in this chapter is one that has been identified as an important European 'megacorridor' (Priemus, 2001; Trip *et al.*, 2001). Hall (1996) reports that higher-level urban development is becoming concentrated into quite small axial belts such as Boston – New York – Philadelphia – Baltimore – Washington in the United States, the Tokaido corridor of Japan, and the transport corridors connecting the major cities of North-West Europe (such as the A12). Hall also notes that at the macro scale there is increasing concentration into metropolitan areas and corridors whilst, at the metropolitan level, there is simultaneous dispersal of homes and jobs. In The Netherlands, the Dutch Ministry of Spatial Planning states that urbanisation and employment development tend to grow along arterial roads and transport axes that are part of the European network. Examples are corridors between the Randstad, the Ruhr and the Brussels – Antwerp – Gent region.

Theoretical Background on the Effects of Transport Infrastructure on Economic Development

The links between transport infrastructure and economic development have been the subject of study since at least the 19th Century. Since the 1970s, more sophisticated theories of transport and development have been developed and there is now a vast literature (for a review, see for example Anas *et al.*, 1998). These more recent theories considered the influence of a range of physical and social characteristics on housing and employment location in urban regions. In general, the research evidence since the 1970s suggests that transport is often a second order consideration for location and relocation decisions for many types of employment, provided that there is already a reasonable standard of transport infrastructure (Banister and Berechman, 2000). This is mainly because transport costs are often a small part of total costs for many firms.

Empirical evidence also supports the view that transport is often a second order consideration for employment location and relocation. For example, Marquand (1980) surveyed firms relocating in assisted areas in the UK between 1972 and 1976, and found that transport facilities were ranked fourth in importance in relocation decisions. Similarly, a study of business relocation in Germany by Frerich (1974) found that proximity to a motorway was mentioned by 42 per cent of respondents, but it was only the fourth most important factor for relocation. A study by the National Economic Development Council (1985) in the UK found that proximity to roads is important (and more so than proximity to rail), but that relocation near existing operations was a more important consideration. Balduini (1974) examined the influence of motorway development on business location in Italy and found that it was the dominant factor in only 10 per cent of decisions, mainly in the south of the country. A study of motorway development in France by Bonnafous (1979) found no clear links between road investment and new development.

Research in the United States by Chandra and Thompson (2000) shows that road infrastructure may increase economic activity within a certain distance from the road, but this is at the expense of the economic activity of more distant locations. Linneker and Spence (1996) conclude from their study of road infrastructure and economic development in the UK that areas with relatively high levels of accessibility actually experienced decreases in employment between 1981 and 1987, whilst areas with lower accessibility gained employment. They report that the underlying negative relationship between accessibility and employment growth runs counter to similar earlier studies such as those by Dodgson (1974) and Botham (1980). It must be noted, however, that Linneker and Spence's case study, the M25 motorway (London's orbital motorway), is surrounded on both sides by greenbelt land (where development is generally not permitted), which therefore reduces the potential for employment growth in close proximity to the road.

Overall, evidence for the effects of accessibility on employment and economic activity is quite mixed: some research suggests that proximity to transport infrastructure increases employment and economic growth but other research does not. According to Boarnet (1997), it is difficult to find direct evidence of a cause and effect relationship between changes in accessibility and economic productivity. Perhaps less controversial is the argument that accessibility may have impacts on the location of specific types of employment such as transport and communication industries (see for example Bruinsma *et al.*, 1997). However, in a review of literature on land use impacts of motorways, Giuliano (1989) reports that impacts, regardless of the indicator used, appear to be decreasing over time.

Empirical Context

Introduction to the Case Study Area

Empirical analyses of employment growth along transport infrastructure were performed to test the hypothesis that corridor development is occurring. These analyses included testing the variation of employment development with various proximity indicators. Statistical analysis and geographical information technology were used to do this.

As stated, the study area is the transport corridor along the A12 motorway in The Netherlands, between The Hague and the German border. It connects two of the largest cities in The Netherlands (The Hague and Utrecht) and a number of smaller cities (as well as important German cities in the Rhine-Ruhr region further to the east). Hence, it is an important regional, national and international transport corridor, for road and rail. It runs through both urban and rural parts of the country. The western part of the corridor is more densely populated than the eastern part, although employment and housing are now booming in the east. The study area is a strip of land 30kms wide (15kms along both sides of the A12 motorway).

Dependent Variables

The data analysed in this study were derived from detailed digital land use maps and automated registers, including employment data, data on urbanisation, road networks, and public transport data. Table 7.1 contains a complete list of variables used in the analyses.

The analyses include employment data as dependent variables. These data come from the register of business 1991 and 1997 (LISA Foundation). The register contains the number of persons in employment according to post code. Although the register contains the type of business, these data were not used in this study: only total employment (irrespective of employment type) was examined.

The data were assigned location indicators with the aid of the x-y co-ordinates of post codes. As density measures are sensitive to differences in shape and size, administrative and statistical divisions (e.g. districts or post code areas) proved inadequate. This problem was addressed by converting the data into grid cells measuring 250 by 250 meters. A problem with every spatial division is the sharp and relatively arbitrary delineation of regions. Shifting the boundaries will often influence the values. However, a grid-based Geographical Information

Table 7.1   Descriptive statistics of the variables

	Frequency	Min	Max	Mean	Std. Dev.
Provinces					
South Holland	2460				
Utrecht	2179				
Gelderland	3098				
Regions					
Randstad West	1200				
Green Heart	1911				
Randstad East	778				
Central Region	3041				
Achterhoek	807				
Urbanisation					
Type of urbanisation					
Not urbanised	6535				
Highly urbanised	336				
Moderately urbanised	300				
Less urbanised or suburb	226				
Village	340				
Nature reserve	1158				
Proximity to infrastructure					
Distance to A12 motorway		0	15	7.32	4.29
Distance to any motorway		0	12	3.16	2.54
Distance to motorway exit		0	13	3.99	2.46
Distance to railway line		0	12	3.08	2.55
Distance to railway station		0	14	4.4	2.75
Distance to intercity or main railway station		0	35	10.77	5.79
Distance to The Hague		0	143	66.36	39.06
Distance to Rotterdam		0	131	60.06	35.51
Distance to Utrecht		0	90	38.06	20.87
Distance to Arnhem		0	121	51.06	33.31
Dependent variables					
Employment in 1991		0	14814	188.03	672.83
Employment in 1997		0	14068	206.43	671.11
Absolute employment Change 1991-97		-3285	3016	18.4	181.59
Growth	2132				
Stabilisation	2326				
Decline	3279				
Valid cases	7737				

System (GIS) provides the possibility to calculate a 'spatially moving average' for each cell (the average of the value of the cell itself plus the values of the eight adjoining cells). As a consequence, for each of the eight variables, the initial values of the cells are replaced by the average value of the cell and its eight neighbours, an area of 750 by 750 meters. This procedure smoothes out abrupt transitions over cell borders and compensates for the arbitrary spatial configuration of post code areas, which were originally created for mail delivery purposes. Moreover, the generalised patterns give a better insight than a detailed mosaic of cells (for a discussion of this method, see also Maat and Harts, 2001).

The main variable of interest in the chapter is the 'absolute employment change per cell', which is simply calculated as the employment in 1997 minus the employment in 1991. In identifying the spatial changes in employment, it would have been useful to look at both absolute and relative changes. However, many cells with employment in 1997 had no employment in 1991, which makes it impossible to calculate relative employment change per cell. Hence, relative employment change was only examined for larger areas (where there was some employment in 1991).

Independent Variables

The potential explanatory variables were all computed per grid cell of 750 by 750 meters. They were grouped into several categories: location in relation to infrastructure, the extent of urbanisation and region. Each category is described below.

Location of Employment in Relation to Infrastructure   Since the effects of proximity to infrastructure on employment are the main focus of this chapter, proximity indicators are essential to this research. We hypothesise that, if corridor development exists, employment growth will be higher in close proximity to transport infrastructure. The indicators used in the research include: the distance to the A12 motorway; the distance to any motorway; and the distance to any motorway exit. A positive relationship between job growth and distance to motorway exits (see Figure 7.1) may indicate corridor development in clusters. In addition, a number of proximity indicators for public transport infrastructure were also examined: the distance to a railway line; the distance to a railway station; and the distance to a major (inter-city) railway station.

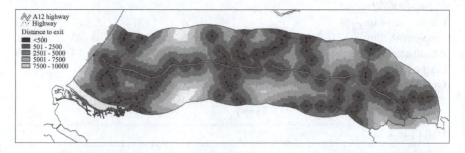

Figure 7.1   Distance to motorway exits

The Extent of Urbanisation   Although we might expect employment development near infrastructure, it is still likely to be related to urbanisation. Location, in relation to urbanised area, was examined using dummy variables indicating the extent of urbanisation: highly urbanised, moderately urbanised, less urbanised and non-urbanised areas (Figure 7.2). A dummy variable indicating nature reserves (where development is not possible) was also used. Four other urbanisation indicators used in the research were distances from the cell to the centre of the four main cities in the corridor (The Hague, Rotterdam, Utrecht and Arnhem).

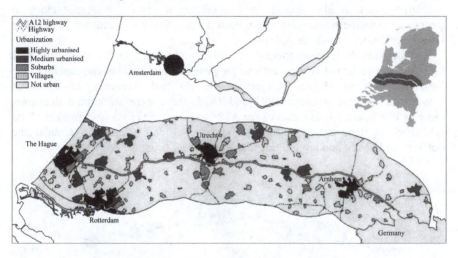

Figure 7.2   Urbanisation along the A12 corridor

Region   Variables were created to indicate province and region. The case study area covers three provinces (South Holland, Utrecht, Gelderland) and five regions (West Randstad, Green Heart, East Randstad, Central Region and Achterhoek). The West Randstad is a densely populated region and includes the cities of The Hague and Rotterdam. The Green Heart is a less urbanised area and contains a large proportion of land that is protected from development. The East Randstad is densely populated and includes the city of Utrecht. The Central Region is less urbanised and includes countryside, nature reserves and the city of Arnhem. Finally, the Achterhoek (literally the 'back corner') is the region that borders Germany.

Empirical Analysis

Descriptive Spatial Analysis

Figure 7.3 shows how employment is distributed along the A12 corridor. As expected, the majority of employment is concentrated in urban areas. The distribution of employment follows the corridor at least to some extent. Figure 7.4 shows employment change between 1991 and 1997 along the A12 corridor. The central urban areas of large cities experienced noticeable losses in employment, as did two less urbanised areas (in which horticulture is an important employment sector): one to the south of The Hague (Westlands) and the other to the north of Gouda (Boskoop). Areas that experienced noticeable increases in employment between 1991 and 1997 include a cluster of relatively new settlements to the south of Utrecht (Nieuwegein, Vianen and Houten). In general, employment growth appears to be mainly concentrated in the medium-sized cities and the suburbs of the large cities. It also appears that employment growth is higher close to motorway exits, particularly in the regions around Ede and Veenendaal, between Utrecht and Arnhem and the Achterhoek.

Looking from west to east at 1997 employment levels along the A12 corridor (Figure 7.5), it is apparent that the peaks of employment correspond to the larger cities (The Hague, Rotterdam, Utrecht and Arnhem). In terms of employment change between 1991 and 1997, there were substantial decreases close to The Hague (within 2km of the A12) and west of Gouda (within 5km of the A12), whilst there were substantial increases around Zoetemeer, Gouda, the outskirts of Utrecht and around Ede and Veenendaal (Figure 7.6).

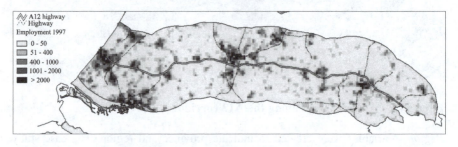

Figure 7.3   Employment in 1997

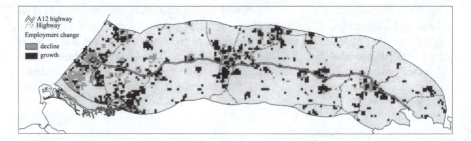

Figure 7.4   Employment change between 1991 and 1997

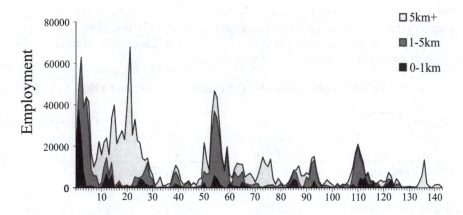

Figure 7.5   Employment along the A12 corridor

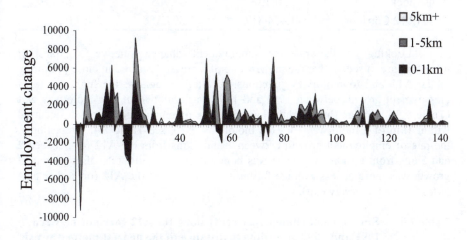

Figure 7.6   Employment change between 1991 and 1997 along the A12 corridor

Descriptive Tabulation Analysis

When employment patterns along the corridor are examined by region, some clear differences are apparent. Of the five regions in the corridor, the western region (West Randstad) had the largest number of jobs in 1997: the region contained almost half of all the jobs in the corridor (Table 7.2). However, the rate of employment growth between 1991 and 1997 was the lowest of all five regions (West Randstad experienced just 3 per cent growth in employment between 1991 and 1997, whilst employment growth across the whole corridor was 10 per cent). In contrast, the Achterhoek, which contained a small proportion of employment in 1997 (just 4 per cent of employment in the corridor), experienced very rapid increases in employment between 1991 and 1997 (28 per cent growth). Overall, it appears that the rate of employment growth between 1991 and 1997 is related to the position along the A12: the rate of growth was lower than average in the western part of the corridor and highest in the east.

Table 7.2   Employment along the A12 corridor in 1991 and 1997

Region	Total Employment 1991	Total Employment 1997	Employment Change 1991-1997 (%)
West Randstad	703,943	727,872	3
Green Heart	150,286	166,738	11
East Randstad	291,571	355,286	22
Central Region	257,770	302,297	17
Achterhoek	50,707	64,965	28
Total (A12 Corridor)	1,454,817	1,597,158	10

Looking at the rate of employment change relative to transport infrastructure, it seems that the highest rate of increase occurred in close proximity to the A12 and to motorway junctions. In all five regions, the highest rate of employment growth between 1991 and 1997 was within 1km of a motorway exit (Table 7.3). Similar (but slightly lower) levels of employment growth occurred within 1km of a motorway (not the motorway exit), see Table 7.4. Interestingly, the rate of employment growth between 1 and 5kms from the A12 (or between 2 and 5kms from a motorway exit) was below average, whilst rate of employment growth was more or less average further than 5kms from the A12 (or further than 5kms from a motorway exit).

Table 7.3   Employment change (per cent) along the A12 corridor between 1991 and 1997 according to distance to the nearest motorway exit

| Region | Distance to the nearest motorway exit | | | | |
	0-1 km	1-2 km	2-5 km	>5km	Total
West Randstad	19	2	-2	-2	3
Green Heart	27	16	0	14	11
East Randstad	32	18	8	26	15
Central Region	53	30	12	15	17
Achterhoek	55	37	20	17	28
Total (A12 Corridor)	25	11	4	9	10

Table 7.4   Employment change (per cent) along the A12 corridor between 1991 and 1997 according to distance to the nearest motorway

Region	0-1 km	1-2 km	2-5 km	>5km	Total
	Distance to the nearest motorway				
West Randstad	11	-3	-2	5	3
Green Heart	26	7	1	15	11
East Randstad	33	12	1	27	15
Central Region	28	18	12	16	17
Achterhoek	49	28	18	21	28
Total (A12 Corridor)	19	6	3	13	10

Models: Regression Analysis

Stepwise linear regression was used to estimate the absolute change in employment between 1991 and 1997. Although this method is essentially non-theoretical, this process provides a good technique for exploratory analysis to help identify important variables. However, the model for the entire study area and all dependent variables (Table 7.5) showed weak results. Four variables proved to be significant, explaining only 3.7 per cent of the variation in employment change. The most important explanatory variables were urbanisation indicators. Distance to motorway exits was significant, but added hardly any explanation.

Table 7.5   Regression analysis results for the entire study area (location indicators only)

Variable	Coefficient	t-statistic
Constant	23.727	5.839
Urby2: moderately urbanised cities (dummy)	146.081	13.766
Urby3: suburb (dummy variable)	91.034	7.513
Dmexit: distance to motorway exit	-3.868	-4.620
Urby4: village (dummy variable)	40.759	4.115

$R^2 = 0.037$
N $= 7737$

It can be hypothesised that existing jobs attract new jobs (the so-called clustering of employment). Thus, the second model (Table 7.6) not only includes location indicators, but also total employment in 1991. This model explains 9.5 per cent of the total variation. The moderately urbanised cities dummy variable remains the most important explanatory variable, but the number of jobs in 1991 is also important. This variable has a negative sign, which suggests that existing employment areas have a negative influence on new jobs. Distance to the motorway remains significant but less important.

Table 7.6   Regression analysis results for the entire study area (all indicators)

Variable	Coefficient	t-statistic
Constant	31.422	7.675
Urby2: moderately urbanised cities (dummy)	205.510	19.278
Job91: employment in 1991	-0.077	-22.109
Urby3: suburb (dummy)	143.362	11.939
Urby1: highly urbanised cities (dummy)	127.411	11.246
Urby4: village (dummy)	64.364	6.650
Dmexit: distance to motorway exit	-4.739	-5.746

$R^2 = 0.095$
N = 7737

Much better regression coefficients are obtained when employment change is split into growth and decrease. It is assumed here that employment growth is influenced by variables different to those that influence employment decline. Although separate models for growth and decline explain the variation in employment change better, this does not ignore the fact that there is a partial relationship between growth and decline, since some businesses move from declining areas to growth areas.

In regression analysis, where employment change is split according to growth and decrease (Table 7.7), employment decline is mainly explained by the number of jobs in 1991 ($R^2 = 0.63$). Three variables are also significant, although their relevance is negligible. Employment growth (Table 7.8) is also mainly explained by employment in 1991 ($R^2 = 0.27$). The results from these analyses (a coefficient of -0.158 for decline and a coefficient of +0.116 for growth) suggest that an agglomeration effect exists. The more jobs in 1991, the larger the decrease in declining areas. However, in areas experiencing an increase in employment between 1991 and 1997, the more jobs in 1991, the larger the increase. The number of jobs in 1991 seems to have a larger effect on decreases than increases. The R^2 value for the decline model is much higher than for the increase model.

Table 7.7   Regression analysis results for areas experiencing employment decline

Variable	Coefficient	t-statistic
Constant	-7.463	-2.734
Job91: employment in 1991	-0.158	-60.234

$R^2 = 0.630$
N = 2131

Table 7.8   Regression analysis results for areas experiencing employment increase

Variable	Coefficient	t-statistic
Constant	68.451	11.028
Job91: employment in 1991	0.116	20.429
Urby2: moderately urbanised cities (dummy)	136.967	10.587
Urby1: highly urbanised cities (dummy)	139.216	9.193
Dmexit: distance to motorway exit	-8.726	-6.520

$R^2 = 0.260$
N = 3278

The models tend to show that the type of urbanisation is important for employment change, so the data were then split into urban and non-urban categories and similar regression analyses were repeated for employment growth and decline in both urban and non-urban areas. The number of jobs in 1991 was still the main predictor in all models. However, distance to the motorway for the growth model in urban areas also shows some significance.

Since the regions are rather different from each other with respect to urbanisation and employment development, separate models for each region were also investigated. The models show that in the Randstad (both west and east) and in the Green Heart, the number of jobs in 1991 had a negative effect on employment development. In the Central Region the number of jobs in 1991 had no significant effect on employment change. In the Achterhoek, however, the variable explains 41 per cent of the variation in employment change (positively). Furthermore, locations in moderately urbanised areas and suburbs grew faster in every region, but the variable is not included in the Achterhoek model. Distance to motorway exits is not very important. This variable has some significance only in the western part of the Randstad, the Central Region and the Achterhoek where it appeared that the closer to the motorway exit, the more employment growth.

Conclusions and Implications

The impact of corridors on economic development has been discussed for some time. There is a generally held belief that employment development has been developing along corridors over recent years. However, there is still little empirical evidence relating proximity to transport infrastructure and employment change. This chapter has attempted to identify some empirical evidence from a major transport corridor in The Netherlands.

The chapter examined recent spatial patterns of employment change in relation to transport infrastructure. The hypothesis of the research was that the rate of employment growth is higher near transport infrastructure, given the right interchange and urbanisation conditions. In order to test this hypothesis, a number of indicators of proximity, urbanisation and land use were developed using GIS. Data at a small scale were derived and analysed using three main techniques: descriptive spatial analysis; descriptive tabulation analysis; and regression analysis. The findings of the descriptive spatial analysis indicate that there were significant decreases in employment between 1991 and 1997 in the central areas of large cities and significant increases in employment in the more moderately urbanised (smaller) cities and suburbs. The descriptive tabulation analysis indicates that there has been much more employment growth in the eastern regions of the case study area than in the western regions (which are generally much more urbanised and contain the majority of employment in the corridor). The regression analysis gave weak results when all cases and only proximity variables were used. Using employment in 1991, slightly better results were obtained. Substantially better results were obtained when the cases were split according to the direction of employment change (increase or decrease) and region. Here, important variables included in the regression models were employment levels, urbanisation conditions and proximity to transport infrastructure (distance to a motorway exit).

The implications of this preliminary study appear to be that proximity to transport infrastructure does have some effect on employment, although it is not particularly strong. This study presents evidence suggesting that employment growth is much higher within very close proximity to transport infrastructure (within 1km of a motorway or a motorway junction). However, proximity to existing employment areas appears to be a more important factor for employment growth (perhaps confirming the concept of clustering) as well as urbanisation (presumably for reasons of access to markets and labour). It is likely that a more complex picture emerges if different types of employment are examined, and it may be that transport infrastructure is more important for the growth of jobs in certain sectors than others. This is certainly an interesting issue to explore in more detail in the future.

Acknowledgements

This research is developed from a study of urban development in the Netherlands (Harts *et al.*, 2002; Maat and Harts, 2001), which was funded by the Dutch National Spatial Planning Agency.

References

Anas, A., Arnott, R. and Small, K.A. (1998) 'Urban Spatial Structure', *Journal of Economic Literature*, vol. 36(3), pp. 1426-1464.

Balduini, G. (1974) *Effets de Localisation Industrielle des Autoroutes Italiennes de l'IRI*, ECMT, Paris.

Banister, D. and Berechman, J. (2000) *Transport Investment and Economic Development*, University College London (UCL) Press, London.

Boarnet, M.G. (1997) 'Highways and Economic Productivity: Interpreting Recent Evidence', *Journal of Planning Literature*, vol. 11(4), pp. 476-486.

Bonnafous, A. (1979) 'Underdeveloped Regions and Structural Aspects of Transport Infrastructure', in W.A.G. Blonk (ed.), *Transport and Regional Development*, Saxon House, Farnborough, pp. 45-62.

Botham, R. (1980) 'Regional Development Effects of Road Investment', *Transport Planning and Technology*, vol. 6(1), pp. 97-108.

Bruinsma, F.R., Rienstra, S.A. and Rietveld, P. (1997) 'Economic Impacts of the Construction of a Transport Corridor: A Multi-level and Multi-approach Case Study for the Construction of the A1 Highway in the Netherlands', *Regional Studies*, vol. 31(4), pp. 391-402.

Chandra, A. and Thompson, E. (2000) 'Does Public Infrastructure Affect Economic Activity? Evidence from the Rural Interstate Highway System', *Regional Science and Urban Economics*, vol. 30(4), pp. 457-490.

Dodgson, J. (1974) 'Motorway Investment, Industrial Transport Costs, and Sub-regional Growth: A Case Study of the M62', *Regional Studies*, vol. 8(1), pp. 75-91.

Forkenbrock, D.J. and Foster, N.S.J. (1996) 'Highways and Business Location Decisions', *Economic Development Quarterly*, vol. 10(3), pp. 239-248.

Frerich, J. (1974) *Die Regionalen Wachstums – und Struktureffekte von Autobahnen in Industrieländern*, Verkehrswissenschaftliche Forschungen Bild 28, Duncker and Humblot, Berlin.

Garreau, J. (1991) *Edge City: Life on the New Frontier*, Doubleday, New York.

Giuliano, G. (1989) 'Research Policy and Review 27, New Directions for Understanding Transportation and Land Use', *Environment and Planning A*, vol. 21(2), pp. 145-159.

Hall, P. (1996) 'The Global City', *International Social Science Journal*, vol. 48(1), pp. 15-23.

Harts, J.J., Maat, K. and Ottens, H. (2002) 'An Urbanisation Monitoring System for Strategic Planning', in S. Geertman and J. Stillwell (eds), *Planning Support Systems in Practice*, Springer Verlag, Berlin, pp. 315-329.

Krugman, P. (1991) *Geography and Trade*, MIT Press, Cambridge, M.A.

Linneker, B.J. and Spence, N.A. (1996) 'An Accessibility Analysis of the Impact of the M25 London Orbital Motorway on Britain', *Regional Studies*, vol. 26(1), pp. 31-47.

Maat, K. and Harts, J.J. (2001) 'Implications of Urban Development for Travel Demand in the Netherlands', *Transportation Research Record*, 1780, pp. 9-16.

Marquand, D. (1980) *Measuring the Effects and Costs of Regional Incentives*, Government Economic Services Paper 32, Department of Trade and Industry, London.

Ministry of Economic Affairs (1997) *Ruimte voor Economische Dynamiek. Een Verkennende Analyse van Ruimtelijk Economische Ontwikkelingen tot 2020 (Space for Economic Dynamics)*, Ministry of Economic Affairs, The Hague, The Netherlands.

National Economic Development Council (NEDC) (1985) *A Fairer and Faster Route to Major Road Construction*, NEDC, London.

Priemus, H. (2001) 'Corridors in The Netherlands: Apple of Discord in Spatial Planning', *Tijdschrift voor Economische en Sociale Geografie*, vol. 92(1), pp. 100-107.

Quigley, J.M. (1998) 'Urban Diversity and Economic Growth', *Journal of Economic Perspectives*, vol. 12, pp. 127-138.

Scott, A.J. (1998) *Regions and the World Economy. The Coming Shape of Global Production, Competition and Political Order*, Oxford University Press, Oxford.

Trip J.J., Romein, A. and de Vries, J. (2001) *Megacorridors in the North West Metropolitan Area. Background Report and Theoretical Framework. Corridesign Research Report*, OTB Research Institute for Housing, Urban and Mobility Studies, Delft.

VROM-Raad (1999) Corridors in Balance: From Unplanned Corridor Formation to Planned Corridor Development, Advies 011, VROM Council, The Hague.

Chapter 8

The Compact City as a Means of Reducing Reliance on the Car: A Model-Based Analysis for a Sustainable Urban Layout

Mamoru Taniguchi and Taichiro Ikeda

Introduction

Many transport demand management measures have been used to improve urban transport. These measures have included park-and-ride, flextime commuting, and the use of toll fees. In general, these schemes focus solely on transportation and not on urban layout. Though these types of measures could effectively improve specific urban transportation problems, they are unlikely to curb the trend of growing reliance on the car.

Several studies have suggested that a compact urban layout is essential for solving these problems. If urban layouts were well planned, society would be more sustainable. However, there is little quantitative information describing an optimum or preferable compact urban layout. Hence, it is useful to carry out statistical analyses, based on accurate estimates of travel requirements and land use information to establish the basic parameters of a sustainable urban layout.

The objectives of the study reported on in this chapter are to define important factors of a compact urban layout at two different scales; the 'city' scale and the 'neighbourhood' scale. The city scale defines the municipal level, and the neighbourhood or 'residential' scale denotes a smaller spatial area. If municipalities were analysed from a macro viewpoint, city scales would be appropriate. However, improvement projects leading to compact urban layouts require micro information on a neighbourhood scale as well. The National Person Trip Survey (NPTS, Ministry of Construction, 1993) that was carried out in Japan is adopted as the trip data source for both analyses. A total of 67,067 residents of 78 cities participated in the NPTS.

In the city scale analysis, one objective is to determine the relationship between trip patterns and urban characteristics, such as population density and other regional characteristics. The basic approach of this analysis is similar to that of Newman and Kenworthy (1989), who concluded that per capita petrol consumption varies inversely to population density. In addition, the city scale analysis uses a multiple regression model to examine public transportation services, road infrastructure, historic background, and regional characteristics.

An objective of the neighbourhood scale analysis is to determine the relationship between the characteristics of each residential area and the patterns of car use, with a focus on fuel consumption. A statistical analysis based on the scale of residential zoning has not previously been undertaken. For the neighbourhood scale analysis, because the total number of residential zones in the NPTS is about 2,000, it was necessary to designate groups of these zones. The characteristics of each residential zone, such as location, population density, land use control, transportation conditions, and distance from a city center, were examined as index factors to designate the groupings. Then a multiple regression model was calibrated to explain the patterns of car use in each group of residential zones. The dependent variable of this model is per capita petrol consumption in each group. The independent variables are population density, location, land use control, conditions of public transportation, and mix of land uses. An objective of the model is to find which characteristics are important at the neighbourhood scale. Based on the findings here, new guidelines can be devised for improving residential areas that effectively assume a compact urban form and hopefully lead to reduced reliance on the car.

Previous Studies on Urban Form and Car Use

Thomson (1977) was one of the first researchers to discuss the relationship between urban layout and its transportation networks. Though many publications have encouraged a more compact urban layout for sustainable development since then, only a few studies have quantitatively addressed the relationship between urban layout and car use. Newman and Kenworthy (1989) calculated the relationship between urban population density and annual fuel consumption per capita on a municipal scale. Their results clearly show that cities with low densities rely on car transportation. Jenks *et al.* (1996), Naess (1996), de Roo and Miller (2000), and Williams *et al.* (2000) have also investigated the relationship between urban layout and transportation, and their findings shed new light on potential improvements to urban layouts.

Though these findings suggest that compact urban forms and high population densities are perhaps desirable, few quantitative guidelines for urban improvement projects have been developed. Moreover, other factors affecting urban form, with the exception of population density, have not been statistically investigated until now. Case studies of cities with higher population densities than European cities are also required.

For these reasons, this study has the following characteristics:

1.   It uses a statistical approach. Current studies that outline preferences for a compact urban layout are required to present reliable and quantifiable information. This study uses a multiple regression model as a statistical technique, which is based on a sufficient number of trip samples with

accurate land use information to confirm the basic factors of a compact urban layout.

2. It considers factors other than population density. This study includes analyses of potentially important factors, such as public transport services, road infrastructure, historic context, and regional characteristics.

3. It uses a two-scale analysis. An objective of this study is to clarify important factors of compact urban layout at two scales: city and neighbourhood. The neighbourhood level is mostly areas under 1000ha.

4. It can suggest guidelines for improvement. Based on the findings, new guidelines can be developed for improving residential areas by developing compact urban forms that lead to a reduction in reliance on the car. Since cities with higher densities serve as good models, this study focuses on cities in Japan that are more densely populated than European cities.

Data and Methods

In Japan, Metropolitan Person Trip Surveys (MPTS) have been conducted in major cities and metropolitan areas for the past three decades. Though they provide rich information, they are inappropriate for use here. This study requires trip data from many cities based on the same standard over an identical survey period. As a result, trip data from the National Person Trip Survey (NPTS) is preferable to the usual MPTS.

The Ministry of Construction of Japan has conducted three NPTS so far. The first survey was conducted in 1987 in 131 cities; the second survey was conducted in 1992 in 78 cities (Figure 8.1); and the third survey was in 1999 in 98 cities. This study adopts the 1992 data for analysis instead of the latest 1999 data because the 1999 survey does not include all information in several cities: sample cities of the NPTS were selected to cover a variety of urban areas. Specifically, the following three characteristics were considered:

- the population of the city;
- the population of the metropolitan area that the city belongs to; and
- the location (e.g. central or periphery) of that city in the metropolitan area.

In this study, 'local' cities mean those that are not a part of the three major metropolitan areas of Tokyo, Osaka, and Nagoya.

In the NPTS, each household filled out a two-page survey. Part of it dealt with household attributes, and the other sought information about trips by each family member. The NPTS also includes questions about the possibility of car use for each family member.

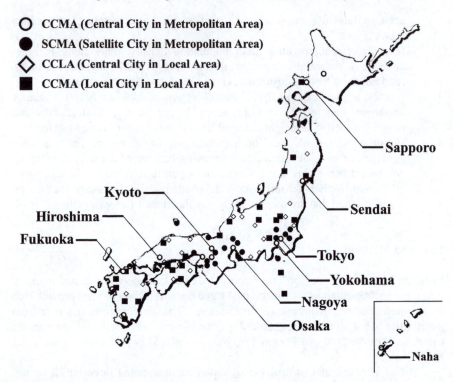

Figure 8.1   Sample cities (1992 National Person Trip Survey)

Questionnaires were distributed to at least 360 households in each sample city. During the 1992 survey, the total number of household questionnaires was 29,502, and that of personal questionnaires was 80,997. Investigators visited all the selected households to distribute and collect the questionnaires. The number of household and personal questionnaires collected was 25,009 and 67,067, respectively. The effective personal return rate was 82.8 per cent. It is statistically guaranteed that this collection rate is large enough to record basic transportation characteristics, such as average trip length in each city (Ministry of Construction, 1993). The special strengths of the NPTS data were that many cities were surveyed with the same standards over the same period of time. Because of the restriction of land use data, 11 out of 78 cities were excluded from the city scale analysis, and six out of 78 cities were excluded from the neighbourhood scale analysis. Consequently, 67 cities were used in the city scale analysis, and 72 were used for the neighbourhood scale analysis.

The quantity of fuel consumed during each trip (q) was estimated using the following equation (Kaneyasu and Kanaizumi, 1972).

$$q_{[cc/km]} = 0.290x_{[s/km]} + 49.3$$

x : (vehicle speed)$^{-1}$

The ' x ' is calculated from the trip distance and time required, which were obtained from the NPTS. The fuel consumption volume on weekdays is converted into energy use with the following coefficient (Hayashi *et al.*, 1995): fuel 1,000cc: 720g, fuel 1kg: 44.1MJ.

Both the city and neighbourhood scale analyses used multiple regression models to evaluate the factors of urban layout and their effects on fuel consumption. Namely, the dependent variable (Y) of the regression model is per capita petrol consumption. Several types of regression equations were tested, and the following log-linear model had the best fit of all models:

$$\ln Y = a_1 X_1 + a_2 X_2 + \ldots + a_n X_n + b$$

The Results of the City Scale Analysis

Figure 8.2 shows the relationship between population density and petrol consumption in each city. As seen in this Figure, population density is a very important factor in explaining the consumption of fuel at the city scale. On the other hand, Figure 8.2 also indicates that population density is not the only factor used to explain petrol consumption. If cities where the population density is around 50 persons/ha are examined, fuel consumption ranges from 5,000 to 12,000MJ. To determine the influence of other factors on fuel consumption, is necessary to introduce multiple regression analysis.

To build this model, about 30 explanatory variables were examined that relate to urban layout, land use intensity, historical and geographical background, and transportation conditions. The selected variables are shown in Table 8.1. The parameters and t-values in Table 8.2 show clearly the relationship between urban form and petrol consumption. The key findings are:

1.   Transportation infrastructure, such as the number of railway stations and lengths of roads that are authorised by city planning, significantly affects petrol consumption.
2.   Topographical factors are also important. Linear port cities, which entail topographical restrictions for urban land use, are found to discourage car use.
3.   Cities in large metropolitan areas, such as Tokyo and Osaka, tend to have relatively low fuel consumption.
4.   Castle cities and historic cities, such as Kyoto, tend to have relatively low fuel consumption. The urban layout and road networks in cities such as this are ill-suited for unrestricted car use.
5.   It is very interesting that cities damaged in WW II now show a high rate of petrol consumption. A possible reason could be that urban planning after the War made car use much easier than in other cities.

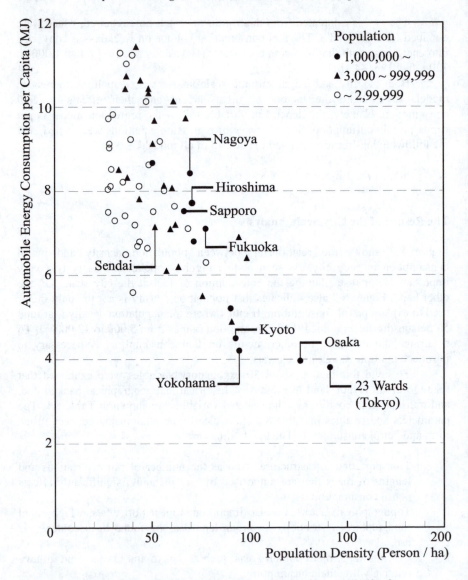

Figure 8.2   Population density and petrol consumption per capita in Japanese cities

Table 8.1   Definition of the variables

Explanatory variables		City	Neigh-bour-hood	Definitions and comments
Population	Population density	•	•	Persons per ha
Location	Distance from city centre		•	Km
Transport conditions	No. of railway stations	•		Includes LRT and AGT
	Length of roads authorised by city planning	•		Km
	Distance from a bus stop		•	Distance between the centre of the zone and the nearest bus stop (km)
	Satellite city in a metropolitan area: railway-inconvenient (D)		•	Distance to the nearest railway station is more than 2km, or train service at station is less than 260 services per day
	Central city in a local area: railway-convenient (D)		•	Train service at nearest station is more than 160 services per day
	Local city in a local area: railway-convenient		•	Distance to the nearest railway station is less than 2km, and train service at nearest station is more than 90 services per day
City type	Central city in a metropolitan area (D)		•	Cities designated by ordinance or cities with a population of > one million
	Central city in a local area (D)		•	Prefectural capitals and cities with a population of > 150,000
	Local city in a local area (D)		•	Local cities with a population of < 150,000 (excluding prefectural cities)
City Characteristic	Tokyo Met area (D)	•		
	Osaka Met area (D)	•		
	Northern Kanto Region (D)	•		
	Castle and historical city (D)	•		Excluding those damaged by WW II
	Damaged by WW II (D)	•		Cities where > 60% of urbanised area was damaged
	Middle sized prefectural capital	•		Cities with population 300,000 – 700,000
	Linear port city (D)	•		

Land use	The rate of secondary industry	•	
	Sprawl (D)	•	Residential area/DID area X 100 ≥ 10.0
	Residential zoning (D)	•	Zones in which >60% of land is assigned to R-1, R-11 or R-111
	Neighbourhood commercial zoning (D)	•	Zones in which >60% of land is assigned to C-11
	Light industrial zoning (D)	•	Zones in which >60% of land is assigned to I-1
	Industrial zoning (D)		Zones in which >60% of land is assigned to I-11
Compound Factors	LCLA + large UCA (D)	•	Zones at LCLA in which the UCA covers >50%
	CCMA or CCLA + UCA (D)	•	Zones at central sites in which the UCA covers 25% - 50%
	Local area + UCA (D)	•	Zones at the local are in which the UCA covers 25% - 50%
	Adjoining station + high and R-11 (D)	•	Zones adjoining railway station in which R-11 use exceeds 60%
	CCMA + mixed-use residential zoning (D)	•	Zones a the CCMA, with high population density, and mixed-use residential zoning
	Non CCMA + Mixed-use residential zoning (D)	•	Mixed-use residential zoning (excluding Metropolitan area + mixed-use residential zoning)
	CCMA + R-1 (D)	•	Zones at the CCMA in which R-1 use > 60%
	Local area + R-1 (D)	•	Zones at the local area in which R-1 use >60%
	Metropolitan area + adjoining station + R-1 (D)	•	Zones at the Metropolitan area adjoining the railway station in which R-1 use > 60%

LRT: Light Rail Transit; AGT: Automated Guideway Transit; (D): Dummy; LCLA: Local City in a Local Area; CCMA: Central City in a Metropolitan Area: CCLA: Central City in a Local Area

R-1: Exclusively residential zone for low-height buildings (class 1) and exclusively residential zone for low-height buildings (class 2); R-11: Exclusively residential zone for high and medium height buildings (class 1) and exclusively residential zone for high and medium height buildings (class 2); R-111: Residential zone (class 1), residential zone (class 2) and semi-residential zone; C-1: Neighbourhood commercial zone; C-11: Commercial zone; l-1: Light industrial zone; l-11: Industrial zone and exclusively industrial zone; UCA: Urbanisation Control Area

All distances in the Table are measured from the centre of each residential zone

Table 8.2   Factors affecting petrol consumption at the city scale

Explanatory variable	Standardised parameter	t-value
Population density	-0.420	-4.43
Osaka Met. Area (D)	-0.279	-4.30
Tokyo Met Area (D)	-0.188	-2.55
Northern Kanto region (D)	0.142	2.46
Castle and historical city (D)	-0.040	-0.63
Damaged by WW II	0.247	3.99
Middle sized prefectural capital (D)	0.208	3.43
The rate of secondary industry	-0.108	1.65
Linear port city (D)	-0.200	-3.53
Length of roads authorised by city planning	0.337	2.81
Number of railway stations	-0.335	-2.75
Sprawl (D)	0.080	1.40
Segment		24.50
Adjusted R2	0.807	

(D): Dummy

Results of the Neighbourhood Scale Analysis

As stated above, because the total number of residential zones in NPTS is as high as 1,996, it was necessary to designate groups of residential zones for an effective neighbourhood scale analysis. The characteristics of each residential zone, such as the location, population density, land use control, transportation conditions, and distance from the city center, were examined as index factors to designated groups of residential zones. Consequently, 138 groups of residential zones are designated, and each of them exhibits a variety of trip patterns by residents.

The neighbourhood scale model also examines a variety of explanatory variables, as shown in Table 8.1, such as land use intensity, infrastructure conditions, transportation conditions, and others. The explanatory variables were finally adopted after checking to avoid multi co-linearity. The parameters and t-values in Table 8.3 show a clear picture of the relationship between urban layout, neighbourhood scale development, and petrol consumption, as follows:

1.   In spite of other factors that are considered, population density is still the most significant variable in explaining petrol consumption.
2.   If a neighbourhood is located close to a city center, fuel consumption decreases. The distance from a city center, which translates exactly into

      compact residential development, is then very significant. This means that infill-type development is an effective measure to reduce fuel consumption.

3.   Railway-convenient zones in a 'local' area discourage car use. On the contrary, railway zones that are inconvenient in a satellite city in a metropolitan area encourage car use.

4.   The type of city that each neighbourhood belongs to significantly affects the rate of fuel consumption. If a neighbourhood is located in an area outside the Tokyo, Osaka and Nagoya Metropolitan environs, petrol consumption increases considerably.

5.   Residential and neighbourhood commercial zoning tends to increase petrol consumption.

6.   Compound factors occupy a very important place in this model. They show the possibilities of combinations of different policies to have an impact on petrol consumption. For example, mixed-use residential zoning is a very interesting factor. In a central city in a metropolitan area, mixed-use residential zoning has a negative impact. On the contrary, in a non-metropolitan area, mixed-use residential zoning indicates a positive impact. These results show that the popular idea that mixed use is desirable for fuel efficient transport is not always true, especially outside a metropolitan area.

7.   If a neighbourhood adjoins a railway station, fuel consumption decreases. This is also a typical example of a compound effect.

8.   An agglomeration of low-rise residences has a different effect in metropolitan areas and in areas outside Tokyo, Osaka and Nagoya. In the case of the latter areas, an exclusive agglomeration of low-rise residences tends to increase fuel consumption.

      Based on these findings, practical guidelines which encourage a compact city to reduce car use, can be developed.

Conclusion

The results of this study provide many indications about how to improve urban layouts to diminish reliance on the car. Urban density is not the only factor that influences fuel consumption. The results of this study show that petrol consumption could be controlled by improving many factors in a city or neighbourhood. Land use regulations, transport conditions and infrastructure are important. The positive effect of infill development is also confirmed. Moreover, some factors that were believed to have a straightforward relationship with car use and petrol consumption show different effects in different locations, and a combination of counter-measures was found to be very effective. The next stage in the research is to turn these findings into specific design guidelines.

Table 8.3   Factors affecting petrol consumption at the neighbourhood scale

Explanatory variables		Standardised parameter	t-value
Population	Population density	-0.392	-5.26
Location	Distance from the city centre	0.299	3.48
Transport conditions	Distance from a bus stop	0.125	2.13
	Satellite city in a metropolitan area: railway-inconvenient (D)	0.156	2.43
	Central city in a local: area: railway-convenient (D)	-0.107	-1.82
	Local city in a local area: railway-convenient (D)	-0.085	-1.46
City type	Central city in a metropolitan area (D)	-0.177	-2.21
	Central city in a local area (D)	0.336	4.41
	Local city in a local area (D)	0.284	3.16
Land use	Residential zoning (D)	0.373	4.38
	Neighbourhood commercial zoning (D)	0.266	4.49
	Light industrial zoning (D)	0.168	2.33
	Industrial zoning (D)	-0.222	-3.30
Compound factors	LCLA + large UCA (D)	0.152	2.47
	CCMA or CCLA + UCA (D)	-0.100	-1.62
	Local area + UCA (D)	0.154	2.66
	Adjoining station + high and R-11 (D)	-0.109	-1.89
	CCMA + mixed-use residential zoning (D)	-0.103	-0.96
	Non CCMA + Mixed-use residential zoning (D)	0.185	3.15
	CCMA + R-1 (D)	-0.169	-3.06
	Local area + R-1 (D)	0.130	2.40
	Metropolitan area + adjoining station + R-1 (D)	-0.196	-3.63
Segment			8.65
Adjusted R2		0.652	

Note: All acronyms as for Table 8.1

Acknowledgements

The authors are indebted to Takeomi Murakawa for his assistance in this study.

References

Hayashi, Y., Kato, H., Kimoto, J. and Sugawara, T. (1995) 'Estimation of Reduction in CO_2 Emissions by Modal Shift Policy in Urban Passenger Transport', *Infrastructure Planning Review*, vol. 12, pp. 277-282.

Jenks, M., Burton, E. and Williams, K. (1996) *The Compact City: A Sustainable Urban Form?* E and FN Spon, London.

Kaneyasu, K. and Kanaizumi, A. (1972) *Koutsuu Kougai (Transportation Pollution)*, Gijyutu-shoin, Tokyo.

Ministry of Construction (1993) *The Report of the 2nd National Person Trip Survey*, Ministry of Construction, Tokyo.

Naess, P. (1996) 'Workplace Location, Modal Split and Energy Use for Commuting Trips', *Urban Studies*, vol. 33(3), pp. 557-580.

Newman, P. and Kenworthy, J. (1989) *Cities and Automobile Dependence, An International Sourcebook*, Gower Technical, Aldershot.

Roo de, G. and Miller, D. (2000) *Compact Cities and Sustainable Urban Development: A Critical Assessment of Policies and Plans from an International Perspective*, Ashgate, Aldershot.

Thomson, J.M. (1977) *Great Cities and Their Traffic*, Victor Gollancz Ltd., London.

Williams, K., Burton, E. and Jenks, M. (2000) *Achieving Sustainable Urban Form*, E and FN Spon, London.

Chapter 9

Patterns of Drivers' Exposure to Particulate Matter

Birgit Krausse and John Mardaljevic

Introduction

Health studies indicate that exposure to air pollutants can have adverse effects on human health, particularly in urban areas where there are high pollution levels. Pollution concentrations show large variations over small spatial and temporal scales. Therefore, in order to evaluate human exposure, it is necessary to investigate the pollution characteristics of the micro-environments where people spend significant amounts of time.

Particles are commonly measured as mass concentrations (μgm^{-3}) of PM_{10} or $PM_{2.5}$, i.e. particles up to a diameter of 10 or 2.5µm, respectively. More recent studies have focussed on smaller particles, so called ultra-fines, which are smaller than 1µm in diameter. Due to their small size and low mass, these particles hardly contribute to mass concentrations, but comprise the bulk of particle number concentrations ($\#cm^{-3}$).

Epidemiological studies found that both short-term and long-term exposure to particles can cause severe health problems and it is generally understood that there is no lower threshold for particulate pollution health impacts, i.e. even at low particle concentrations there are negative impacts on health (e.g. Pope, 2000; Weijers et al., 2001). This said, the Committee on the Medical Aspects of Air Pollutants (COMEAP) concluded that, since there is no strong evidence on the relative effects of different particles in the respirable range, the measurement of PM_{10} is reasonable for policy purposes (COMEAP, 2001). Other studies come to the conclusion that PM_{10} and even $PM_{2.5}$ do not represent the most dangerous particle fractions (i.e. greatest health risk), and recommend focusing on smaller fractions and concentration measurements, i.e. ultra-fine particles (e.g. Weijers et al., 2001; Pope, 2000). This is supported by Harrison et al. (1999), who found that PM_{10} mass measured a short distance from the road is more representative of the local background concentration, while counts of ultra-fine particles are highly sensitive to local traffic conditions. This indicates that people who spend a significant amount of time on or near roads and other transport sources are exposed to higher concentrations of small particles. Until recently, particle concentration measurements have commonly focussed on the larger particle size fractions. However, such measurements are a poor indicator of exposure, when investigating transport related micro-environments, because they omit the ultra-fine particles (Charron and Harrison, 2003). Taking these considerations into account, the study described here investigated particle mass concentrations for PM_{10} and $PM_{2.5}$ as well as number counts of ultra-fine particles.

Because a great number of people travel by car to and from work, school etc., the car itself can be considered a particular micro-environment where people are exposed to particulate matter on a regular basis. A number of studies have been carried out which investigated the exposure of commuters to certain air pollutants in order to quantify exposure and identify differences in travel mode, i.e. bus, bicycle and car (e.g. Adams *et al.*, 2001; Dickens, 2000; Gee *et al.*, 1999 and Rhodes *et al.*, 1998). Most of these studies used integrated pollution measurements, i.e. they determined hourly averages from total concentration or exposure values, measured over the whole of a typical journey. However, it has been shown by Dickens (2000) that the exposure to pollutants does not only depend on travel mode but also on the type of road layout and location (e.g. motorway, small urban road etc.) and also on vehicle speed. Such commuter studies therefore give an indication of the exposure of individuals on particular journeys but, apart from Dickens (2000), cannot account for exposure variation on different parts of the journey. Findings from these studies can therefore only be of limited use in estimating exposure for journeys other than commuting.

A field study has been carried out in Leicester, UK, to evaluate the exposure of drivers to particle emissions in typical urban traffic conditions. A vehicle equipped with environmental monitoring instruments was used to collect air pollution data inside the driver's compartment. By selecting three urban routes, and splitting them into individual road links with constant physical and dynamic parameters, the investigation provided in-vehicle concentrations and driver exposure for a variety of different types of road and traffic conditions.

This chapter gives an overview of the field study and data collection methodology, and presents results obtained from the data analysis. The analysis methods described include innovative data visualisation techniques as well as summary statistics for grouped data and multiple regression analysis, used to identify the main determinants for drivers' exposure to particulates.

Field Study Design and Methodology

Prior to the data collection phase, requirements were defined, equipment options investigated and a suitable vehicle was configured as a mobile monitoring unit by installing on-board particle monitors and a speed sensor. Based on a number of trial runs, a methodology for the data collection process was developed and refined. The following sections give an overview of the study design and data collection methodology.

Location

In-vehicle particle exposure is likely to be greatest in urban areas where high traffic density is common. Thus the data collection focused on locations in an urban centre. The selected areas include various urban road types to allow the investigation of driver exposure depending on road categories. The study was carried out in the urban centre of Leicester, a town in the East Midlands region of the UK.

Three routes were devised. They consisted of different road types, such as dual carriageways, residential streets, and one-way systems with bus lanes. All three routes were circular so as to minimise time loss when subsequent collection runs were carried out on a route. Each route comprised between 11 and 14 road links. Generally, the links were based on the road sections of the traffic flow model TRIPS (Citilabs, 2002) used in Leicester, so that traffic flow and speed information from the model could subsequently be used in the data analysis phase. However, since the model network lacked detail for certain parts of the study area, two links were added to complete the routes.

Route 1 (Uppingham Road) is located in a residential area characterised by single lane streets, bus routes and on-street parking. Route 2 (Abbey Lane) includes dual carriageway access routes, leading into the centre of Leicester, as well as part of the inner ring road. Route 3 (City Centre) follows a one-way system through the centre of Leicester, which has mainly canyon type streets, i.e. narrow streets with high buildings on either side which limit dispersion of pollutants.

Link numbers were allocated as follows: 1-11 for route 1, 21-31 for route 2 and 51-62 for route 3. Since traffic conditions and road layout of a link can vary significantly depending on the direction of travel, each link was treated as two links, one in a clockwise and one in an anti-clockwise direction. For this purpose, a marker (i.e. '1') was added to the link number for clockwise links. With route 3 being a part of a one-way system, the field study was thus based on a total of 57 links.

Equipment

The data collection required a mobile monitoring unit which could be equipped with all necessary monitoring devices. At the same time it needed to be a 'typical' vehicle in order for the results to be as representative as possible for a normal driver's exposure conditions. The vehicle chosen was a Peugeot Partner electric van, which is based on a typical hatchback chassis but powered by an electric motor. The van has not been modified in any other way, and with regard to ventilation and other parameters that may affect pollutant intake, it is considered equivalent to a typical domestic hatchback. The vehicle was equipped with various monitoring devices as well as additional batteries to power the equipment.

Although particles of all size ranges have been associated with adverse health effects it is now generally suspected that ultra-fine particles may be more dangerous than particles in the PM_{10} or $PM_{2.5}$ ranges (e.g. Pope, 2000; Weijers *et al.*, 2001). It was therefore decided to measure mass concentrations of the coarse particles (i.e. PM_{10} and $PM_{2.5}$) as well as concentrations of ultra-fine particles in order to obtain a more general understanding of the nature of particle exposure in vehicles. Two particle monitors were used. The OSIRIS environmental dust monitor is an optical device which can measure four size ranges of coarser particles simultaneously (i.e. total particulate matter, PM_{10}, $PM_{2.5}$ and PM_1), either as mass or number concentrations. The monitor can detect particles in the size range from 0.4 to 20μm. In this study, these particles were measured as mass concentrations. The P-Trak monitor is an ultra-fine condensation particle counter which can detect particles with sizes ranging from 0.02μm to greater than 1μm and provides number concentration measurements. The minimum logging interval for both particle monitors is one second. Regular calibration of the monitors was maintained following the recommendation of the manufacturer. Additionally, frequent zeroing checks were carried out for the P-Trak monitor and the flow rate consistency was regularly confirmed for the OSIRIS.

To relate in-vehicle particle concentrations to traffic flow patterns, such as queuing, it was necessary to record the speed of the vehicle. For this purpose, a TinyTag data logger was used to store data from the frequency-voltage converter which was connected to the on-board speedometer. This voltage data, representing instantaneous speed, was converted to mph during data processing. The conversion function was established based on a calibration procedure carried out on a 'rolling road'.

Initial test runs revealed that particle concentrations can vary significantly over periods of just a few seconds, and that this can be related to specific events such as a close approach to a car directly in front. It was decided therefore to record all parameters at the smallest logging interval supported by the equipment, i.e. one second, and maintain them in the database at this frequency. If longer averaging intervals were required for specific analytical purposes, the high resolution raw data could be averaged over longer periods. It was also crucial to ensure that the data from all monitors and recording devices would be time-synchronised. This was achieved by using a laptop to set up the monitors and a stopwatch, together with a voice recording device, to pinpoint events on the time line.

Data Collection

Data collection runs were scheduled to coincide with the peak traffic periods between 8.00 and 9.00am and 5.00 and 6.00pm. These times were chosen because they represent the most typical condition for the majority of regular commuters. These periods may also be when vehicle occupants are at greatest risk of exposure to elevated levels of pollutants because the traffic density is highest. In order to account for variations in traffic flow, caused by the majority of vehicles going towards the city centre in the morning and out of it in the evening, data was collected, where possible, on all routes in both directions, clockwise and anti-clockwise.

Prior to each data collection run, the equipment was synchronised and local weather conditions, and vehicle ventilation and heater settings were recorded in a log book. No attempt was made to alter window and ventilation settings during data collection in order to acquire concentration data for each combination of settings, but rather the 'personal comfort' approach was applied in which temperature and ventilation were adjusted by the driver to his or her requirements.

During each data collection run, the instrumented van was driven along the selected routes using the 'floating car method', where the vehicle 'floats' in the traffic stream, passing only as many vehicles as pass the test vehicle (Department for Transport, 2002). This ensures that the driver's behaviour is largely determined by prevailing traffic conditions, rather than personal driving habits. The recorded drive cycles can therefore be considered to be 'typical' for the traffic conditions on the road sections studied.

While on route, in-vehicle concentrations of particulate matter were continuously logged, simultaneously with speed. A stopwatch, synchronised with the monitors, and a voice recording device were used to record 'event data' which included the age and type of the vehicle in front as well as incidents, such as entering or leaving a link or joining a traffic jam.

A data collection run typically consisted of visiting two of the three routes. Routes 1 and 2 were each completed twice during a visit, clockwise on one occasion and anti-clockwise on the next, while route 3 is a one-way system and could therefore only be driven in one direction. At the end of the data collection run, the data files from the individual monitors were downloaded onto a laptop and combined in a text file to form a complete data set. This was accomplished using the device specific software in combination with custom written VBA (Visual Basic for Applications) macros. All event data was transcribed to a spreadsheet and converted into a standard time format so that it could be read by custom written routines which were used to automate data extraction for analysis.

Data Analysis

The data collection phase took place between April 2002 and April 2003. Covering almost a whole year, the measurements provide sufficient data for a formal statistical analysis and an investigation into the effects of meteorological conditions on particle concentrations. However, due to time constraints and road works being carried out on route 1 (Uppingham Road) during autumn and winter 2002, slightly less data was collected during the winter months (October–March) than the summer months (April–September). The final data set comprises in-vehicle concentration and speed data from 133 data collection runs. A 'run' typically consists of two consecutively completed loops on one route during the same morning or evening session.

Temporal Dynamics of Drivers' Exposure

In order to visually inspect time-series data from multiple runs simultaneously, a novel method of plotting such data was devised, using programmable data analysis software. For each run, the time-series is plotted as a colour-coded data strip where every individual measurement (i.e. one per second) is shown as a vertical line. The colour of the line represents the particle concentration on a scale from dark for low values to light for the highest concentrations. Link divider lines are included in black, but due to scale can be difficult to distinguish from the data. The length of the shaded part of the strips is proportional to the duration of the run. The remainder where there is no data is shaded grey. The data strips from multiple runs can be compiled into one synoptic plot. This approach facilitates the identification of significant patterns across large samples of the time-series data which can be lost when the data are reduced to summary metrics.

Figure 9.1 shows an example of a plot for ultra-fine particle concentrations from 21 data collection runs (the plots are best viewed in colour). All runs shown were carried out in an anti-clockwise direction on route 1 during morning rush hour. In this case, a run is defined as one complete loop of the route, i.e. driving along all 11 road links once. For each run, the date of data collection and the value for the total exposure experienced are included on the left and right hand sides of the plot respectively. The time-series data included in the Figure show only approximately one tenth of the complete field study data set. Similar types of plots were generated for the time-series data from other routes and for all particle size fractions.

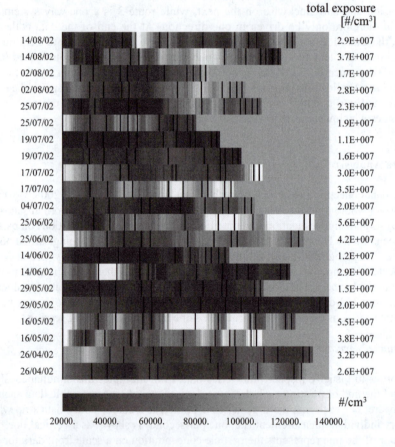

Figure 9.1   Synoptic plot for ultra-fine particle concentrations: time-series data from 21 field study runs carried out on route 1 during morning rush hour

As one would expect, the time taken to complete the same loop varied for each run. During the longest run it took just over 11 minutes to complete, while the shortest run lasted only about half that time. The plots show that concentrations of ultra-fine particles vary significantly over the duration of a run. Typically, long periods of low values are interspersed by peaks which can reach values of up to one order of magnitude higher and last several minutes. Comparisons with plots for $PM_{2.5}$ and PM_{10} data (not shown here) revealed that only ultra-fine particle count data clearly show these distinct periods of high and low concentrations, whereas time-series for the coarser particles exhibit more short-term variability. Interestingly, elevated PM_{10} and $PM_{2.5}$ concentrations were usually matched by a peak in concentrations of ultra-fine particles, whereas not all ultra-fine peaks could be linked to increased concentrations in the time-lines for the larger particles. This suggests that measurements of PM_{10} or $PM_{2.5}$ concentrations cannot, on their own, be used to indicate driver exposure to ultra-fine particulate matter.

A detailed investigation of the collected speed and event data revealed that peaks in ultra-fine particle concentration can usually be linked to the vehicle directly in front or events happening in the traffic stream. Peak values often coincide with the data collection vehicle following buses, or old vans or cars, which either have larger engines or are less likely to be well maintained. High concentrations of ultra-fine particles are also recorded when queuing at traffic lights. Occasionally, however, concentrations stay low when queuing but suddenly increase rapidly during the subsequent acceleration period. This is thought to be related to vehicles emitting more particles when accelerating, as opposed to idling, or increased air exchange between the vehicle cabin and the outside air, with the vehicle effectively 'sweeping in' high pollutant concentrations that have accumulated in the ambient air during queuing. These observations generally also apply to PM_{10} and $PM_{2.5}$ concentrations. However, not all events linked to peaks in the ultra-fine particle concentrations also have an effect on the coarser size fractions.

Plots for all particle size ranges also displayed a pattern whereby concentrations on some runs were generally higher than on others, with runs from the same day having similar concentration levels. In Figure 9.1, for example, during both runs on May 16th, concentrations stayed high throughout, as did they on June 25th. Other days, such as April 26th and May 29th had very low values. It is likely that these patterns are caused by variations in atmospheric conditions, affecting background concentrations and the dispersal of local emissions.

The exposure values at the right hand side of each data strip give an indication of how total exposure is affected by pollutant concentrations and journey time. The exposure experienced during a short journey with very high particle concentrations may by far exceed that experienced during a long journey at low concentrations.

Summary The time-series plots indicate that traffic conditions and meteorological parameters have an influence on drivers' exposure. However, these effects vary for the different size fractions of particles, with concentrations of ultra-fine particles being more strongly coupled with traffic-related changes than PM_{10} and $PM_{2.5}$. This indicates that the temporal dynamics of in-vehicle concentrations of particulate matter can only be accurately assessed when all particle size fractions are taken into consideration. Moreover, the plots show that drivers' exposure does not only depend on concentrations of pollutants but is also determined by traffic conditions. Queuing, in particular, which can significantly extend journey times, results in higher exposure values.

These observations are based on visual inspections of time-series data and therefore offer only a limited scope for generalisation. In order to investigate whether these findings can be confirmed by using averaged metrics for the whole data set, several statistical analysis methods were applied to the data. The following sections describe these methods and discuss the results.

Descriptive Statistics

In order to obtain a general overview of the field study data, summary statistics were calculated for various sub-sets of it. Grouping the data depending on when and where they were collected, and calculating basic descriptive statistics for the sub-sets of data that were generated indicated that parameters such as 'location', 'season' and 'time of day' may affect particle concentration values. Table 9.1 shows geometric mean and standard deviation values for all sub-sets. Data collected in clockwise and anti-clockwise directions are presented separately since the difference in traffic conditions was very pronounced, i.e. they caused different traffic flows, and thus particle concentration patterns.

Table 9.1   Field study data set showing number of samples, geometric mean and standard deviation, GM(GSD), for all runs grouped by location, direction of travel, season and time of day

Direc-tion[a]	Summer am			Summer pm			Winter am			Winter pm		
	ns #	UF[b] # cm^{-3}	PM$_{2.5}$ µg m^{-3}	ns #	UF[b] # cm^{-3}	PM$_{2.5}$ µg m^{-3}	ns #	UF[b] # cm^{-3}	PM$_{2.5}$ µg m^{-3}	ns #	UF[b] # cm^{-3}	PM$_{2.5}$ µg m^{-3}
Route 1 – Uppingham Road												
cw	16	73,395	19.9	20	60,144	14.2	8	93,128	18.3	8	57,650	12.9
		(1.6)	(1.9)		(1.7)	(2.0)		(1.7)	(1.5)		(1.6)	(1.8)
acw	15	50,879	13.5	16	46,147	9.7	8	75,959	15.6	8	54,583	13.6
		(1.8)	(1.6)		(1.6)	(1.6)		(2.0)	(1.9)		(1.8)	(1.8)
Route 2 – Abbey Lane												
cw	15	87,979	25.3	16	61,496	14.7	13	115,623	23.5	13	92,930	21.7
		(1.5)	(1.9)		(1.6)	(1.5)		(1.5)	(1.5)		(1.5)	(1.8)
acw	16	80,204	18.3	16	65,657	13.4	13	100,774	20.1	12	87,567	19.1
		(1.5)	(1.5)		(1.7)	(1.8)		(1.6)	(1.5)		(1.6)	(1.7)
Route 3 – City Centre												
acw	33	62,617	16.0	32	48,345	11.2	16	81,433	19.6	14	70,510	19.0
		(1.7)	(1.9)		(1.7)	(1.7)		(1.7)	(1.6)		(1.7)	(2.1)

[a] cw: clockwise, acw: anti-clockwise
[b] UF: ultra-fine particles

Average particle concentrations range from 46,000cm^{-3} to 120,000cm^{-3} for ultra-fine particles, and from 11.2µgm^{-3} to 25.3µgm^{-3} for PM$_{2.5}$. Average concentrations recorded for PM$_{10}$ were between 28.7µgm^{-3} and 77.9µgm^{-3} (not shown here).

Generally, the average values for exposure to PM$_{10}$ and PM$_{2.5}$ observed during the field study are comparable to results published by Adams *et al.* (2001) and Dickens (2000). Average particle counts measured by Dickens (2000) were lower by one to two orders of magnitude, but this may be due to a different size detection range of the equipment used. This is supported by the fact that average in-vehicle concentrations of ultra-fine particles measured in London as part of the DAPPLE project (DAPPLE, 2004) using a P-Trak monitor, were around 95,000cm^{-3}, i.e. well within the range of the field study results.

According to the values shown in Table 9.1, ultra-fine particle concentrations are, on average, higher during morning rush hour and during the winter months compared with evening and summer runs, respectively. Average mass concentration values for particles in the PM$_{10}$ and PM$_{2.5}$ ranges show the same diurnal trend, with concentrations being higher in the morning, but an inverse seasonal behaviour. Summer concentrations of these particles are clearly higher than winter concentrations. This may be due to concentrations of the larger particles being more closely linked to background particle concentrations, which are likely to be higher in the dustier summer months. Ultra-fine particles, however, depend more on local emissions, which may be higher in the winter months due to cold-start emissions and adverse meteorological conditions.

It is also apparent from Table 9.1 that average concentrations on route 2 are generally higher than on the other two routes. This is true for ultra-fine particles as well as mass concentration values. This observation is confirmed when link average values are considered, as shown in Figure 9.2. Minimum and maximum geometric mean concentrations are plotted for the links on the three field study routes, separated into clockwise and anti-clockwise links. Ultra-fine particle results are shown in black using the primary y-axis, while PM$_{10}$ and PM$_{2.5}$ values are plotted in white and grey, respectively, using the secondary y-axis.

The Figure illustrates that all three particle ranges show similar trends. Although the ranges overlap in some cases, average particle concentrations are generally higher for the links on route 2. This could be due to this route being part of Leicester's central ring road, i.e. having a higher proportion of road links with dual carriageway layout than the other two routes. These links would be expected to have higher traffic flows and possibly higher speeds, leading to higher primary emissions.

This initial broad look at the field data indicates that meteorological and location specific factors, which are known to affect emissions of particulate matter, can also be shown to influence in-vehicle concentrations and thus drivers' exposure. They therefore confirm the observations from the visual inspection of time-series plots. The findings further suggest that concentrations of ultra-fine particles differ from the more commonly measured PM$_{10}$ and PM$_{2.5}$ fractions in terms of dynamic patterns and seasonal variability.

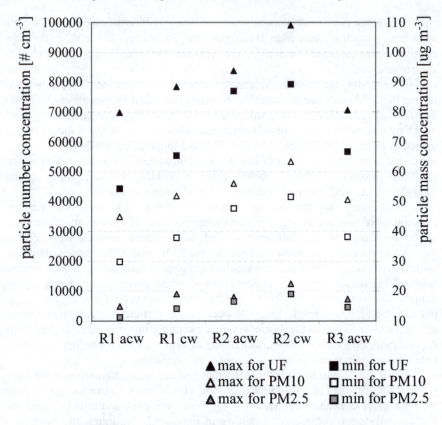

Figure 9.2   Maximum and minimum link averages for three particle size fractions, grouped by route and direction

Determinants of Drivers' Exposure

To investigate whether these general observations can be substantiated by applying more advanced statistical methods to identify specific parameters affecting drivers' exposure and to establish how strong the underlying relationships are, the data set was subjected to a formal statistical analysis. Multiple linear regression with backward elimination was carried out separately for three dependent variables: average total exposure (ATE), average total exposure per km (ATEK) and average concentration (AC).

The values for ATE were derived by calculating the sum of all measured concentration values collected on a particular link during one run and then taking the average of all runs carried out during the same morning or afternoon session. Since a link would typically be visited twice during one run, an 'average total exposure' value could be calculated from all visits during one run, which is more representative of conditions on that link than the average value for an individual visit, which may be exceptionally high if an extreme pollution episode occurred. To investigate drivers' exposure independently of the length of the link, 'average total exposure per km' was calculated as a second dependent variable. These values were obtained by dividing the average total exposure values by the link length. The third dependent variable 'average concentration' was obtained by calculating the average of all concentration values measured on a link during one run.

A range of meteorological and link specific parameters were used as independent variables, i.e. potential determinants. Meteorological data, provided as hourly averages, included temperature (T), wind direction (WD) and wind speed (WS). (The wind direction measurements were converted into a categorical variable coded with eight categories: $0°$ to $45°$ [NNE], $33-45°$ to $90°$ [ENE]).The main link specific parameters were modelled flow (tFL) and speed data (tSP) for each link (these parameters are output variables from the TRIPS model, provided by the Pollution Control Group at Leicester City Council), link length (LL), road function (RF) and link end description (LED). Road function was coded into five categories: local; high street; inter-urban; arterial, in; and arterial, out. 'Link end' was also categorised and coded as: no signal; left turn; signal; right signal; and right turn without signal. Further included were the variables 'season' (S) and PM_{10} 'background concentrations' (PM_BG), which was measured as hourly averages from a fixed site monitoring station.

Both dependent and independent variables were cleaned and prepared for data analysis to ensure that the applied statistical methods would provide valid results. This process involved the removal of all records with missing data, logarithmic transformation of the dependent variables (to ensure normal distribution) and the removal of outliers. The final data set included 1626 individual observations, consisting of one value each for every dependent and independent variable.

The results of the multiple linear regression analyses for all three dependent variables are shown in Table 9.2. They include the multiple correlation coefficients R^2 and the main determinants remaining after backward elimination. The most significant variables are marked in bold type.

Table 9.2   Results of multiple linear regression for all size ranges, multiple correlation coefficient R^2 and main determinants

Particle type	N	Average total exposure (ATE)		Average total exposure per km (ATEK)		Average concentration (AC)	
		R^2	Determinants[a]	R^2	Determinants[a]	R^2	Determinants[a]
UF	1626	0.39	LL, **LED**, S, WS, WD	0.36	LL, **LED**, S, WS, WD	0.40	**T**, WS, WD
PM_{10}	1704	0.35	LL, tSP, **LED**, PM_BG	0.33	LL, **RF**, LED, PM_BG	0.34	**PM_BG**, T, WS, WD
$PM_{2.5}$	1704	0.38	LL, **LED**, PM_BG, WD	0.36	LL, LED, PM_BG, **WD**	0.44	**PM_BG**, WS, WD

[a] LL: link length, RF: road function, LED: link end description, PM_BG: PM_{10} background concentrations, S: season, T: temperature, WD: wind direction, WS: wind speed

Results for Ultra-Fine Particles (UF)   The final models for ultra-fine particles all have multiple correlation coefficients $R^2 > 0.35$, which means that more than 35 per cent of the variability in the measured values can be explained by the models. The same determinants were identified for ATE and ATEK with the first model showing a slightly higher multiple correlation coefficient of $R^2 = 0.39$. The main determinants for both models are, in order of importance, link end description, link length and meteorological conditions, i.e. season, wind direction and wind speed.

The strong influence of link length on total exposure values in the first model is to be expected since it takes more time to complete longer links if all other parameters are the same, which leads to higher total exposure values. The model derived for ATEK has a lower correlation coefficient but still explains more than 35 per cent of the variability of the dependent variable. Interestingly, even though the actual length of the link has been cancelled out, link length still remains as a significant predictor variable in the model. However, it is now negatively correlated to the dependent variable, which means that high exposure values per km are expected for shorter links. The parameter with the strongest influence on both ATE and ATEK however is link end description, showing the influence of junction layouts, in particular traffic lights, on exposure values. Of the categories included, 'right signal' and 'right turn' were found to have the strongest effect on exposure values.

Unfortunately, no published results from directly equivalent studies are available for comparison. However, a personal exposure study by Adams *et al.* (2001), who used average $PM_{2.5}$ journey exposure levels, derived a model that explained about 34 per cent of the variability in exposure values, with 'route' being the most influential factor, explaining more than 20 per cent. This could represent the influence of queuing. The finding that link length is negatively correlated to 'total exposure per km' further supports this observation. Since road links are, by definition, typically terminated by a junction (i.e. change of flow or number of lanes), short links are associated with proportionally more queuing time than long links, which leads to higher exposure values per distance travelled.

The variables relating to meteorological conditions included in the two models are season, wind direction and wind speed. Even though they are less influential than link end description and link length, the results confirm that meteorological conditions have an effect on exposure values (see discussion below).

The main determinants identified for AC do not include any road specific parameters but are solely based on meteorological conditions, i.e. temperature, wind speed and wind direction. Contrary to the results for $PM_{2.5}$ presented by Adams *et al.* (2001), however, wind speed was found to be less influential than temperature, which reinforces the notion that exposure to ultra-fine particles does not follow the same pattern as exposure to particles in the $PM_{2.5}$ range.

The variables 'wind speed' and 'wind direction' are included in all three models. Wind speed was found to be negatively correlated to average concentration values, which suggests that pollutant dispersion lowers drivers' exposure by diluting emissions before they enter the vehicle, despite the close proximity to the emission sources, i.e. vehicle exhausts. The observed link between lower wind speeds and elevated concentration and exposure values is consistent with results from a study by Charron and Harrison (2003) who showed that this relationship also exists for roadside concentrations of ultra-fine particles. A detailed investigation has shown that wind direction is identified as a main determinant due to an underlying relationship with wind speed, where winds coming from a westerly direction tend to be stronger than from other directions. The inclusion of wind direction does not therefore add any information, but merely confirms the influence of wind speed on particle concentrations and exposure.

In the AC model, temperature is negatively correlated with the dependent variable, i.e. low temperatures are linked to high concentration values, which could be due to increased cold-start emissions under cooler conditions. This is in accordance with the effect of season in the ATE and ATEK models. Season, which takes the values 'zero' for winter and 'one' for summer, is negatively correlated to the dependent variable, linking elevated exposure values to winter conditions. In addition to temperature affecting cold-start emissions, this may also include other effects such as adverse driving conditions affecting traffic flow and queuing times, and wetter conditions leading to increased formation of small particles from precursor gases. This notion is supported by findings from the study by Charron and Harrison (2003) who reported that rain seemed to be linked to elevated outside concentrations of fine particles. However, such a relationship with temperature has not been reported for personal exposure, either by Adams *et al.* (2001), who removed seasonal influences by analysing summer and winter data separately, or any other comparable study based on particle concentration measurements. This could be because drivers' exposure is a special case of commuter exposure, where, for example, the ventilation settings chosen by the driver during different weather conditions may affect particle concentrations inside the car.

The fact that the final AC model only includes temperature, wind speed and wind direction emphasises the difference between 'concentration' and 'exposure'. Average concentrations are mainly affected by meteorological conditions, whereas exposure values seem to be more strongly related to road specific parameters. However, if concentration values were to be used to assess exposure, factors such as 'queuing time', which has been identified as a determining factor by the two other models, would have to be considered, i.e. the calculation of exposure values from concentration averages would have to take the time spent on a link or route into account. This time factor, and hence the exposure result, would be higher for links with longer queuing periods, if all other parameters were the same.

As mentioned before, all three models explain more than 35 per cent of the variability in the dependent variables. This is a reasonably good fit considering that the time series plots shown above indicate that in-vehicle concentrations of ultra-fine particles are strongly influenced by emissions from the vehicle in front and that no parameter representing this was included in the analysis. As a study by Johnson and Ferreira (2001) shows, such a parameter may well have led to a better model. Their study aimed to predict levels of sub-micrometer particles that are contributed to road side concentrations by traffic flows, and found that their basic model's accuracy could be increased from 58 per cent to 75 per cent by incorporating information on fleet composition, temperature and wind speed.

However, differences in fleet composition on individual road links can only be derived from a more elaborate data set which is not readily available for the field study area at this time.

Results for PM_{10} and $PM_{2.5}$ For comparison, and in order to investigate the extent to which drivers' exposure to larger, more commonly measured, particles can be used as a surrogate for ultra-fine particle exposure, multiple linear regression analyses were also carried out for PM_{10} and $PM_{2.5}$ mass concentration data.

The results, presented in Table 9.2, show that the main determinants for drivers' exposure to particles of the larger size fractions are similar to the ones identified for ultra-fine particle exposure. For all three size fractions, link length and link end description are included in the ATE and ATEK models. The significant difference, however, is that the third variable included in the two models for the larger size fractions is PM_{10} 'background concentration', while the models for ultra-fine particles use 'season' and 'wind speed' instead. This is not surprising, considering that the ultra-fine particle concentrations were measured as number concentrations ($\#cm^{-3}$) while PM_{10} and $PM_{2.5}$ particles were measured as mass concentrations (μgm^{-3}), which is also the unit of the independent variable for 'PM_{10} background concentrations'. However, this also means that PM_{10} background concentrations from fixed site monitors may be used to predict drivers' exposure to larger particles, but do not have a statistically significant relationship with drivers' exposure to smaller particles. This is consistent with results from a large number of studies (e.g. Weijers *et al.*, 2001; Charron and Harrison, 2003) that report that mass concentration measurements are not suitable for the evaluation of personal exposure to particulate matter from transport sources.

The dependence of exposure values on meteorological parameters, found for ultra-fine particles, is confirmed for $PM_{2.5}$ particles by the inclusion of wind speed in the ATE and ATEK models. Interestingly, however, the equivalent PM_{10} models did not include any meteorological parameters, whereas the ultra-fine models include wind speed as well as season and wind direction. Particle concentrations in the $PM_{2.5}$ range can therefore be said to have characteristics of both the larger size ranges (i.e. dependence on background concentrations) and the smaller particles (i.e. susceptibility to wind direction). They may therefore be slightly more suitable as indicators for ultra-fine particle concentrations than PM_{10} measurements.

It should be noted that the strong significance of road layout parameters in the PM exposure models, which affect queuing time, may have masked the less significant effect of wind speed on exposure values. This is supported by the fact that the main determinants identified in the AC models, where the influence of queuing time is removed, included wind speed as one of the more influential parameters.

In fact, wind speed is included as a significant variable with a negative correlation in all average concentration models, which shows that findings from studies such as those by Harrison *et al.* (1997) and Deacon *et al.* (1997) who identified strong negative correlations between outdoor concentrations of $PM_{2.5}$ and wind speed, are also relevant for assessing drivers' exposure. As discussed above, the inclusion of wind direction as a main determinant can be linked to its relationship with wind speed and does not offer any further information.

Summary Meteorological and road specific parameters have been identified as the main determinants for drivers' exposure to ultra-fine particulate matter. In-vehicle concentrations are mainly determined by temperature and wind speed. While drivers' exposure clearly depends on these concentrations, and is thus also subject to meteorological influences, it is additionally dependent on road and traffic related parameters. Queuing times, in particular, appear to be linked to increased exposure levels.

The main determinants for driver exposure to PM_{10} and $PM_{2.5}$ particles include the same link specific parameters as the models for ultra-fine particles, but also make use of PM_{10} background concentration measurements. However, these background measurements are not useful for the prediction of drivers' exposure to ultra-fine particles, which seems more closely related to meteorological parameters. The results for the average concentration models confirm that meteorological parameters have a strong effect on average concentrations for all particles. Wind speed, in particular, seems to have an influence on particle concentrations and exposure, with higher values expected at lower wind speeds.

Conclusions

The field study carried out in Leicester, UK, produced a large data set of drivers' exposure measurements. The data was collected on three routes, which were split into individual road links to allow the investigation of driver exposure dependent on road types. Measurements were made for a wide range of representative meteorological conditions (i.e. summer and winter). The data set therefore provided a sound basis for the investigation of various aspects of drivers' exposure.

Synoptic plots of time-series data from the study illustrate the short-term variability of in-vehicle particle concentrations. In combination with event data, the plots revealed that elevated in-vehicle concentrations can be linked to certain events happening in the traffic stream, such as following an old car or queuing at lights. Investigating multiple runs showed that drivers' exposure is also strongly connected to journey time. Queuing at traffic lights, as well as low speeds during traffic congestion, can lead to high total exposure values. The visual inspection of time-series data also indicated a dependence of in-vehicle concentrations on meteorological parameters. This was confirmed by the subsequent statistical analysis. Descriptive statistics for grouped data showed that high average concentrations tend to occur during the winter months, probably linked to meteorological conditions adverse to particle dispersion, such as low wind speeds and temperatures. These statistics also indicated that driver exposure depends on route-specific parameters.

A multiple linear regression analysis, aimed at identifying the main determinants of drivers' exposure generally confirmed these observations. Meteorological parameters were shown to have a strong effect on in-vehicle concentrations of ultra-fine particles. Driver exposure also depends on these parameters but is additionally influenced by road specific parameters, typically those associated with queuing times. For the coarser size fractions, i.e. PM_{10} and $PM_{2.5}$, the determinants were similar but were more closely linked to PM_{10} background concentrations and less dependent on meteorological conditions. In fact, the model for driver exposure to PM_{10} did not contain any meteorological determinants, while $PM_{2.5}$ exposure seemed to take an intermediate position, i.e. showing similarity to ultra-fine exposure as well as to PM_{10} exposure.

Generally, however, the results showed that drivers' exposure to ultra-fine particles cannot be inferred from PM_{10} or $PM_{2.5}$ measurements. The time-series plots demonstrated that peaks in the ultra-fine concentrations often did not have an equivalent in the plots for the other size fractions, and that the size fractions exhibited different short-term variability. The descriptive statistics showed that ultra-fine particle concentrations have different patterns of seasonal variability than PM_{10} and $PM_{2.5}$.

These findings strongly suggest that the coarser size fractions cannot be used as a surrogate for ultra-fine particles in the assessment of drivers' exposure. In order to obtain a complete picture of the pollution levels experienced inside vehicles and how they may affect people's health, all size fractions of particles have to be investigated. Ultra-fine particles are suspected of having a greater detrimental health impact than the coarser size fractions. Accordingly, further studies on the dynamics of human exposure to ultra-fine particles are advised.

Acknowledgements

The authors would like to acknowledge support from De Montfort University, the Engineering and Physical Sciences Research Council (EPSRC) and the Pollution Control Group of Leicester City Council which provided much of the data for the study.

References

Adams, H.S., Nieuwenhuijsen, M.J. and Colvile, R.N. (2001) 'Determinants of Fine Particle ($PM_{2.5}$) Personal Exposure Levels in Transport Microenvironments, London, UK', *Atmospheric Environment*, vol. 35, pp. 4557-4566.

Charron, A. and Harrison, R.M. (2003) 'Primary Particle Formation from Vehicle Emissions During Exhaust Dilution in the Roadside Atmosphere', *Atmospheric Environment*, vol. 37, pp. 4109-4119.

Citilabs (2002) *TRIPS (TRansport Improvement Planning System)*, software web site, http://citilabs.com/v.trips/trips.html.

COMEAP (Committee on the Medical Effects of Air Pollutants) (2001) *Statement on Long-term Effects of Particles on Mortality*, Committee on the Medical Effects of Air Pollutants, Department of Health, http://www.doh.gov.uk.

DAPPLE (2004) Dapple Project web site, http://www.dapple.org.uk.

Deacon, A. R., Derwent, R. G., Harrison, R.M., Middleton, D.R. and Moorcroft, S. (1997) 'Analysis and Interpretation of Measurements of Suspended Particulate Matter at Urban Background Sites in the United Kingdom', *The Science of the Total Environment*, vol. 203, pp. 17-36.

Department for Transport (2002) *The Transport Statistics Bulletin, Traffic Speeds in English Urban Areas*, Department for Transport, London.

Dickens, C.J. (2000) *In-Car Particle Exposure*, A Report Produced for the Department for the Environment, Transport and the Regions, AEA Technology, Abingdon, Oxon.

Gee, I.L., Coleman, B. and Raper, D.W. (1999) 'Commuter Exposure to Respirable Particles Inside Vehicles in Manchester, UK', *Proceedings of Indoor Air 1999*, 8-13 August, Edinburgh.

Harrison, R.M., Deacon, A.R., Jones, M.R. and Appleby, R.S. (1997) 'Sources and Processes Affecting Concentrations of PM_{10} and $PM_{2.5}$ Particulate Matter in Birmingham, U.K.', *Atmospheric Environment*, vol. 31, pp. 4103-4117.

Harrison, R.M., Jones, M. and Collins, G. (1999) 'Measurements of the Physical Properties of Particles in the Urban Atmosphere', *Atmospheric Environment*, vol. 33, pp. 309-321.

Johnson, L. and Ferreira, L. (2001) 'Modelling Particle Emissions from Traffic Flows at a Freeway in Brisbane, Australia', *Transportation Research Part D*, vol. 6, pp. 357-369.

Pope III, C.A. (2000) 'Epidemiology of Fine Particulate Air Pollution and Human Health: Biologic Mechanisms and Who's at Risk?', *Environmental Health Perspectives*, August 2000, vol. 108(4), pp. 713-723.

Rhodes, C., Sheldon, L., Whitaker, D., Clayton, A., Fitzgerald, K., Flanagan, J., DiGenova, F., Frazier, C. and Hering, S. (1998) *Measuring Concentrations of Selected Air Pollutants Inside California Vehicles, Executive Summary of Final Report*, (ARB Contract No. 95-339), California Air Resources Board, USA.

Weijers, E.P., Even, A., Kos, G.P.A., Groot, A.T.J., Erisman, J.W. and ten Brink, E.M. (2001) *Particulate Matter in Urban Air: Health Risks, Instrumentation and Measurements, and Political Awareness, Research Report*, Netherlands Energy Research Foundation, Petten, Netherlands.

Part C:
Sustainable Transport Policies
and their Implementation

Chapter 10

The Gordian Knot:
Resisting Sustainability in Urban
Transport in Australia

Nicholas Low

Legend has it that Gordius was a Phrygian peasant who got himself elected king. He dedicated his electoral bandwagon to Jupiter and fastened the yoke to a beam with a rope tied in a knot so intricate that, he boasted, no-one could untie it. Alexander the Great, the Macedonian, who happened to be passing in a warlike way through Phrygia found himself challenged by Gordius and his comrades. Alexander was told that whoever could untie the knot would reign over the whole of the east. Well then, said Alexander, 'thus I perform the task' and drew his sword and cut the knot in two.

Introduction

Urban transport in Australia is shackled to a culture of road building by a discursive knot of story-lines upheld and promulgated by longstanding institutional structures. The great cities of Australia are sprawling, unsustainable monsters created by the continual construction of motorways. Contrary to popular belief, road building is not the servant of low density urban form but its master. New roads, and especially the ring roads now being built around Sydney and Melbourne, are pushing urban development to the periphery. Edge cities are growing not by accident, as seems to have happened *without* planning in the USA, but *by design* in Australia. Both Sydney and Melbourne have extensive suburban railway systems which now could be supplied with well co-ordinated feeder bus systems to encourage more intensive development around railway stations: 'transit cities' (Mees, 2000). Sydney has about 838kms and Melbourne 672kms of track. Better public transport and a more sustainable urban form, however, will not be provided unless courageous politicians at Federal and State levels are prepared to cut through the Gordian knot, acknowledge that further road building is not a sustainable option for Australian cities, and fund urban public transport at least to the level of roads. There are signs that change is in motion. The success of Brisbane's bus way has prompted Sydney to follow suit at a larger scale in its Western suburbs. Following the success of the Northern Suburbs line, Perth is planning another new rail line. But the Australian case deserves attention more because it can tell us something about the policy *inertia* that is both deep-seated and prevalent in many countries, not only Australia. It is important for planners to think not only about solutions to the problems of sustainability but what stops them being implemented: what barriers stand in their way?

Stephen Trudgill (1990) explored barriers to a better environment, but the barriers addressed were: lack of consensus, inadequate knowledge, technology, and socio-economic and political barriers. He did not make the link between discourse and institutions that informs Hajer's work which we find particularly helpful in understanding what stops us from solving environmental problems (Trudgill, 1990). Linking the framework of Hajer (1995) with that of Latour (1987) and Callon (1987), we use the term 'discourse network' to describe the specific set of story-lines and arguments that co-ordinate action in a particular policy domain. The 'knots' in the network are the related discursive threads of argument, the 'nodes' are institutional structures binding people together, sometimes in particular places, for close communication (Latour, 1987). Our broader theoretical framework is developed in two recently published papers (Low and Gleeson, 2001; Low, 2002). The focus of this chapter is the knot of story-lines, but first it is important to consider a few institutional facts by way of context.

Institutional Barriers

While the planning, management and construction of transport systems (both road systems and public transport) in Australia is the responsibility of State governments, the federal ('Commonwealth of Australia') government provides a large amount of funding for transport. Federal roads programs are often high profile political items aspiring to a nation-building rhetoric. There is also some spending on urban public transport hidden in the road program, but it is of small significance (see Table 10.1).

What is important is that there has been, and remains, an enormous imbalance in federal expenditure in favour of roads compared with urban public transport. Laird (2001) calculates that between 1974 and 1998 about $38.5 billion was spent on roads while only $1.5 billion was spent on urban public transport. If money is available from the federal level it is a particularly 'brave' State Government minister who will refuse it. In fact, of course, it is never refused. Instead the funds go to support large and powerful State agencies whose principal task is building roads and who therefore mainly employ road engineers, the apex of whose skill is the design and construction of motorways.

These road building departments (The Department of Main Roads in Sydney and the Country Roads Board in Melbourne) have a long and distinguished history and *esprit de corps* (Davison, 1995). Their names have been changed several times over the last thirty years (the New South Wales Department is now the Roads and Traffic Authority [RTA], while its counterpart in Victoria is called VicRoads). But the departments have retained their own distinctive culture, built around road construction and influenced by the interchange of ideas and personnel with the road planners of the USA. The RTA in Sydney and VicRoads in Melbourne are critical nodes in the discourse network supporting continued road building.

Table 10.1   Commonwealth (federal) road and urban public transport expenditure ($ million) 1987/1988 to 1999/2000

Year	Principal road Programs	Other road-related programs	Total roads	Urban public transport
1987/88	*1194.3	8.3	1202.6	49.2
1988/89	*1192.5	15.1	1209.6	24.7
1989/90	1335.1	22.9	1359.0	0
1990/91	1381.4	*172.3	1553.7	42.2
1991/92	1092.3	*541.9	1634.2	86.2
1992/93	1451.2	*632.5	2083.7	93.2
1993/94	1014.8	537.4	1552.2	0
1994/95	816.1	719.5	1535.6	0
1995/96	831.3	770.3	1601.6	0
1996/97	801.2	821.7	1622.9	0
1997/98	814.9	820.8	1635.7	0
1998/99	874.1	837.6	1711.7	0
1999/2000	766.9	854.6	1621.5	0
Total	12184.7	6754.9	18939.6	295.5

*Includes some federal funding for urban public transport
Source: Webb (2000)

The historical development of Australia's transport institutions has shaped the stories about transport that have been promulgated. Occasionally politicians have intervened either to restrict or enhance road building, to re-badge the bureaucratic agencies, to pull new projects such as the Sydney Harbour Tunnel or the Sydney and Melbourne Ring Roads out of the bureaucratic hat to impress the voters. But road building has been effectively quarantined from the influence of the agenda of ecological sustainability, with its own story-lines. The consequence is that if current performance continues, by 2010 Australia is likely to experience a 67 per cent increase in emissions in the transport sector above the 1990 level, with by far the largest contribution coming from road use (Allen Consulting Group, 2000). What could possibly justify such an appalling performance?

Discursive Barriers

Research conducted in 2001 with funding from the Universities of Melbourne and Western Sydney surveyed the transport policy literature produced in Sydney and Melbourne since the early 1960s to identify the story-lines used to justify road building. Sydney (2001 population: approx. 3.9 million) and Melbourne (2001 population: approx. 3.4 million) are Australia's two largest cities and are, respectively, the capitals of the State of New South Wales and the State of Victoria. The main focus of the study was the outer ring roads proposed and partially constructed around the two cities, and two sections of these roads in particular: the Scoresby 'transport corridor' in Melbourne (the Eastern section of the ring, the Scoresby Transport Corridor, or Mitcham to Frankston motorway), and the Western Orbital in Sydney. But the study also included a large volume of background documentation on transport policy from the late 1960s to the present day.

Case studies of the publications of non-state actors were also carried out. These included road service organisations (National Roads and Motorists' Association [NRMA] in Sydney and the Royal Automobile Club of Victoria [RACV] in Melbourne) and oppositional groups (the Public Transport Users' Association [PTUA] in Melbourne, and in Sydney, Action for Public Transport [APT], Truth About Motorways [TAM], and Ecotransit). Only a brief overview can be provided here of what turned out to be a substantial content analysis of some 25 planning and transport reports for Melbourne and 15 reports for Sydney, voluminous environmental impact statements of sections of the ring roads and substantial documentation from supportive and oppositional interests.

The Engineer's Tale

The story-line that has become standard doctrine around the world is *predict and provide* (though this has been less potent in England since the Department of Transport report of 1989). The message is: discover the trend in the use of different modes of transport in a population and project it forward a given number of years. Then design a transport system to fit the projection. This story-line is supported by the collection of simple quantitative data and manipulation of numbers inside what to the public and their political representatives are 'black boxes' called 'models'. Predict and provide was the master story-line of the 1969 Melbourne Transportation Study (MTC, 1969) and the 1974 Sydney Area Transportation Study (SATS, 1974). Both were heavily influenced by American transport consultants. The story has the persuasive advantage of appearing scientific because it depends on quantitative methods. Those who argue against it are represented as unscientific and even emotional. The internal logic of the transport models is not easy to penetrate. Our examination of the logic of the key 'economic' justification contained in the environmental effects statement for the Scoresby Freeway (DoI, 1989) is founded upon 'predict and provide':

- there will be a 'consumer surplus', *because*
- total trips made in the corridor will increase, *because*

- additional trips will be induced, *and*
- there will be no reduction in the level of existing trips, *because*
- there will be no demand management, *and*
- the improved transport system will release a latent demand for travel.

Much of the alleged economic benefit which is presumed (erroneously) to compensate for both the financial cost to the community of building the freeway and the deleterious effects on the global and local environment, public health and so forth, are derived from the assumption that there is a latent demand to travel which cannot be reduced by demand management measures.

In Sydney, on the other hand, the city's more complex and uneven physiography means that there is simply less space to accommodate both urban growth and new roads. Predictive models were still being used by Sydney road planners until the late 1980s, but this changed significantly following a study for the RTA in 1991 which 'pointed out in unequivocal terms that if the existing trends continued there would be significant environmental, operational and financial impacts 20 years hence' (DoP, 1995, p. 17). In plainer language, environmental damage would occur and no amount of financially feasible road building would prevent congestion increasing. Since then, transport planning discourse in Sydney has evidenced an uneasy tension between the need to accommodate demand by providing new roads and the need to reduce private vehicle travel.

The dominant 'predict and provide' story-line is supported by four other stories. The first is implied in all transport plans claiming to solve congestion (and most do). We call it the 'free movement' story-line. 'Congestion' is a word that suggests an abnormal condition (Allen, 1990). This abnormal condition is a disease, some threatening disturbance of a bodily system. Because it is 'abnormal' the opposite pole is suggested: a 'normal' condition which in this case is free-flowing road traffic. Free movement by car, even though it occurs nowhere in cities is, however, depicted as 'normal'.

The second important supporting story-line can be found in transport planning documents in both cities from the early years: 'balanced' or 'integrated transport'. This seems to suggest that there should be an even or equal balance between different modes of transport. If 'equal' balance is a tautology, 'unequal' balance is an oxymoron. Though some early reports (e.g. the *Melbourne Transportation Study*, MTC, 1969) paid lip service to increased investment in public transport, it was in the context of far more massive investment in roads. An equal balance between public transport and roads has never been contemplated, let alone an equal balance between roads and walking and/or cycling. 'Balanced' has therefore been superseded by the word 'integrated'. Whereas 'balanced' was close to an outright lie, 'integrated' is more difficult to pin down.

Finally, when all else fails, transport planning reports revert to the 'technical fix' story-line. Even if petrol engines have to be phased out for environmental reasons or because of oil shortages, vehicles running on electricity and hydrogen will replace them and therefore more and better roads will still be needed. This argument conveniently ignores the remaining ecological and social costs of roads and road traffic as well as the economic costs of converting to hydrogen based transport technology. Interestingly, an article appeared in a recent edition of Royal Auto (the monthly journal of the Royal Automobile Club of Victoria, by Horrell, 2002) that applauded hydrogen fuel cell technology but acknowledged that a clean way would have to be found to produce the enormous quantity of hydrogen required, and no such way currently exists.

The Economist's Tale

From economics comes the story-line that all travel results from people seeking opportunities to enhance their lives by engaging in spatially separated activities: 'travel as opportunity'. The story-line is not often stated, it does not need to be, but it is necessary to such economic concepts as the consumer surplus which is used in benefit-cost analysis. It is also associated with the view that private vehicles are the modern way to travel. The latter is to be found strongly stated in those reports with a more ideological tone such as the 1980 Lonie Report to the Victorian State Government which states that 'mobility has become an ingrained part of the 1980 lifestyle' (Lonie, 1980, para 3.10), and that 'the general public has evolved its own transportation system, which is basically a private enterprise one involving specific and personal investments by millions of individuals in mobility' (*ibid.*, para 11.1). Another example is *Transporting Melbourne* which states that, 'The availability of the car has enabled people to live at their preferred locations in suburban or rural environments while at the same time being able to participate in a full range of urban activities' (DoI, 1996, p. 62). This story privileges private vehicle transport as being consistent with a market perspective in which the unit of political analysis is the individual and there is no such thing as society.

Two important points about this story-line are, first, that it positions those who oppose road building as seeking to take away freedom of movement and self-expression; second that it supports an important related story that investment in infrastructure brings economic growth. In the benefit-cost analysis of the Scoresby Freeway, the alleged economic benefits were derived largely from the aggregate of small parcels of time saved in travel as a result of investment in the infrastructure (including extra travel induced by building the freeway). However if travel is reduced, for instance by demand management measures, economic benefit is also reduced. If, say, a person substitutes time working at home for time spent travelling to work, or a business saves money by rationalising pick-up and delivery, this would count as a disbenefit, which is obviously absurd.

In recent years the story's focus has shifted from commuter trips to freight movement, claiming that the prosperity of the city depends on the constant intra-urban flow of freight on the road system. Just-in-time logistics is held to be unalterable even though it contributes to wasteful extra trips, and loads costs on to the road bill, health bill and the environment. Our study indicated that this story-line, contained in successive Sydney and Melbourne reports, especially in the environmental effects justifications for the Sydney Orbital and Scoresby Freeway, does much of the persuasive work supporting continued investment in roads, e.g. 'many more jobs will be created in local industries through improved access to the Sydney Orbital road and rail freight network and reduced transport costs' (NSW

Government, 1998, p. 25). 'Recent studies [*we are not given the reference*] have shown that investments in regional roads can generate community benefits which are six times the cost of the projects' (*ibid*). Such beliefs will be familiar to Europeans from the European Commission paper that gave rise to the Trans-European Network (EC, 1993), though Black (2001) regards the story-line as a myth.

Finally an economic story-line that stems from transport practice in Australia and shores up 'predict and provide', is the 'separate markets' story: 'The rich mosaic of overlapping land uses, historical patterns of development, redevelopment opportunities, and growth areas leads to a multitude of distinct travel markets, each with its own needs and requirements' (DoI, 1996, p. 13). In this story, each mode of transport has its own market which it serves. The possibility of one mode substituting for another is denied (for instance better public transport relieving road congestion at least as effectively as road construction). While this story-line is prevalent in Melbourne, it is less dominant in Sydney. There seem to be fewer cases in which there is postulated to be no choice but to use a car, or where public transport is not seen as a substitutable for the car.

Both the shift of emphasis from passenger transport to freight and, in Sydney, the diminishing insistence on the use of cars for commuter journeys, we believe may be evidence of the impact of the environment lobby. In the former case, the argument has shifted to position critics of roads as opposed to economic growth (roads are essential to business and jobs); in the latter case there is a dawning recognition that increased use of public transport is at least as effective in reducing congestion as building more roads.

Interestingly, there has been very little (if any) discussion of road pricing in the transport infrastructure policy literature. Pricing is, of course, a favourite economists' solution to congestion; but since it does not lead to increased road building it has been almost entirely ignored. If sustainability and its associated story-line about the necessity of demand management gains ground, then this solution can be expected to emerge more strongly into the policy sphere.

The Town Planner's Tale

These days it might be thought that planners interested in sustainable or ecological cities, 'smart growth', urban or transit villages, urban consolidation and the reduction of car dependency would be opposed to the standard story-lines of road engineers and transport economists. But there are three intertwined story-lines found in urban planning documents in Sydney and Melbourne that weaken the planners' resolve. The first is the story that low population density can only be served efficiently by road transport; the second is 'locational equity', the third is about a balance between mobility and amenity. These stories are underpinned by the argument that the balance of costs and benefits for residents varies in different locations in the city and people should not suffer disadvantage because of where they live. In short, people living in the outer suburbs deserve better transport (in fact they are sometimes correctly seen as transport disadvantaged) and this better transport can only be provided by building better roads: 'Urban sprawl has made it difficult to provide an efficient system of public transport in outer areas' (DPE

1987, p. 10). Because public transport cannot effectively serve areas of low gross density, 'residents are forced to rely on private transport' (DoP, 1993, p. 14; DoP, 1995, p. 16).

Sydney has a significantly higher level of public transport use than Melbourne and has had a 'concentrated' urban strategy since 1988 (DEP, 1988) so the low density justification of roads has not been so dominant. Melbournians, in particular, are frequently told by planners that they live in an exceptionally low density city. Despite the fact that urban sprawl was first brought to the city by the railways, only road transport is believed to serve today. Planning documents generally try to have the best of both worlds. On the one hand they acknowledge the continuing growth of the city at low densities and argue that a grid of roads best serves such development. On the other hand, a major theme of metropolitan planning over the years has been the densification of population around service cores: 'district centres' served by railway stations.

Planners are perforce concerned with residential amenity. Not only is this a longstanding concern of planning, but institutionally the function of planning control in Australia is located predominantly at local authority (municipal) level, where amenity and its connection with property values is most at issue. When it has to be acknowledged that building new transport infrastructure destroys local residential amenity, planners in alliance with their road engineer colleagues resort to the argument that a balance must be sought between the 'values' of mobility and amenity. The argument runs as follows: mobility is necessary for modern life; mobility can best be achieved by the use of the private car; but cars reduce amenity (pollution, noise, severance of communities); so the best resolution of this inherent conflict between mobility and amenity is to restrict most traffic movement to arterial roads which will keep traffic out of residential areas and preserve the amenity of residential streets. This was basically the argument of the famous English report of Colin Buchanan (Steering Group and Working Group of the Minister of Transport, 1963). It was first presented in detail in the report of the Melbourne Metropolitan Board of Works in 1981 but it has been regularly referred to when justifying expenditure on arterial roads or 'by-passes' (Lonie, 1980; MMBW, 1981; MoT, 1986; VicRoads 1994).

The story-line appeals to the rhetoric of pragmatic compromise, that is trying to do the best for most people, most of the time. It evokes a utilitarian argument that for the greatest happiness of the greatest number a few small groups may have to lose out: 'The effects of road improvements are such that a small group [*those living in the vicinity of arterials*] may suffer while the majority [*those living in residential streets*] benefit' (MoT, 1986, p. 22). Opponents of this story-line question both whether 'increased' mobility is so necessary to modern life, and whether 'increasing' provision for the private car is the best way of achieving it. But opponents can be portrayed as small groups or interested parties and not the majority which, in fact, they often are. While they never actually argue for the reduction of car use, they may be portrayed as doing so and are thus implicitly stigmatised as a threat to freedom of movement.

These story-lines position public transport advocates as a minority group which also advocates higher density or urban consolidation (in Europe, often referred to as urban compaction). Although it is official policy, consolidation is not popular in the 'leafy suburbs' of Melbourne and Sydney (see e.g. Lewis, 1999). Mees (2000) however argues that Melbourne is not an exceptionally low density city and points out that the metropolis possesses a much more extensive heavy rail network than metropolitan Toronto (of comparable urban density) where public transport patronage is much higher. Overall, Toronto's urban density is only 30 per cent higher than Melbourne's, whereas its public transport patronage is 130 per cent higher (Mees, 2000, p. 210). The reason: better service and better co-ordination of transport modes in Toronto.

What then of 'sustainability'? Certainly the language of sustainability has been adopted. Yet the implication that traditional policy settings must change has not penetrated the transport establishment. In the case of the Melbourne Scoresby Corridor, in the environmental effects statement, sustainability was simply traded off against supposed economic benefits. The consultants showed in their report that the full freeway option was the least sustainable, yet they recommended adoption on the grounds that business benefits would flow from it. Sustainability was dealt with differently in the case of the Sydney Orbital. The environmental effects report is considerably less detailed than the Melbourne one. So building the ring road was claimed to be quite compatible with sustainability (DOTRS, 2000). The argument is that an increase of traffic in the system would be avoided by demand management measures. There is little information about what these measures will be and how they are to be monitored. Why is a new orbital road needed at all if demand management works? Even though this may signal a decisive shift of story-line, it made no difference to the solution adopted, which was another motorway.

The richness and subtlety of the story-lines of the transport planning texts cannot accurately be conveyed by such a brief exposition. There are subtle slippages in the stories, when one argument is about to fail the text moves its ground to another. There are implicit and explicit stigmatisation and positioning of oppositional voices (which sometimes advance cogent arguments), and there are many more subplots in the story-lines than can be related here. There is both some truth and much falsehood in the claims made in transport reports and, on the whole, remarkably little empirical evidence adduced for anything. This does not, of course, stop the stories in favour of road building being constantly disseminated to the public and to politicians by the road service organisations. Compared with the readership of the NRMA's *The Open Road* and the RACV's *Royal Auto*, which are both distributed free to all members, i.e. probably most car owners, the propaganda mustered by the environmental groups has very little coverage, relying heavily on generating enough controversy to be taken up by the commercial media.

Conclusions

If we are eventually to have ecologically sustainable cities it is not enough to make plans, create new architectures, invent new technologies, build new capacities and rationally implement solutions. All are important, but insufficient. Understanding is needed not only of what should be done, but of what stops it being done. This has much to do with what people with power believe to be right and true. We need a better understanding not only of the natural environment, but of human society and its dynamics.

Most people act on their beliefs, but these beliefs come from somewhere. Individual 'preferences' to which markets are supposed to respond do not spring spontaneously into being. Belief systems are socially constructed and institutionally embedded. They can and do change, but much more needs to be understood about how they change and how they resist change.

The research reported here represents just a first step in developing this understanding in one policy field (transport), in one country (Australia). The approach can be, and we think needs to be, both deepened to explore in much greater detail the social articulation and impact of beliefs, and extended into other policy domains and other countries. The research suggests that without bold political action it will be difficult to change the paradigm of transport planning in Australia. It will not be simply a matter of instituting new policies, but also of demolishing ingrained modes of behaviour associated with professional interests and popularly supported funding programs, and of changing and radically reconstructing bureaucracies around new story-lines. Inspired, determined and politically risky leadership ('Alexander's sword') seems to be needed to make substantial modifications of the old paradigm. Yet the paradigm is changing slowly and incrementally. To perceive this change, planners need to take a longer term perspective not only of the future (already suggested by concepts such as intergenerational equity as well as time scales of environmental change) but also of the past, especially of our own history.

Note

The research reported here was undertaken by the author, with Professor Brendan Gleeson (School of Environmental Planning, Griffith University, Queensland, Australia) and Ms Emma Rush (The University of Melbourne, Australia). The author takes full responsibility for this chapter. The research was supported by the University of Western Sydney and the University of Melbourne. The author would also like to acknowledge the contribution of Ms Kamini Pillai for clarification of the institutional structures for transport planning.

References

Allen Consulting Group (2000) *Greenhouse Emissions Trading*, vol. 1, Allen Consulting Group, Melbourne.

Allen, R.E. (1990) *The Concise Oxford Dictionary of Current English*, Clarendon Press, Oxford.

Black, W.R. (2001) 'An Unpopular Essay on Transportation', *Journal of Transport Geography*, vol. 9, pp. 1-11.

Callon, M. (1987) 'Society in the Making: The Study of Technology as a Tool for Sociological Analysis', in W. Bijker, T. Hughes and T. Pinch (eds) *The Social Construction of Technological Systems*, MIT Press, Cambridge, M.A. pp. 83-103.

Cosshall, W.J. (2002) 'In Defence of the Car', *The Age*, Melbourne, 17 August, p. 6.

Davison, G. (1995) 'Dream Highways: Automobilising Melbourne 1945-1975', *Proceedings of Urban History Planning Conference*, vol. 1, 27-30 June, Canberra.

DEP (Department of Environment and Planning) (1988) *Sydney into its Third Century: Metropolitan Strategy for the Sydney Region*, Department of Environment and Planning, Sydney.

Department of Transport (1989) *National Road Traffic Forecasts (Great Britain)*, Her Majesty's Stationery Office, London.

DoI (Department of Infrastructure) (1996) *Transporting Melbourne, A Strategic Framework for an Integrated Transport System in Melbourne*, Department of Infrastructure, Melbourne.

DoI (Department of Infrastructure) (1998) *Scoresby Transport Corridor Environmental Effects Statement*, vol. 1, Sinclair, Knight, Merz and the Department of Infrastructure, Melbourne.

DoP (Department of Planning) (1993) *Sydney's Future: A Discussion Paper on Planning the Greater Metropolitan Region*, Department of Planning, Sydney.

DoP (Department of Planning) (1995) *Integrated Transport Strategy for the Greater Metropolitan Region*, Department of Planning, Sydney.

DOTRS (Department of Transport and Regional Services) (2000) *Proposed Western Sydney Orbital Environmental Impact Statement*, DOTRS, Roads and Traffic Authority, Sinclair, Knight, Merz and PPK, Sydney.

DPE (Department of Planning and Environment) (1987) *Shaping Melbourne's Future, The Government's Metropolitan Policy*, Government Printer, Melbourne.

EC (European Commission) (1993) *Growth, Competitiveness and Employment*, Office for Official Publications of the European Commission, Luxembourg.

Hajer, M. (1995) *The Politics of Environmental Discourse, Environmental Modernisation and the Policy Process*, Clarendon Press, Oxford.

Horrell, P. (2002) 'The Hydrogen Revolution', *Royal Auto*, vol. 70(8), Royal Automobile Club of Victoria, Melbourne.

Laird, P. (2001) 'Federal Funding of Australian Land Transport, Appendix C', in P. Laird, P. Newman, M. Bachels and J. Kenworthy, *Back on Track, Rethinking Transport Policy in Australia and New Zealand*, UNSW Press, Sydney.

Latour, B. (1987) *Science in Action, How to Follow Scientists and Engineers Through Society*, Harvard University Press, Cambridge, M.A.

Lewis, M. (1999) *Suburban Backlash, The Battle for the World's Most Livable City*, Bloomings Books, Melbourne.

Lonie, W.M. (1980) *Victorian Transport Study, Final Report*, Ministry of Transport, Melbourne, Victoria.

Low, N.P. (2002) 'Ecosocialisation and Environmental Planning: A Polanyian Approach', *Environment and Planning A*, vol. 34(1), pp. 43-60.

Low, N.P. and Gleeson, B.J. (2001) 'Ecosocialisation or Countermodernisation? Reviewing the Shifting "Story-Lines" of Transport Planning', *International Journal of Urban and Regional Research*, vol. 25(4), pp. 784-803.

Mees, P. (2000) *A Very Public Solution: Transport in the Dispersed City*, Melbourne University Press, Melbourne.

MMBW (Melbourne Metropolitan Board of Works) (1981) *Hierarchy of Roads Study: Steering Committee Final Report*, MMBW, Melbourne.

MoT (Ministry of Transport) (1986) *METRAS: Strategy Development Final Report*, Ministry of Transport (Metropolitan Arterial Road Strategy), Melbourne.

MTC (Metropolitan Transportation Committee) (1969) *Melbourne Transportation Study, vol. 3, The Transportation Plan*, Metropolitan Transportation Committee, Melbourne.

NSW (New South Wales) Government (1998) *Action for Transport 2010: An Integrated Plan for New South Wales*, Government of NSW, Sydney.

SATS (Sydney Area Transportation Study) (1974) *A Transport Plan for Sydney*, Sydney Area Transportation Study, Sydney.

Steering Group (and Working Group of the Minister of Transport) (1963) *Traffic in Towns, A Study of the Long Term Problems of Traffic in Urban Areas*, Her Majesty's Stationery Office, London.

Trudgill, S. (1990) *Barriers to a Better Environment, What Stops us Solving Environmental Problems?* Belhaven Press, London.

VicRoads (1994) *Linking Melbourne*, VicRoads, Melbourne.

Webb, R. (2000) *Commonwealth Road Funding Since 1990*, Economics, Commerce and Industrial Relations Group, Parliamentary Library, Canberra.

Chapter 11

Creating Liveable Streets: Developing Traffic Management Guidelines for Western Australia

Carey Curtis

Introduction

Australia, like the United States, the United Kingdom and Europe, has seen a decade of policies for sustainable transport (Department of the Environment and Heritage, 1992; Department of Transport *et al.*, 1996; Western Australian Planning Commission, 1997a; Queensland Transport, 1998; National Transport Secretariat, 2003). The vision of most transport policies is for a reduction in private car travel and the development of an integrated transport system where public transport and non-motorised transport are realistic alternatives for most trips. One of the means of achieving this is through better integration of land use planning and transport. Planners, urban designers and transport engineers have a key role in this approach by designing neighbourhoods at a scale and form that support walking and cycling, and public transport accessibility.

Turning this vision into reality exposes a tension between the professions and their traditional ideologies. For example, in designing for shared or liveable streets and vibrant active public places, some argue that road safety objectives are being sacrificed. Conventional traffic management practice since the 1970s has been dominated by road safety objectives. Car-centric traffic engineering standards for street layout, design and intersection control are still promoted by some, and this often undermines attempts to create sustainable urban environments.

To achieve better integration between land use and transport planning we must ensure that we are not hindered by this tension between the professions. Collaborative working is required. All professions must be involved and have a clearly articulated role to play. An integrated strategy involves not only the physical relationship between land use and transport uses and networks, but also the institutional relationship between professions. The coordination of agencies, services and operations is required to ensure the benefits of one group's initiatives are fully utilised by other groups. In this way we can ensure true integration of land use and transport and then benefit from the implementation of a total package of measures.

Traditionally the various professions have worked separately and sequentially, rather than sitting down together to discuss each others' objectives and question their compatibility. The outcomes have been poor. There are many examples of functionally separated land uses with little thought as to how people can travel between them. For example, wide road reserves in quiet residential communities make simply crossing the street to talk to a neighbour difficult. Often little thought is given to the orientation of buildings in relation to the pedestrian network, or even ensuring that the pedestrian network is connected.

The urban system is complex and each group of professionals has an input into this system. But working independently means that even apparently shared objectives, such as creating mixed-use, vibrant, liveable urban areas, can be undone by the lack of understanding of the impact of our individual design solution on others' solutions. This suggests that we need to work together to produce shared solutions that will result in better environmental outcomes.

This chapter highlights the work carried out for the Western Australian government on the development of new traffic management guidelines aimed at creating liveable streets: traffic calmed and accessible by all modes of transport. The chapter starts by reviewing the main objectives and approach put forward under conventional traffic management practice in Australia. Then the chapter examines the development of a new approach by the Western Australian government with the objective of creating 'liveable neighbourhoods'. Using examples, the chapter examines the traffic management guidelines now being trialled.

The traffic management guidelines present a new challenge to conventional transport planning and engineering practice. The chapter discusses the processes which were utilised, including the 'enquiry-by-design' process, in an attempt to achieve agreement about future practice. The prime means of achieving this is through greater multi-disciplinary working rather than a polarised debate. The chapter reviews the debate arising from that challenge and highlights other issues that might hinder the use of the guidelines to create more liveable streets.

Planning and Transport Strategies in Western Australia

The Perth metropolitan area is characterised by low-density development, with the urban area stretching 120 kilometers along the Indian Ocean coastline. There is an extensive road network, comprising a central freeway linking northern and southern suburbs to the Perth Central Business District (CBD), and a system of arterial distributor roads dissecting the urban area at approximately one kilometre intervals (Curtis, 2001). The planned road network was influenced by American transport planning ideas (i.e. predict and provide) with transport consultants from America employed on key regional transport studies during the 1970s (Gleeson *et al.*, 2003). The consequence of Perth's dispersed urban form is shown by the following data. Annual private car travel per capita was 12,029km in 1990 compared to a European average of 6,601km (Newman and Kenworthy, 1999). The estimated mode share for all personal trips in 1991 was 76 per cent by car, 10 per cent walking, 6.4 per cent by public transport, 5.7 per cent by bicycle and 2 per cent by other modes (Curtis, 2001). Given the high level of car dependence, it is not surprising that approximately 5,000 hectares of land is dedicated to car parking in the Perth metropolitan area.

Set against this background of car dependency, Western Australia has been pursuing a sustainable transport strategy since the late 1990s that aims for a balanced approach to transport provision and use. *The State Planning Strategy* (Western Australian Planning Commission, 1997a) and the *Metropolitan Transport Strategy* (Department of Transport *et al.*, 1996) propose strategies that seek a move away from car dependence and towards providing for transport choice. The *Metropolitan Transport Strategy* sets targets for mode share, seeking a shift from car driver trips to public transport, cycling, walking, car sharing and alternatives to travel, such as teleworking (Figure 11.1).

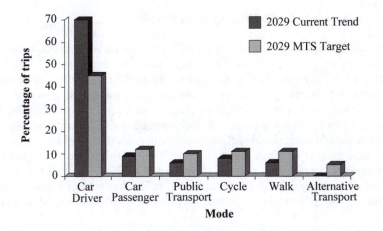

Figure 11.1   Metropolitan transport strategy mode share targets

In both strategies it is evident that land use and development planning are part of the package of measures put forward and have a key role to play. By better integration of land use planning and transport, land use activities can be accessible by all modes of transport. One such approach advocated by planners and urban designers is the *Liveable Neighbourhoods: Community Design Code for Western Australia* (Western Australian Planning Commission, 1997b). This has its roots in Federal and State government initiatives to reduce the spread of urban areas and to move towards more sustainable sub-division of land (Curtis and Punter, 2004). It is a planning concept based on new urbanism, an approach to land use development based on ideas emerging from North America since the late 1980s. It has been evident in Australian planning policy for just over a decade: see for example the *Australian Model Code for Residential Development* (Commonwealth Department of Housing and Regional Development, 1995); *Victorian Code for Residential Development* (Department of Planning and Housing, 1992); and *Shaping Up:*

Shaping Urban Communities to Support Public Transport, Cycling and Walking in Queensland (Queensland Transport, 1998).

A major component of the Western Australian planning concept of 'liveable neighbourhoods' (Western Australian Planning Commission, 1997) is the approach to the 'movement network', and within this street design and intersection control. To provide more detail to planners, designers and engineers, an accompanying document *Liveable Neighbourhoods: Street Layout, Design and Traffic Management Guidelines* (Western Australian Planning Commission, 2000) was produced. These guidelines set out to create a street layout that provides for legibile and walkable neighbourhoods, and street design and intersection control aimed at calming vehicular traffic and safely providing for the movement of pedestrians and cyclists.

Past Approaches to Traffic Management Practice

Perth, the capital city and major metropolitan region in Western Australia, has a long history of traffic planning. There have been two broad phases. Traditional practice from early sub-division through to the 1970s resulted in a 'one-size fits all' approach to the design of the street network. Land was sub-divided mostly with 20 metre road reserves (or 22 yards/one chain) with limited forward thinking to the differing mobility needs and access requirements for different land uses. The second phase of conventional traffic management practice arrived during the 1970s, again as a product of American engineers. It comprised a hierarchical tributary street network designed to meet the objectives of mobility (by car) and access to land uses, balancing through traffic and local traffic. At the heart was the notion of segregating the different modes of transport for safety and efficient movement.

The Traditional Approach to Traffic Management

The following Figures show some examples of 'traditional' practice. All are 20 metre road reserves but have very different functions and land use activities. Figure 11.2 shows an arterial road linking the Perth CBD with the port city of Fremantle. It caters for through traffic, including public transport, but also a neighbourhood shopping centre. There is little space to cater for all of these purposes. Figure 11.3 shows a neighbourhood connector using the same road reserve width. This road connects different neighbourhoods and is flanked with residential land uses, however, the households are separated by a vast road reserve. The positive outcome of this traditional approach today has been the possibility of re-arranging road space so that bicycles are allocated an on-road bike lane, as can be seen in this Figure. Finally, Figure 11.4 shows the 20 metre reserve functioning as a local access street.

Figure 11.2   Traditional practice: arterial road

Figure 11.3   Traditional practice: neighbourhood connector

Figure 11.4   Traditional approach: local access street

The Conventional Approach to Traffic Management

A useful summary of the 'conventional' approach to traffic management planning is provided by Brindle (1996; 1999). He notes that the guidelines on town layout are familiar as long standing 'good planning practice'. These guidelines promoted a range of practices that have become the mainstay of conventional traffic management. Key features include the need for clear separation of traffic functions and access functions. This is achieved through the planning of a hierarchical street pattern, where through traffic is catered for at the periphery of the residential cell, and local access within the residential cell. Not only are places laid out according to their traffic function, but also the network is designed for segregation of motorised and non-motorised traffic. Intersections are designed to minimise traffic conflict and facilitate motorised traffic movement. The main area of difference between conventional traffic management practice and the new approach at this general level of classification is in the approach to the segregation of traffic: from segregation of modes under the conventional approach, to shared road space under the new guidelines.

Street Network In the conventional approach, the hierarchical street network is generally designed around the premise that different land use functions should be separated (Figure 11.5). Therefore, local residential neighbourhoods are sited between arterial roads in large single land use components. Retail uses are grouped in one large land parcel (i.e. 'big box' shopping centres) and these, together with schools serving large catchments, are invariably separated from residential areas by an arterial road. This means that for individuals to undertake their daily activities, they find the land uses they need to access are spread over a larger area, usually beyond walking and cycling distance. Invariably this leads to increased car use. More cars on the network increases road safety concerns for non-car users. A vicious cycle is created as increased car use leads to fewer people walking and cycling.

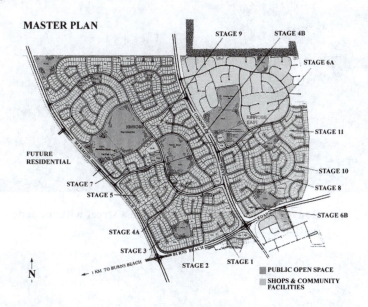

Figure 11.5   Conventional approach to street network design

Source: Reynolds and Salmon, 1998

Street Cross-Section Design The conventional approach designs the street cross-section with the primary aim to provide for unimpeded flow for cars and other vehicles. This is achieved by segregating different types of road user. Therefore pedestrians and cyclists are not provided for on the road. Instead the intention is to give them separate pathways. However, the experience in Western Australia has been that cyclists are almost never catered for, and in residential areas pedestrian footpaths are rarely provided along local access streets, leaving only the carriageway for pedestrian access (Figure 11.6). The design provides wide streets as this is thought to both reduce crashes and increase the carrying capacity of the road network. Providing for high carrying capacities was predicated on the belief that this would reduce congestion.

Figure 11.6   Conventional approach: local access street without pedestrian footpaths

Figure 11.7   Conventional approach: residential distributor road showing lack of direct access from adjoining properties

Access Management In the interest of safety, the district and local distributor roads are segregated from the activity arising from adjoining developments. Direct vehicle access to properties is limited or prohibited. On-street parking is also eliminated in the interests of safety. In a residential environment the approach is to prohibit direct driveway access onto the distributor road. Figure 11.7 shows this approach with houses set back from the street and concealed by walls and vegetation. The result is that natural surveillance is reduced, as is land use activity and interest for pedestrians. In the commercial district, the district distributor road functions as an urban expressway with frontage and roads or service lanes adjacent to commercial properties (Figure 11.8). Large frontage car parks are built, creating even wider spaces for pedestrians to negotiate.

Figure 11.8   Conventional approach: distributor road in a commercial district showing lack of direct access from adjoining properties

Intersection Design The conventional approach requires that intersections are designed primarily to facilitate motorised vehicles so that efficient flow is maintained and conflicting vehicle movements are reduced. In these circumstances there is no priority for pedestrians or cyclists, and discontinuous street networks are inefficient to service by bus.

Brindle (1999) provides a review of conventional practice guidelines. From 12 key sources he categorises 41 generalised guidelines. By assessing these guidelines against the need for a more sustainable transport approach it becomes clear that very few aspects of conventional practice promote sustainable transport. Consistently across his 12 sources, only six items appear to support the notion of sustainable transport, and these are mainly found in the more recent sources. These items include the idea of planning to limit total travel, and planning to minimise the need to drive locally. There is mention of the need to locate land uses to maximise public transport efficiency (but even here much would depend upon the definition of efficiency). Street cross-section design suggests adapting mixed-function roads for other road users and designing residential access streets for low speeds (but 'low speed' is not specified).

The New Western Australian Traffic Management Guidelines

By comparing the new guidelines to the past practice, it is possible to illustrate the different ideologies described above. This also serves to highlight the challenge that the new guidelines pose to the current practices of the different professions. New *Traffic Management Guidelines* were released as part of the 'liveable neighbourhoods' initiative, which was introduced by the State Government as a new Community Design Code in 1997 (Western Australian Planning Commission, 1997b) for a trial period of testing and review. After the first stage of the trial, modifications were made and a second version was released in June 2000. The new Traffic Management Guidelines (Western Australian Planning Commission, 2000) accompanied the second version.

The *Liveable Neighbourhoods Community Design Code* (Western Australian Planning Commission, 1997b) is a tool to be used for assessing structure plans and sub-division in new urban development areas. The stated intention is to deliver sustainable development in accordance with the *State Planning Strategy* (Western Australian Planning Commission, 1997a). The key design approach is to plan for communities based on a system of 'walkable neighbourhoods'. These neighbourhoods are then limited to a catchment of a 400 metre radius (deemed to be a five minute walk). The aim is to cluster these neighbourhoods around a town centre.

A major component of the design code is its approach to traffic management. The traffic management guidelines accompanying the design code are designed to achieve three broad objectives. The first is to provide a highly connected network of streets. This allows for compatible land uses to be located within a walkable catchment. In so doing, the aim is to provide a viable alternative to car-based travel, which would in turn reduce traffic congestion on arterial roads. The second objective seeks to set out land use in 'perimeter blocks', designed to provide an active street frontage. The idea is that this will provide for passive surveillance and so improve the personal safety of pedestrians. Finally, parking provision is located on-street. This provides for shared public parking and better use of parking spaces between developments. In so doing, it also enables more intensive use of lots and improved pedestrian amenity.

Curtis and Aulabaugh (2001) noted that the *Traffic Management Guidelines* (Western Australian Planning Commission, 2000) were unique amongst traffic management guidelines in the extent and detail with which they dealt with interconnected streets. Their review of other guidelines had noted a move in this direction, particularly in those produced by the Institute of Urban and Regional Development, Berkley, USA.

The *Traffic Management Guidelines* feature three interrelated design categories: street layout, street cross section design, and intersection control. Each of these categories has its own set of aims within the overall context of achieving good urban design. These are considered in turn below.

Street Layout

The aim is to provide a network which provides high levels of accessibility to centres of activity and local uses without returning to the problems of through traffic that arose in the traditional traffic management approach of the grid network. The network has a design based on an orthogonal grid with interconnected streets, but like the conventional approach it maintains a hierarchy within the grid. There is direct connection between some lower order and higher order streets in the network. The neighbourhood centre is not located in the centre of the 'cell'. Instead, arterial streets and local streets (neighbourhood connectors) form the spine of the neighbourhood rather than being at the edge of the neighbourhood. Town and neighbourhood centres are located at the junction of these streets (Figure 11.9). This approach means that centres can serve local people arriving on foot or bike, as well as through traffic. This also provides an economic solution for retail catchments whilst maintaining the capability of providing for travel choice.

Curtis and Aulabaugh (2001) compared the new and conventional approaches. They note that where shops and community facilities are located at the centre of the residential cell, long travel distances are the result. These are more usually undertaken by car. Traffic congestion occurs during the peak periods at the intersections between the local distributor and arterial. In the new approach, the interconnected street provides a choice of possible routes for vehicles, so spreading the traffic and avoiding congestion. The design builds in a hierarchy in order to avoid through traffic and 'rat running' within residential areas. The interconnected street system also provides a choice of routes for pedestrians and cyclists, making the network more permeable for them. In the new approach, culs-de-sac are rarely used since they reduce this permeability. The conventional network created poor accessibility for buses, putting bus stops at the periphery of the residential cell on distributor roads. The new approach enables buses to penetrate the neighbourhood.

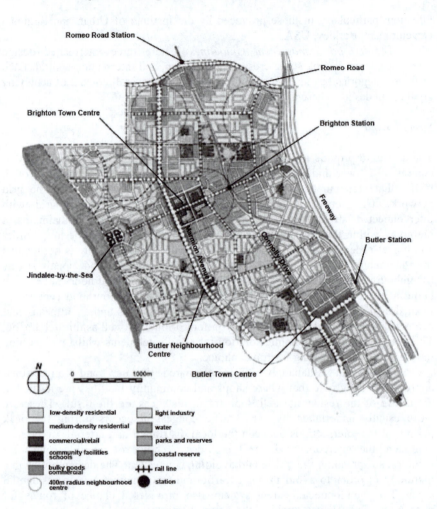

Figure 11.9   *Traffic Management Guidelines* **approach: street network layout for Brighton, Perth demonstrating the extent of connectivity**

Source: Western Australian Planning Commission, 2000, in collaboration with City of Wanneroo and Satterley Property Services.

The new street network aims to integrate land uses and activities with transport by matching particular land uses along a street to appropriate street types designed to cater for different traffic functions. So a street which transitions from residential uses to a primary school, or row of small neighbourhood shops, would not be uniform in its cross-section design, as it is in the traditional approach. Figure 11.10 shows the way in which street types within the network are selected in relation to land use activity as well as traffic volumes. Neighbourhood connectors link neighbourhoods to each other, to the town centre and to the regional road system: higher intensity land uses would be located here. A choice of wider and narrower access streets through residential areas depends upon densities and car parking controls.

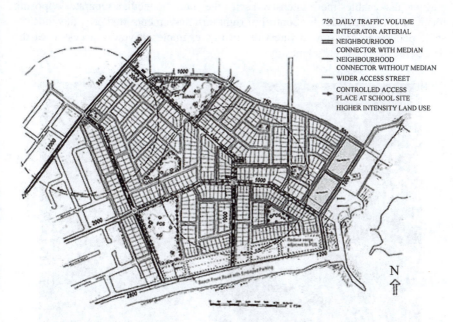

750 DAILY TRAFFIC VOLUME
══ INTEGRATOR ARTERIAL
══ NEIGHBOURHOOD
　　CONNECTOR WITH MEDIAN
── NEIGHBOURHOOD
　　CONNECTOR WITHOUT MEDIAN
⋯ WIDER ACCESS STREET
→ CONTROLLED ACCESS
　　PLACE AT SCHOOL SITE
　　HIGHER INTENSITY LAND USE

Figure 11.10　Street layout and land use relationship

Source: Western Australian Planning Commission, 2000

In designing this interconnected street system, one of the tensions is road safety, with the potential for through-traffic on local streets. This issue was explored through workshops by the team drafting the guidelines. It became clear that to overcome this problem would require a careful and iterative design process involving close liaison between urban designers, planners and traffic engineers. Unlike the conventional planning process, this has required detailed design issues to be addressed earlier in the planning phase, at early concept planning. To achieve both the objectives of safety and of transport choice, a range of devices are used, including configuration of street blocks, street cross section design, and restricting some movements at intersections.

Street Cross-Section Design

In catering for pedestrian and cycle travel it is important to plan active, liveable streets, which have variety and points of interest. The 'liveable neighbourhoods' traditional boulevard is shown in Figure 11.11. In this example of a neighbourhood connector, mixed-use properties front the street providing interest to the pedestrian and natural surveillance. The new guidelines provide for on-street parking (but only on roads where vehicle speeds are 60km/hr or below) in order to calm traffic and provide some protection for pedestrians from moving vehicles. On-street parking also enables more intensive use of the site. The median separates opposing traffic streams, provides for control of right turn movements, and provides for two-stage pedestrian crossing at intervals. In this example, driveway access is at the rear of the property, via a laneway.

Figure 11.11 'Liveable neighbourhoods' traditional boulevard

In the conventional approach for residential environments the street cross-section uses a wide street but this creates an unsatisfactory integration with land use. Buildings are too distant across the street, and neighbourly interactions and life on the street are reduced. The problem with the conventional approach is that it replaces road safety dangers with personal safety dangers. Interestingly, it has recently been suggested that widening streets and reducing congestion actually reduce safety: Noland (2000) notes that road infrastructure safety improvements actually lead to increases in fatalities and injuries whereas congested roads lead to fewer casualties.

In retail or commercial environments, the new guidelines seek to design at the human scale. The divided distributor is provided with building frontage but no access or service lanes, and no on-street parking. The median prohibits right turns to large commercial car parks found at the rear of the perimeter block development (except where openings and right turn storage lanes are provided). On-road cycle lanes are provided. The experience for pedestrians and cyclists is significantly better. Compare this with conventional planning practice, where wide road reserves, high vehicle speeds and frontage car parks create unfriendly places for pedestrians and cyclists, and liveability is lost.

Intersection Design

The new guidelines aim to provide for the efficient movement of pedestrians and cyclists by giving them priority in intersection design and ensuring design solutions do not place them in danger. Kerb radii are reduced in order to shorten pedestrian crossing distances and limit vehicle turning speeds. In areas of high pedestrian and cycle demand (i.e. in or near town centres) the use of traffic signal controls rather than dual lane roundabouts is required. In residential environments, small, single-lane roundabouts designed for 20-30kph vehicle speeds are recommended. Whereas stop and/or give-way controls at four-way intersections of access streets is advocated, in order to minimise the proliferation of roundabouts in interconnected street systems.

Implementation Issues

The new traffic management guidelines have been in existence since 2000. To attempt to assess implementation issues presents a challenge because there are few examples of completed developments that have been assessed under the guidelines. There are, however, several areas of new development which have been designed using the same 'new urbanism' principles that can provide an indication of the ease of implementation. The author's involvement in early testing of the guidelines with other transport professionals makes it possible to highlight some of the emerging issues. In-depth interviews were also conducted with those involved in designing and assessing recent planning applications.

Professional Working Practices and Integration

As noted above, traditionally the various professions have worked separately and sequentially without discussing each others' objectives and questioning their compatibility. In fact, it is rare for planners or urban designers to get involved with the design details of street networks. The approach taken in the development of the guidelines was to use an 'enquiry-by-design' workshop. This drew together a multi-disciplinary team of planners, urban designers, engineers, public transport planners and transport planners for a period of three days, to test the guidelines. The aim was to consider and design possible solutions to a set of problems for a specific place. The group, working in a number of smaller multi-disciplinary teams, undertook an iterative process of design exercises, starting with the strategic context of the site, and gradually working down to finer details. At each stage the designs were reviewed by the whole group, discussed and modified if needed. Working in this way provided a greater awareness and understanding of the objectives of different professions. It became clear which solutions achieved the shared objectives of the whole group and which served only one professional group's objectives. Together workable solutions were found. It was on this basis that agreement was reached on the adopted guidelines.

However, in practice, the debates over design solutions for 'real world' development proposals demonstrate that there is clearly resistance amongst the wider group of conventionally trained engineers and transport planners. For example, not all are convinced about a number of the design details. At the network level, traffic volume thresholds for controlled access highways are still contested. Street cross-sections have overly large reserve widths in some instances, not in keeping with the land use activity solutions. 'Friction free' public transport routes are preferred by transport service providers, not routes with roundabouts, T-junctions, tight corners and so on. So there is still a preference by public transport planners to stay away from residential cells. In intersection design, the attempts to slow motorised vehicles, and reduce cross sections for ease of pedestrian crossing are resisted: 12m kerb radii instead of 6m radii are still being used. Four-way intersections are also contested, with engineers still preferring a proliferation of roundabouts.

Design Details

There are clearly misunderstandings about the role, place and features of some design details. Laneways are a good example. They are intended to be used as rear access to residential property, enabling it to front directly onto a public space such as a park, in order to improve amenity and natural surveillance. More often than not, the property is dissected by a front access street as well as being served by a rear laneway. Hence, there appear to be a proliferation of streets. This brings criticism from the development industry who claim the traffic management guidelines are costly in terms of road provision. Another issue is that the common treatment of laneways suffers from very poor design, lacking in balconies and street configuration to ensure overlooking. This is shown clearly in Figures 11.12 and 11.13.

Development Industry Issues

The development industry sees a number of teething problems with the new guidelines. The assessment process is clearly more complex. It requires a move towards performance-based assessment rather than a simpler prescriptive list of standards which can be 'ticked off'. Therefore, it is argued by the industry that development assessment takes longer and is consequently more costly. This is not substantiated by the assessors.

The iterative approach to design solutions means that even at the early concept phase designers are involved in very detailed design issues. This adds to the initial development costs, but there are possible cost savings at later stages. In addition, developers are stressing the importance of good quality design in providing them the market edge.

Figure 11.12 Rear laneway treatment providing natural surveillance

Figure 11.13 Poorly designed rear laneway treatment

At present there is a choice of assessment route for development proposals. Applications can be assessed under conventional policies, or developers can elect for assessment under the new codes. This has led to a perception of uncertain outcomes. Developers perceive a risk of choosing the new codes route. Some concerns include local authority and state government personnel lacking training and understanding of the new guidelines, and so continuing to impose conventional practice on design proposals.

Some developers perceive a market demand for the conventional, low-density layouts complete with culs-de-sac. For this group, there is a resistance to change. The culs-de-sac approach is seen as a safer solution, tried and tested on the market. Interestingly culs-de-sac are now seen as a personal security benefit rather than a road safety issue because they form a quasi gated community.

Conclusions

The neighbourhood and suburb design that has resulted under traditional planning practice raised concerns about through traffic and road safety. Conventional traffic management practice, since the 1970s, addressed these problems by providing a hierarchical road network where there was segregation of through and local traffic as well as of the different modes of transport. It is now considered that this practice has created unliveable streets, resulting in poor outcomes, particularly when now considered against an agenda for more sustainable land use and transport outcomes. The conventional approach to road safety has promoted segregation rather than integration. There has been an increase in the number of journeys made by car at the expense of other modes of transport, and there have been increases in trip distances by car per capita. This exacerbates problems for the vulnerable modes of walking and cycling, and even access to bus routes.

Brindle (1996; 1999) shows that the traffic management guidelines and practices in Australia have, for the most part, continued a philosophy developed well before the objective of sustainability was introduced. But as the new guidelines demonstrate, when the conventional tributary street layout is replaced with an interconnected or permeable street network, with appropriate attention given to traffic and access functions, land use activity and intersection controls, there is better integration between land use and the transport network. Furthermore, active, liveable streets can be provided.

Speed reduction is also an important component of the physical design solution. Designing streets to reduce speeds provides a safer environment for pedestrians and cyclists, while still supporting the car and buses. The challenge is to ensure land use activity adjusts to a new pattern of development, based on walkable catchments rather than unsustainable car-based catchments. Such car-based catchments are driven by economies of scale rather than environmental or social sustainability.

Early evidence from the completed 'new urbanism' type developments, and the limited implementation of the guidelines to date, indicates a need for wider awareness, knowledge and training in order to avoid the expensive mistakes that are occurring. This, in turn, should help to reduce some of the development industry's concerns.

The experience of multidisciplinary team working in developing and testing the guidelines before their release was of great benefit in giving different professions the opportunity to test and challenge each others' objectives and work towards shared goals. There is a need for this approach to be replicated through a change in design practice in the development stage of planning. Detailed and iterative integrated land use and traffic management plans must be developed early in the development phase. While this may incur some extra costs, these must be set against the wider benefits to the community.

Acknowledgments

The use of material from the *Liveable Neighbourhoods: Street Layout, Design and Traffic Management Guidelines* (Western Australian Planning Commission, 2000) is acknowledged. The guidelines were prepared by a multidisciplinary team that included the author. The issues presented in this chapter arise from the researcher's experience as a member of the team, and from in-depth interviews conducted with practitioners from state and local government and private industry.

References

Brindle, R. (1996) *Living with Traffic: Twenty-seven Contributions to the Art and Practice of Traffic Calming 1979–1992*, ARRB Transport Research Ltd, Melbourne.

Brindle, R. (1999) 'Planning for Safer Environments: Some Knowns and Unknowns', *Proceedings, New South Wales Local Government Road Safety Conference*, August, Sydney.

Commonwealth Department of Housing and Regional Development (1995) *AMCORD, A National Resource Document for Residential Development*, Commonwealth Department of Housing and Regional Development, Canberra.

Curtis, C. (2001) *Future Perth: Transport*, Western Australian Planning Commission, Perth.

Curtis, C. and Aulabaugh, B. (2001) 'Does Zero Road Toll Create Unliveable Neighbourhoods?' *Australasian Transport Research Forum 2001*, Hobart, Australia.

Curtis, C. and Punter, J.V. (2004) 'Design-Led Sustainable Development: The Liveable Neighbourhoods Experiment in Perth, Western Australia', *Town Planning Review*, vol. 75(1), pp. 116-150.

Department of Planning and Housing (1992) *Victorian Code for Residential Development: Subdivision and Single Dwellings*, Department of Planning and Housing, Melbourne.

Department of the Environment and Heritage (1992) *National Strategy for Ecologically Sustainable Development: An Overview*, Australian Government, Canberra.

Department of Transport, Main Roads Western Australia, Ministry for Planning, Fremantle Port Authority, Westrail and Metrobus (1996) *Metropolitan Transport Strategy*, Government of Western Australia, Perth.

Gleeson, B., Curtis, C. and Low, N. (2003) 'Barriers to Sustainable Transport in Australia', in N. Low and B. Gleeson (eds) *Making Urban Transport Sustainable*, Palgrave Macmillan, Basingstoke.

National Transport Secretariat (2003) *National Charter of Integrated Land Use and Transport Planning: An Initiative of the Local Government and Planning Ministers Council*, National Transport Secretariat, Brisbane, Australia.

Newman, P. and Kenworthy, J. (1999) *Sustainability and Cities: Overcoming Automobile Dependence*, Island Press, Washington.

Noland, R.B. (2000) 'Traffic Fatalities and Injuries: Are Reductions the Result of "Improvements" in Highway Design Standards?', *Transactions of the 80th Annual Meeting of the Transportation Research Board*, Washington.

Queensland Transport (1998) *Shaping Up: Shaping Urban Communities to Support Public Transport, Cycling and Walking in Queensland*, Queensland Government, Brisbane.

Reynolds, H.R. and Solomon, P.L. (1998) *The Property Development Process: Western Australia*, Victor Publishing, Perth.

Western Australian Planning Commission (1997a) *State Planning Strategy*, Ministry for Planning, Perth.

Western Australian Planning Commission (1997b) *Liveable Neighbourhoods Community Design Code*, State Government of Western Australia, Perth.

Western Australian Planning Commission (2000) *Liveable Neighbourhoods: Street Layout, Design and Traffic Management Guidelines*, State Government of Western Australia, Perth.

Chapter 12

Integrating Land Use Policy into Regional Transport Planning: The Metropolitan Planning Process in the Central Puget Sound Region of Washington State, USA

Rocky Piro

Introduction: Integrating Land Use and Transport Planning

While the development of regional transport plans in North American urban regions typically relies on models that assign generalised population and employment characteristics to large analysis zones, efforts to incorporate actual land use policy are more limited. The central Puget Sound area of Washington state (USA) uses traditional urban transport modelling, but the region also took steps to incorporate land use and growth management policy in the most recent update of its Metropolitan Transportation Plan. This chapter examines how land use policies and provisions, both local and regional, have been integrated into the transport plan update. The chapter relies on the impressions of the author, who managed the growth strategies work on the update, rather than on detailed scrutiny of documents. The benefits, at both the local and regional levels, of linking land use policy with regional transport planning are discussed here. Limitations to the process are discussed, as well as opportunities for further refinement and improvement. The relevance of this process to other urban regions is also described.

The Setting: The Central Puget Sound Region of Washington State

The central Puget Sound region of Washington state includes four counties: King, Kitsap, Pierce and Snohomish. More than 80 cities and towns are located in the four-county area, including the major cities of Seattle, Tacoma, Everett, Bremerton and Bellevue. The region is very diverse geographically. The Cascade mountain range, with its vast resource lands and national forests, runs through the eastern portion of the region. Puget Sound, an inlet of the Pacific Ocean, bisects the region. Communities on the west side of the Sound are linked to Seattle and the rest of the area by car and passenger ferries. Numerous hills and bodies of water contribute to the natural beauty of the region, but provide serious challenges for mobility and transport.

Based on the 2000 federal census, the urbanised portion of the region is home to 3.3 million people. It is anticipated that the population of the region will increase to 4.7 million by the year 2030: nearly a 50 per cent increase (Puget Sound Regional Council, 2000a). Over the past three decades, similar rates of growth have contributed to increased congestion and deteriorating mobility in the region. From 1980 to the mid-1990s, vehicle miles travelled in the region were increasing at a rate four times that of population growth (Puget Sound Regional Council, 2000b). At the same time, more and more land is being consumed for urbanisation, creating longer and longer distances to be travelled for many trips. The land area dedicated to urban uses expanded at two and a half times the rate of population growth between 1970 and 1990 (Diamond and Noonan, 1996). While the region's population has grown, there has been no major expansion of the area's highway system in three decades. The region is served by five transit agencies that provide local and regional bus services. Two serve Snohomish County, and separate agencies serve each of the other three counties. A high-capacity transit agency was created in the late 1990s to develop light rail, commuter rail, and an express bus service. Transport studies of metropolitan regions consistently rate central Puget Sound as being one of the most congested areas in the United States (Texas Transportation Institute, annual reports).

The responsibility for developing the region's transport plan currently rests with the Puget Sound Regional Council, the growth management and transport planning agency for the central Puget Sound area. The Council's authority comes from both federal and state legislation, as well as through the provisions of an interlocal agreement signed by counties and municipalities in the urban region. The Council has the challenging role of working with more than 80 units of local government that have almost exclusive responsibility for land use within their jurisdictional boundaries. At the same time, the Council must address state and federal mandates for transport planning which require cross-jurisdictional approaches for addressing transport system needs and issues.

Background of Planning Efforts in the Central Puget Sound Region

In the late 1980s, the central Puget Sound region set out to revise its federally required regional transport plan. A parallel effort was also underway to develop an updated development strategy to guide growth in the region. Staff at the regional planning agency (then the Puget Sound Council of Governments [PSCOG]) along with planning staff from local jurisdictions, began to advance the notion of combining these two parallel planning efforts into a single integrated regional strategy. Elected officials concurred and the resulting product was *VISION 2020* (Puget Sound Council of Governments, 1990) adopted in 1990.

One of the hallmarks of *VISION 2020* is its recognition that the development of land significantly impacts the transport system, and vice versa. Co-ordinating land use with transport planning therefore became a major component of the region's transport strategy. The cornerstone of *VISION 2020* is its emphasis on developing urban centres within a defined urban growth area. Between 1992 and 1994 the four counties adopted countywide policies that took the urban centres concept in *VISION 2020* and applied criteria for local jurisdictions to use to formally designate areas within their planning boundaries as urban centres. As of 1995, 21 such centres were designated in the region, including 12 in King County, five in Pierce County, three in Snohomish County, and one in Kitsap County. These communities are to have a more compact pattern of development, with a mix of housing and land uses. Such compact communities are intended to allow easier access to transit and will create more walkable environments, thus providing alternatives to car travel (Puget Sound Regional Council, 1995a). The transport component of the strategy calls for linking these centres with efficient, high capacity transit.

The crafters of *VISION 2020* advocated that if even a modest proportion of the region's future development could be strategically directed into more compact urban centres, the result would help to eliminate significant numbers of car trips. Although no formal goals were initially adopted to prescribe how much of the region's projected growth should be directed to centres, the original modelling done for *VISION 2020* accounted for 15 to 20 per cent of future development locating in centres. Locally adopted comprehensive plans anticipate approximately 16 per cent of the region's 20-year population growth (1995 to 2015) to locate in the 21 urban centres (Puget Sound Regional Council, 1997).

In the same year that *VISION 2020* was adopted, the State of Washington substantially revised its planning laws by adopting the Growth Management Act. Among other features, the Act calls for jurisdictions to explicitly address regional planning issues and to co-ordinate land use and transport planning efforts. Subsequent amendments to the Growth Management Act laid out requirements for multi-county planning policies to serve as a framework for local and county planning efforts in the central Puget Sound region. The Act also requires the regional planning organisation to formally certify elements in local comprehensive plans for conformity with state planning requirements and consistency with the regional transport plan (Statute Law Committee, 2002). In 1993, the Puget Sound Regional Council (the successor agency to the Puget Sound Council of Governments) amended *VISION 2020* to serve as the multi-county planning policies called for under the Growth Management Act.

The federal government also took action to advance the importance of integrating land use into transport planning. The 1991 Intermodal Surface Transportation Efficiency Act (United States House of Representatives, 1991) which is the federal transport legislation (known as 'ISTEA') included 16 planning factors, including one that specifically links land use and transport planning. The federal law states that in developing a metropolitan transport plan, an urban region is to consider:

> The likely effect of transportation policy decisions on land use and development, and the consistency of transportation plans and programs with the provision of all applicable short and long-term land use and development plans (*ibid*, [f]).

However, the federal law stops short of actually addressing the nature and character of regional land use or development plans and how consistency between a regional transport plan and any land use and/or development plans is to be achieved.

In response to ISTEA, *VISION 2020* was again updated in 1995 and a more detailed transport component was also developed: the *Metropolitan Transportation Plan* (*MTP*) (Puget Sound Regional Council, 1995b). The *MTP* identified the region's existing land use patterns and addressed growth factors in relation to the area's transport problems and challenges. The plan also continued to reinforce the central theme of linking the region's urban centres with high-capacity transit. To ensure conformity of local transport and land use plans with the region's growth and transport strategy, a policy and plan review process was developed. This review process was developed by the Regional Council in co-operation with local governments and includes provisions for the Council to formally certify that the transport-related provisions in local comprehensive plans are consistent with the *MTP* (see Piro, 1999). Four major policy objectives were included in the *MTP*, these were to:

1.   optimise and manage the use of existing transport facilities and services;
2.   manage travel demand, addressing traffic congestion and environmental objectives;
3.   focus transport investments on supporting transit and pedestrian-oriented land use patterns; and
4.   expand transport capacity, offering greater mobility options.

The third policy area addressed the integration of land use and transport with a number of provisions that support compact, pedestrian-oriented land use development. Growth is encouraged especially in urban centres and a mix of land use and densities is promoted at major transit access points (see Puget Sound Regional Council, 1995b, policies RT8.17 to 8.25).

VISION 2020 has served as the general planning framework for county and municipal efforts to develop comprehensive plans under the Washington State Growth Management Act. The update of *VISION 2020* in 1995 also provided an opportunity to address the designation of urban centres and to formally identify specific centres for local and regional planning purposes. The 1995 update called for each of the four counties to work with their municipalities to designate a limited number of urban centres.

> The policies and descriptions for centers in *VISION 2020* are intended to provide a framework for implementation of the centers strategy. Through countywide planning, local jurisdictions have developed or are expected to work on centers criteria, strategies and incentives specific to local conditions. Identification of centers should occur through countywide planning processes, in consultation with affected interests such as transit and regional agencies, and in a manner that is compatible with the *VISION 2020* center types. (*ibid*, p. 19)

The 1995 update included a table of future density and transit characteristics for four types of centres: regional centre; metropolitan centre; urban centre; and town centre. Recommended minimum densities for numbers of employees and households were listed for each centre type. Broad guidance for minimum transit services was also provided. In addition, four general characteristics for centres as compact communities were included. They should have:

1. safe, connected, bicycle and pedestrian facilities and pedestrian-scaled block sizes;
2. reduced parking supply and higher parking costs in denser localities served by 'good transit';
3. central gathering places and open spaces; and
4. buildings designed and sited to support walking, including entrance locations, active uses at street level, and pedestrian-scale architectural features.

While working with a common planning concept guided by *VISION 2020*, each county took a slightly different approach to the designation of urban centres. At the completion of the work on the 1995 update, 21 locations had been formally designated as urban centres: 12 in King County, one in Kitsap County, five in Pierce County, and three in Snohomish County.

The 21 designated urban centres are the most visible examples of the region's progress in implementing the growth strategy. Although discussion is often focused on these 21 centres, the region continues to recognise that other strategic land use concepts, such as compact communities, urban corridors, mixed-use districts, and transit station areas remain an integral part of the overall vision for growth in the region. When examining the function of centres in the context of how they affect the regional transport system, it is important to acknowledge that other concentrations may act very much like the designated urban centres and can also benefit from the strategies employed for centre enhancement and development.

Updating the Transport Strategy: Need for Further Specification and Clarity

While the 1995 *Metropolitan Transportation Plan* (Puget Sound Regional Council, 1995b) advanced the importance of co-ordinating land use and transport planning, its policies and provisions remained broad and general. The 2001 update of the *MTP* was not intended to be a major revision of the 1995 plan, however, regional and local planners agreed to provide more specificity and detail about the benefits of compact development for mobility and accessibility. The provisions to link land use and transport planning were identified as a key area that needed strengthening.

As part of the work on the update, the Regional Council worked extensively with local agencies and their elected officials to assess opportunities and challenges of identifying certain land use initiatives, based on adopted land use policies, that could be developed into key strategies and planning provisions to positively affect regional accessibility and mobility. The Council's Regional Staff Committee (a group of directors and senior level planning and public works staff from local jurisdictions in the four-county region that provides consultation and guidance to Regional Council staff) played a key role in the initial scoping of topics to address in the 2001 *MTP* update. The Committee encouraged the Council to focus on refining provisions in the regional plan that would help facilitate local growth plans.

With the guidance to clarify ways in which the *MTP* could be used to advance regional and local growth management planning, Regional Council staff arranged for a series of focus group meetings with local staff with expertise in growth planning and transport implementation. Participants were asked to discuss challenges and constraints, as well as opportunities and successes in their work to advance local comprehensive plans. Several themes emerged from these discussions. First, financing was not always adequate to provide the facilities needed to serve new development. Secondly, zoning and development regulations did not always take into account transport considerations beyond parking. Third, and perhaps most significantly, there was frustration that there were inherent tensions in the requirements of the Growth Management Act for jurisdictions to both accommodate additional population assigned through a mandated allocation process and curb or delay development if adequate facilities could not be in service or financed.

Moving into an investigative phase, Regional Council staff researched both short- and long-term trends in population, housing and economic activity in the area, focusing on patterns that shape the use of the region's transport system. The research also explored the relative importance of land use policy and regulation with respect to mobility and accessibility. More than two dozen potential land use strategies were identified for further consideration as work progressed on the update. These strategies included development practices, regulatory reform, and financial tools related to growth management. At the close of the investigative phase, two recommendations were advanced:

1.   Develop planning guidelines to establish regionally consistent expectations of appropriate development that best supports the regional transport system.
2.   Identify key land use strategies that can be used to help alleviate transport problems within certain geographies of the region. (Puget Sound Regional Council, 1999)

Combining Efforts – Using University Research in the Update of the Metropolitan Transportation Plan

An additional study was also conducted by Regional Council staff on urban centres, transit station areas, and other locations of concentrated development. One of the main purposes of this study was to investigate in more detail the benefits of compact development on regional mobility and accessibility. The study examined socio-economic indicators, such as changes in local population, housing and employment. Existing land use, roadway networks, and land subdivision patterns were documented and mapped. Local urban form, including the arrangement of buildings, land uses and activities, was discussed for each study area. The resulting report, *Concentrated Urban Development in the Central Puget Sound Region* (Puget Sound Regional Council, 2000c), concluded that although urban centres have continued to attract concentrations of jobs (approximately 28 per cent of all employment in the region), they are developing well below planned housing targets and densities (currently representing about five per cent of the region's total population).

Aware of research being conducted at the University of Washington on nodes of moderate-density residential concentration in suburban areas, the Puget Sound Regional Council contracted with university researchers to expand the scope of their work. In all, nearly 100 suburban residential nodes, or 'suburban clusters', were identified in the four-county region. The expanded research revealed that these nodes were areas of increasingly dense residential and job growth in the 1990s. The work on suburban clusters was incorporated into the centres report cited above and reinforced the conclusion that both infrastructure deficiencies and urban form will need to be addressed if the central Puget Sound area hopes to achieve its long-term vision of a vibrant region of compact communities linked by an efficient, multi-modal transport network (see Moudon and Hess, 2000).

Incorporating Research on Compact Communities into Regional Modelling

As part of the technical analysis and modelling associated with the update of the *Metropolitan Transportation Plan*, Regional Council staff conducted tests that changed the land use distributions in the regional transport demand model. Working with the results of the *Concentrated Urban Development* (*op cit.*) report, a modest increase in projected population and employment growth was assigned to those model analysis zones having designated regional centres or suburban clusters along transport corridors. These tests were designed to modify the future household and employment distributions for the purpose of fostering greater pedestrian and transit opportunities and improving system-wide and sub-area efficiency. A model run was conducted to understand how this growth configuration might help realise system performance improvements and other regional objectives (see Bakkenta *et al.*, 2000). Model performance indicators showed slight improvements over model output that did not have the re-allocation of households and jobs, lending support for the regional position that increased densities, along with appropriate urban form, can potentially affect the operation of the metropolitan transport system. (It should be noted, however, that the Regional Council's existing 'gravity' model, which uses large zones for analysis, is limited in its ability to simulate finer-scale land use impacts, particularly in compact districts).

From Research to Recommendations

The results of the expanded study and modelling output were presented to the Regional Council's Regional Staff Committee and Growth Management Policy Board for consideration. (The Policy Board consists of elected officials and representatives of environmental, business and community groups and is responsible for overseeing and guiding the Council's growth management work program, including the development of the growth strategies provisions in the *MTP* update.) Both groups embraced the concentrated development study and used it to advance the inclusion of certain growth initiatives in the 2001 update of the *MTP*. Thirteen specific land use and development tools and ten design guidelines were recommended for inclusion in the draft *MTP* analysis document. The Board, together with its sister body for transport planning issues (the Regional Council's Transportation Policy Board) endorsed the release of a draft analysis document for public review in August 2000. However, due to some concerns that growth initiatives might be too prescriptive for local governments, the land use concepts were advanced as useful information rather than as possible requirements (Puget Sound Regional Council, 2000d). Among other things, the draft *MTP* analysis document presents a series of physical design guidelines that were crafted to address densities, mixed-use development, and pedestrian connections in designated urban centres, as well as in other areas of compact development, including suburban clusters and transit station areas.

Additional growth initiatives that promote the development of centres and compact communities were also included in the draft *MTP* analysis document. A series of financial incentives and development strategies designed to make it easier for communities to advance the development of denser, mixed-use centres were described in the document. At this point, these initiatives were being promoted as useful information to assist local planning.

During the public review process, which included presentations to planning commission bodies, staff planning committees and task forces, city and county councils, interest groups, and community groups, there was broad support for including the land use and growth initiatives in the final plan. Much of the debate at this point in the process focused on proposals advanced by private sector groups to significantly expand the region's road network. Other groups advocated re-examining whether the regional transportation plan should shift away from light rail and opt for rapid bus transit as the selected mode for high-capacity transit. Feedback and comments provided during the public outreach process were compiled for the Regional Council's policy board members to review and consider as work advanced on preparing a final version of the plan update.

Destination 2030: Plan Adoption and Implementation Efforts

Following the public review process, the Regional Council worked extensively with its two policy boards and the Regional Staff Committee to prepare a final adoption draft of the update. It was decided to name the updated plan *Destination 2030* (Puget Sound Regional Council, 2001). Little additional work was undertaken on the land use growth initiatives during the final phase of the project. During this period, most of the attention focused on further developing the financial component of the plan, and listing regionally significant transport projects and programmes to include in the final document. The final *Destination 2030* plan was adopted in May 2001, with the entire programme of growth initiatives intact.

Physical Design Guidelines

Ten physical design guidelines were established in *Destination 2030* (*ibid*, Chapter 4). These included encouraging a mix of complementary land uses, encouraging compact growth by addressing planned density, linking neighbourhoods, linking public and semi-public uses near transit stations in designated activity centres, and designing for pedestrians and cyclists. The guidelines are intended to advance fundamental design principles and site development characteristics that are supportive of both growth management and transport planning objectives. It was left up to the Regional Council's policy boards and Executive Board to determine what status and prominence they are given in regional and local growth management planning efforts. It is anticipated that these guidelines could be formally incorporated into the Regional Council's plan review project. As noted earlier, the Council uses this project to examine local plans for conformity with state requirements for transport planning and for consistency with the adopted regional transport plan. Only those jurisdictions whose transport plans have been formally certified are eligible to apply for federal transport money in the Regional Council's Transportation Improvement Program (TIP). Thus it would be a significant step for the Regional Council to adopt physical design guidelines for centres and compact communities.

Best Practices and Tools

Research conducted in the central Puget Sound region, as well as in other urban areas of North America, suggests that traditional land use planning techniques (for example, zoning and development regulations) may not be sufficient for addressing growth management objectives, including improving the link between land use and transport planning. As a result, *Destination 2030* advances a series of regulatory reforms, development strategies, and financial incentives to help the development of urban centres, compact communities, and transit station areas (*ibid*, Chapter 4). The update includes directives for the Regional Council to gather and distribute information on these best practices.

Implementation

Destination 2030 provides the groundwork for strategic implementation actions to help advance projects and programmes that improve the link between land use and transport planning. For example, in 2001 the Regional Council undertook further studies of innovative housing programmes in the region and developed a report to assist local governments in promoting innovations in housing that could contribute to making both local and regional growth and transport strategies more successful. At the same time, a study of the effectiveness of local transport concurrency programmes was initiated. A key focus of this study was whether local adequate facility ordinances were being used in a manner that advances land use and growth management planning efforts, including the development of urban centres as mixed-use, transit-oriented districts.

During the 2001 session of the Washington State Legislature, a number of the financial incentives related to development of urban centres were considered for legislative action. Authorisation for municipalities to use tax increment financing for redevelopment was expanded and is now available to a wide range of municipalities in the central Puget Sound region and elsewhere in Washington state. Yet proposals to allow the creation of transit tax incentive zones did not progress from the committee. The Regional Council is expected to continue to study, and provide information and perhaps incentives, to local jurisdictions on many of the remaining growth initiatives included in *Destination 2030*.

One of the more significant actions taken to further integrate land use and transport planning in the first year after adoption of *Destination 2030* has been the revision of the region's TIP which is the mechanism by which federal money for transport projects and programmes is distributed to local jurisdictions and regional agencies. The Regional Council's past improvement programmes have had criteria that addressed the development of urban centres since 1995. However, these land use based criteria were only one group of criteria among many other factors that were considered in selecting transport projects for funding. In 2002, the Council's Transportation Policy Board significantly altered the policy framework for the TIP and created only two categories for applications: projects and programmes in the region's designated urban centres, and projects and programmes that connect designated urban centres. This change in the programme was deliberately designed to provide more financial support to communities that were advancing local and regional growth management objectives by developing urban centres. In the end, the Council's Executive Board agreed to fund five projects: two in urban centres, and three along corridors connecting two or more centres.

Both the *Destination 2030* effort and the renewed focus on urban centres through the regional improvement programme provided catalysts for a major review of development activity in the region's urban centres. The review covered how the centres are designated and whether criteria for guiding their identities and development should be revised. A study of the 21 designated urban centres, which examines population and employment trends, along with existing and planned land use patterns, is currently underway. A series of recommendations has been incorporated into a review draft of a report that suggests strengthening the Regional Council's role in the designation process. The Council's policy boards will consider these recommendations in the near future. Other plan implementation and monitoring efforts designed to examine growth management implementation as it relates to transport planning are also scheduled.

Finally, the Regional Council is building on the modelling exercises conducted during the update process and is committed to moving from the rather generalised 'gravity' urban transport model used over the past several decades, to a more sophisticated 'activity' based model. It is anticipated that the new modelling effort will allow for more parcel-based types of input that better reflect actual land use policy in more localised districts and sub-areas. Such a model should improve the ability to assess scenarios involving urban centres, transit station areas and other compact communities.

Applicability for Regional Planning: Transferability and Limitations

This study demonstrates a continued evolution of integrating land use policy into regional transport planning and decision making in the central Puget Sound region: an evolution which some might characterise as slow and limited. Yet there has indeed been an advancement of incorporating additional land use and growth management concepts through subsequent phases and updates of the regional transport strategy: an advancement that is steady, even if modest by standards employed outside the North American setting.

The linking of land use oversight, which continues to remain the purview of local government, and transport decision-making, which involves agencies at all levels of government, has been strengthened by the collaborative process used by the Regional Council in developing *Destination 2030*. Such collaboration is not always present in urban regions of the United States. The central Puget Sound region's effort to update its transport strategy benefited from the high level of involvement by local staff, elected officials, and the public, which allowed land use policies and growth management considerations to be incorporated into the analysis of plan options and alternatives.

The nature of how the growth initiatives were brought into the *Destination 2030* plan, i.e. as information and best practices, was limited by ongoing concerns from some local officials of possible local pre-emption of their authority in land use decision making. This limitation is not uncommon for metropolitan planning organisations across the United States, which lack authority to get too involved in local land use decisions. Yet, by establishing the physical design provisions as guidelines with the understanding that the Regional Council's policy boards and Executive Board could decide over time how to apply these guidelines, there is an opportunity for strengthening regional direction to localities.

The revision of the region's TIP to focus primarily on the development of urban centres is significant and makes the Puget Sound region distinct in how it has chosen to distribute federal transport funds. Yet the amount of money that the Regional Council oversees is rather modest compared with total revenue expended on transport improvements by various agencies and governments. It is unclear how significant this one programme is in influencing other programmes and overall transport investments in the region.

For other regions working on the challenge of how to integrate land use and transport planning, the efforts in the central Puget Sound region demonstrate a phased approach that has allowed further linkage of land use and transport to be advanced through regular updates and revisions. Building on a regional planning vision, subsequent stages of planning have produced a broad policy framework, and then more detailed analyses that resulted in a series of growth initiatives. Although these initiatives are advanced as information and best practices, the groundwork was also established to enable local and regional decision makers to determine how to use the initiatives in the period leading up to the next regional update. This incremental evolution could be viewed as demonstrating that fully comprehensive integration of land use and transport planning has not yet arrived in the central Puget Sound region. Yet, given the bottom-up philosophy of government in North America, the Puget Sound process should be viewed as successful, and showing continued promise.

Conclusion

The central Puget Sound region has now experienced more than a decade of growth management. This chapter examined the long term evolution of the region's land use planning strategies as they relate to the development of a more efficient regional transport system. These strategies emerged as a combination of federal, state and regional mandates to manage growth and transport infrastructure development.

At the root of these land use planning efforts is the concentration of future regional growth in compact communities that serve as the urban framework for developing a multi-modal transport network. In the early 1990s, the Puget Sound Regional Council led the region's efforts in creating the *VISION 2020* document. Twenty-one locations were officially designated as 'urban centres' in 1995. These centres represent the region's primary focus of existing and planned activity. Many already hold significant concentrations of employment or housing, and are expected to accommodate a substantial portion of future growth. Further refinement of the regional transport plan in 2001 added clarity to the provisions linking land use and transport and offered tangible growth initiatives for local jurisdictions to use in advancing the development of centres as part of the overall strategy to address the region's mobility and accessibility challenges.

The central Puget Sound region has been a pioneer within the United States in developing a 'centres-based' approach to growth management in general, and transport specifically. The approach has benefited from revisions to Washington state planning law which directs the regional transport planning agency to create a policy framework to guide county and municipal growth management planning efforts. Input from local staff, elected officials and other stakeholders has been important in forming regional planning strategies that are required under federal and state programmes. In a democratic environment with an emphasis on land use decision making at the lowest tier of government, the central Puget Sound region has found a meaningful way to bring land use and growth management concepts into the development of a detailed, multifaceted transport plan. Early implementation efforts since the adoption of the plan indicate that there is growing acceptance of the provisions and guidance provided in the regional plan for local officials and planners.

Note

In 2003 the American Planning Association recognised *Destination 2030* (Puget Sound Regional Council, 2001) with its Outstanding Award for a Plan. This was the first time the Association had honoured a metropolitan transportation plan with this award.

References

Bakkenta, B., Hess, P. Moudon, A. and Piro, R. (2000) 'Multinucleation and Regional Transport Planning', *Association of Collegiate Schools of Planning Conference*, Atlanta, 5 November, 2000.

Diamond, H. and Noonan, P. (1996) *Land Use in America*, Island Press, Washington.

Moudon, A. and Hess, P. (2000) 'Suburban Clusters: The Nucleation of Multifamily Housing in Suburban Areas of the Central Puget Sound', *Journal of the American Planning Association*, vol. 66(3), pp. 243-263.

Piro, R. (1999) 'Effectiveness of Interjurisdictional Growth Management', in D. Miller and G. de Roo (eds), *Integrating City Planning and Environmental Improvement*, Ashgate, Aldershot, pp. 85-107.

Puget Sound Council of Governments (1990) *VISION 2020, Growth and Transportation Strategy for the Central Puget Sound Region*, Puget Sound Council of Governments, Seattle.

Puget Sound Regional Council (1995a) *VISION 2020: 1995 Update, Growth Management, Economic and Transportation Strategy for the Central Puget Sound Region*, Puget Sound Regional Council, Seattle.

Puget Sound Regional Council (1995b) *Metropolitan Transportation Plan, The Transportation Element of VISION 2020, the Region's Growth Management, Economic and Transportation Strategy*, Puget Sound Regional Council, Seattle.

Puget Sound Regional Council (1997) *Urban Centers in the Central Puget Sound Region: A Baseline Summary and Comparison*, Puget Sound Regional Council Seattle.

Puget Sound Regional Council (1999) *Growth Context Paper, 2001 Metropolitan Transportation Plan Update*, Puget Sound Regional Council, Seattle.

Puget Sound Regional Council (2000a) *2001 Metropolitan Transportation Plan Update: Technical Baseline Report*, Puget Sound Regional Council, Seattle.

Puget Sound Regional Council (2000b) *Puget Sound Trends, Growth in Traffic and Vehicle Miles Travelled*, No. T-2, August 2000, Puget Sound Regional Council, Seattle.

Puget Sound Regional Council (2000c) *The 2001 Metropolitan Transportation Plan Alternatives Analysis and Draft Environmental Impact Statement*, Puget Sound Regional Council, Seattle.

Puget Sound Regional Council (2000d) *Concentrated Urban Development in the Central Puget Sound Region*, Puget Sound Regional Council, Seattle.

Puget Sound Regional Council (2001) *Destination 2030*, Puget Sound Regional Council, Seattle.

Statute Law Committee (2002) *Revised Code of Washington, 2002*, Olympia, Washington.

Texas Transportation Institute (annual) *Urban Mobility Report*, Texas Transportation Institute, College Station, Texas.

United States House of Representatives (1991) *Intermodal Surface Transportation Efficiency Act, 1991*, Title 23, United States Code (USC), §134, United States House of Representatives, Washington DC.

Index